SPI
EGE
L&G
RAU

WELCOME TO UTOPIA

SPIEGEL & GRAU

NEW YORK 2010

WELCOME TO UTOPIA

Notes from a Small Town

KAREN VALBY

Published in the United States by Spiegel & Grau,
an imprint of The Random House Publishing Group,
a division of Random House, Inc., New York.

SPIEGEL & GRAU and Design is a registered
trademark of Random House, Inc.

Title-page photograph: © iStockphoto.com

LIBRARY OF CONGRESS CATALOGING-IN-PUBLICATION DATA
Valby, Karen.
Welcome to Utopia : notes from a small town / Karen Valby.
p. cm.
ISBN 978-0-385-52286-1
eBook ISBN 978-1-58836-968-0
1. Utopia (Tex.)—Social life and customs. 2. Utopia (Tex.)—Civilization.
3. Utopia (Tex.)—History—21st century. 4. City and town life—
Texas—Utopia. I. Title.
F394.U75V35 2010
976.4'432—dc22   2009037970

Printed in the United States of America on acid-free paper

www.spiegelandgrau.com

1 2 3 4 5 6 7 8 9

FIRST EDITION

Book design by Dana Leigh Blanchette

For all the old-timers,
especially my dad

WELCOME TO UTOPIA

INTRODUCTION

In 2006 my editor at *Entertainment Weekly* asked me to go looking for an American town without popular culture. He wanted to hear from people not yet swallowed whole by the all-consuming, trend-hungry maw of Hollywood. In my search for the perfect town, I heard from an old college buddy who had grown up ninety miles west of San Antonio, in a ranching community far off any major highway. Back when she was in grade school the only pop culture available to her and her graduating class of thirteen was a shelf of videotapes for rent down at the gas station. That the name of her hometown happened to be Utopia was a gift.

Utopia has no mayor or local government, so there is no one to record the official population, but locals guess that a few hundred people call the town home. Utopia has zero stoplights, one constable, six real estate offices, and seven churches. There are no chain stores, and forget about fast food. Up until the early nineties, if you wanted to watch television you better have liked what was playing on CBS or NBC. Those were the only two channels people in Utopia could get, unless the wind in the Sabinal Canyon wasn't blowing; then you might twist the rabbit ears just right and luck into ABC. There is one honky-tonk radio station, no book or music stores, and the closest movie theater is a fifty-minute drive to the Forum 4 in Uvalde. Diane Causey, the elegant manager of the antiques store Main Street Utopia, spoke to me somewhat wistfully of her town's former cocoon from the outside world: "If we didn't see it on the old black-and-white TV or hear about it on the San Antonio radio station, we didn't know it existed."

In a small town, change is often cast as the enemy. Shortly before I arrived in Utopia, the people had gone to battle against sidewalks. When the community gathered at the Senior Center to discuss the possibility of the highway department building sidewalks along Main Street, the conversation got so heated that it seemed like someone might bust out a shotgun to make themselves heard. "We don't want 'em here in our town," cried one older man, shaking his fist angrily in the air, as if the subject at hand were pedophiles or drug dealers.

But as I stuck around I found that Utopia was hardly some hermetically sealed biosphere. Things were changing—and fast. The recent introduction of broadband and satellite TV had given the 190 kids enrolled from pre-K through the twelfth grade at Utopia School a flung-open window on life beyond their town's borders. The military had extracted classrooms full of Utopia's young men and women and scattered them around war zones several time zones away, transforming the kids and the families they left behind.

The outside world that had been held at bay for so long had suddenly invaded. On one side were Utopia's traditionalists—the old-timers whose lives were tightly braided into the history of the town, whose investment in the community was blood- and bone-deep, and who felt overwhelmed by the suddenly accelerated pace of change; on the other side, Utopia's fifth column, agitating for change and searching for a way out. My initial story was about what felt like a discovery: a deceptively quiet and isolated town forced to reckon with a new reality, full of upstarts and patriots, surrounded by forces of destruction or liberation. All of this playing out on a half mile stretch of Main Street.

Great literature and pop songs are forever being built around this struggle of young people—the artists, or merely the unusual—trying to break free from the familiar. In a small town, everything and everyone is already known. People know where you're going before the screen door slams shut behind you. There's no anonymity, no encouragement to experiment with identity. You can run out of air fast. It's easy to spot someone who grew up in a small town and got out: They have a breathless air about them, their expressions somehow startled and dreamy. Their stories of flight are both mundane and heroic. Whether you grew up in the suburbs or the city, many of us know what it feels like to run from who or what you don't want to be. It's just more romantic if that escape route was down Main Street, bound for the highway.

But what I didn't presume to understand about Utopia was what was going on in the minds of those who chose to stay, the people whose deepest desire was to make a home for themselves down the street from where their parents lived and their grandparents were buried. Roots are rare these days. So many of us have lost a connection to the ground. I've lived in four different cities and twelve different apartments since I graduated from college. My mom is dead. My dad lives in a Washington, D.C., suburb, where we moved after his job was transferred when I was in the sixth grade. My daughter talks to her relatives on Skype. Sometimes I long for a hometown like Utopia. A place like that can tether a person—whether you comfortably grow old and die there or spend the rest of your life cutting yourself free.

Some New York friends made easy cracks about what I might find when I got to town. "Meth labs and abortion clinics," presumed one, pleased by his smug reduction. "Maybe you'll get invited to a book burning," smirked another. These were people, good people, who lacked a proper imagination, revealing themselves to be every bit as provincial as they figured folks from small towns to be. As for Utopians' distorted image of what it might mean to come from New York, I was asked more than once if all my friends there were Eye-talian and if I'd ever witnessed a shooting at a restaurant or been trapped in a blackout, fearing for my life as a subway quickly drained of oxygen. Once I was goaded into defending the merits of pizza (pizza!), only to be told by a horseshoe of unimpressed old-timers that I'd get a better meal if I took the frozen pizza out of the box, tossed it in the trash, and gnawed on the cardboard instead.

I'm sure I shook hands with a few people, some of whom would probably surprise me, who were cooking meth in their kitchens or selling beer to minors out of their garages. Some girls get pregnant young, and their weary mothers bear the brunt of childcare. As anywhere else, there are ignorant people in Utopia, crimes are committed, and there are youthful mistakes that must somehow be made right. But that in the end isn't what defines Utopia, any more than a crook in a slick suit or a bad rush-hour commute captures city life. No matter how sophisticated or righteous we believe ourselves to be, we're all so clueless and careless when confronted with the idea of a world we know nothing about.

That in the end is why I returned to Utopia. I wanted to get past the mythology of the small town and understand it as a real place where actual people live. Utopia is changing, but it's not in a state of crisis. Nobody has been murdered. A prison hasn't moved in or out. Crystal meth hasn't reduced folks at the café to toothless ghosts. Utopia is just a small town, solitary and disconnected for the time being. But within the next generation, it's clear that Utopia will lose much of its sense of history and tradition and flavor. The old-timers die off, the young people leave, and in come new arrivals, retirees and sportsmen with disposable incomes and a city-nourished appetite for expensive views.

Why does that matter? There's the superficial reason: The way a small town functions—like an old machine with every part moving and useful—is unique to observe. But there is something deeper lost when places like Utopia are diluted or abandoned, something that became clear to me only over the long haul. In much of this country it can feel as if we've made the decision to live in disposable, virtual spaces. Our culture, our economy, and our social lives seem at once thrillingly frictionless and depressingly abstract and volatile. The culture of Utopia can at times feel oppressive and exclusionary, but I also saw that the old machine often worked. A small town, at its purest core, thrums with essential models of behavior—of intimacy and compassion and community—that we have to find a way to retain in the new environments we create in our cities and suburbs and virtual worlds. Such interconnectedness keeps us whole and human. It creates a space for the old and the young, the weak and the strong. It links us to one another, and to the land we live on.

After the magazine article was published I went back to Utopia for five months, the first of a series of long stays over the next two years. I rented one of the four rooms at the town motel before eventually accepting a kind woman's offer to bunk at her ranch. At first, many locals were tight-lipped and disapproving, happy to let me know exactly why they hadn't appreciated my portrait of Utopia. They didn't like that I brought up one of the café's waitress's recovery from cocaine addiction—of which she herself was not ashamed. Or that I had quoted a young man who saw no place for himself in a culture of cowboys and country music. The kids in Utopia seemed impressed when I told them I was from New York City. Most everyone else looked at me like I was surely joking, before their faces accordioned shut. "Well, I'm sorry to hear that," I heard snorted on more than one occasion.

After a few weeks of my stumbling through town, a woman who would become a dear friend let me tag along with her to the Methodist church's adult Sunday school, which is held before the service. The older members gather quietly in the fellowship hall's parlor each week, sipping coffee while one of them leads a subdued discussion on the day's Bible passage. My friend whispered in my ear, asking if I'd like to be formally introduced to the group. When I nodded and said of course, she smiled with some sympathy and rubbed my arm before announcing to the room of white-haired Utopians that I was Karen Valby, or, as some might prefer, "*that* Karen Valby." Conversation stopped;

one of the men stood up slowly, grimacing as he removed the cowboy hat from his head. The only thing I could think to do was to start booing myself, thumbs jabbing down at the spotless linoleum floor. A woman on a blue sofa, her hair in a neat permanent and a brooch pinned to her sensible sweater, joined me. She seemed tickled by the opportunity to weigh in on the uninvited guest tromping through Utopia with a tape recorder.

Over time people just sort of gave in to the fact that I was going to keep showing up at church and the store and basketball games. Every morning I ate breakfast at a coffee shop next to a woman whose face pickled whenever she walked in and saw me. After several weeks, she finally acknowledged my presence by turning to one of her friends and introducing me as "that bitch reporter." Every day thereafter she'd sit down for breakfast in the same jeans and plaid shirt she wore to the nearby farm where she took care of horses. "Oh dammit," she'd say, looking over at me with a groan. "The bitch is back." Eventually, though, she invited me to sit at her table and we ate breakfast together. I liked her. I think she liked me okay too, though she'd never say that herself.

On the last afternoon of my initial five-month stay, I was asked to serve as the cake cutter at the twenty-fifth wedding anniversary party for a childless couple who had claimed me as their own. During their speech of thanks to the large crowd of friends and family, the wife called me up to stand alongside them. She waved over the retired postmaster, who shook my hand with winking seriousness before presenting me with a handmade "Certificate of Acceptance as a Genuine Old-Timer." The gesture touched me to the point of tears. When I returned to New York City, I felt overstimulated and adrift for weeks.

I admit that I often failed at remaining impartial with the people of Utopia. My fondness for them is real and true. As friends are wont to do, we frustrated or annoyed or disappointed one another. But I liked these people, who were unused to a stranger sitting at their sides asking about their most private moments. I thought their stories had value and they seemed to like being heard. Interestingly, most of the men I interviewed cried at some point in front of me. They seemed stunned by the richness of their interior lives.

Before long I found myself returning again and again to the stories of four Utopians, each of them experiencing some form of upheaval in their lives and responding differently to the shifting ground beneath their feet. Ralph, the quintessential old-timer, is the retired owner of the General Store, known by friends and neighbors as "the Grouch." Kathy is a tough middle-aged mother of four boys, three of whom have kissed her goodbye and gone off to fight a distant war. Colter is the town misfit, a young man staked to a ranch that has been in his family for five generations, who dreams of leaving the land and his legacy behind. Kelli is the only black student at Utopia School, a sensitive teenager who must somehow graduate with her dreams and dignity intact. The fifth character at play here is of course the town of Utopia itself, whose shared spaces set a cramped stage for everyone's triumphs and tragedies.

The story of how Utopia earned its idyllic name is held dear by locals. A young man named George A. Barker moved to town from Alabama in 1876, on doctor's orders to seek a more soothing climate for his tuberculosis. After basking in the dry air, taking daily swims underneath the cypress trees in the clear-flowing streams of the Sabinal River, breaking the ice if a cold night had blanketed the water with a papery shell, his chest was said to come unclenched. When Barker, the color now restored to his cheeks, became the first postmaster in the town, then still known as Montana, he had the authority to rename his new home, which had proven so therapeutic. And so Barker, inspired by a loose reading of Sir Thomas More's classic, rechristened it Utopia.

There's a temptation, for those who live in small towns or pretend to, or for those of us who want to see only the good in our friends, to simplify and glorify life there. One morning I was eating at a folksy family-run café, the Hicks House, named after the gentleman who had lived in the old Victorian until he died. The owner, Jessie, walked by my table with a brightly painted ceramic chicken that she took outside and perched at the end of the driveway. When Jessie returned she explained that she wanted to alert one of her regulars, Cobey from across the street at the telephone company, that the lunch special was chicken enchiladas. Cobey doesn't like chicken, so she wanted to give him fair warning to seek his noon dinner elsewhere.

Now that's a cute story, and Utopians would rightly puff up with pride and recognition to have their town so depicted. But it's important to remember that the word "utopia" comes from the Greek, and is literally translated as "no place." There's no such thing as an ideal community, not when real people with richly dramatic lives clutter up the picture. A chicken at the end of a driveway is a charming image, but it only tells a little about what is going on in people's hearts and homes up the road.

A preacher new to town described to me the surprising response his first sermon got from the congregation. He had praised the comfort of living in a valley where one felt buffered on all sides by sweetly rolling hills. As he stood by the door afterward, shaking hands with the parishioners, one woman leaned in close and gripped his hand with unexpected pressure. "Those aren't hills, by the way," she whispered sharply in his ear. "Those are our mountains." I'd like to take this opportunity to apologize in advance to the people of Utopia for always calling their mountains hills—and for all the times they tried to show me one view of town when I was busy looking in the opposite direction.

CHAPTER 1

The Coffee Drinkers

In the small hours of the day, when town is so still as to seem suspended behind glass, Ralph Boyce pulls his white Ford pickup to a stop in front of the Utopia General Store. He turns off his engine and sits alone in the darkness outside the colorless brick front, facing the taped notices of deaths and funerals on the glass door. Ralph has been the first person to arrive at the store, probably the first in Utopia to rise out of bed, for over half a century, and he plans on continuing to swing the first set of headlights onto Main Street for the rest of his days. He wakes up without an alarm, feeds his dog, Fudge, and leaves the house by 5:10 or 5:11, depending on when the weather report ends. Ralph is seventy-six years old and he ran the store for thirty-seven years. He retired over a decade ago and doesn't quite know why he keeps showing up before the store even opens. He figures it probably has something to do with tradition. While he waits, Ralph listens to country standards on the AM radio station. If the air outside is mild, he'll lean against his truck and look down the length of his quiet town, feigning patience. It's a strange thing when a man finds himself locked out of his former place of business.

Soon enough a few more old-timers lurch their trucks alongside his, their dust-blasted Chevrolets and Fords and GMCs lining up against one another like cattle in a pen on the unpaved stretch out front of the store. If one of the men's trucks is ever parked in a different order, or even at a different angle, someone will ask him if he's feeling unwell, or if there's trouble at home. The men nod at one another and clear their throats, trickle out a few words on the weather. Around 5:30, the forty-five-year-old owner, Morris, who started working for Ralph at the store when he was a high school sophomore and who now has a son of his own in his sophomore year, pulls up. He unlocks the back door, switching on the blinkering lights, before trudging up the center aisle to the front, where the old-timers wait like cats eager to be let inside after a long night.

"Evenin', Morris," they say, giving the younger man a hard time about sleeping in, as he takes his place behind the register with a tired sigh. When Ralph owned the store he got to work at 4:30, so as far as he's concerned, Morris should count himself rested. But Morris is groggy and likes to wake up in peace, so he lingers up front, sipping from a giant styrofoam cup of water. His register faces a Blue Bell ice cream cooler, above which hang two wooden shelves covered in deer pelts, crowded with pouches of beef jerky and about a dozen mass market paperback thrillers. In a little while some younger men of Utopia will cluster around the register and share stories of dirt and intrigue as they buy their gallons of iced tea and the paper-wrapped slabs of steak they'll cook up for lunch over propane grills on their job sites.

The old-timers, chapped hands shoved in jeans pockets, walk barrel-legged toward the coffeepots in the back by the meat market, boots creaking all the way. Tony Clark, a ranch manager in an old RFD-TV cap, the cloudy outline of a can of snuff pressed into his left shirt pocket, always makes the first pot of coffee while Sid, whose sons and grandson now run the lumberyard he once owned, Albert, a contractor who built Ralph's house, Hose, a rancher and former professional rodeo circuit rider, and John, the school superintendent, bunch together on a plank bench, careful that their legs don't touch. The town welder, John Hillis, who can trace his family's roots all the way back to Utopia's founder, Colonel William Ware, floats between the cash register and the coffeepots, a toothpick settled comfortably in his amused grin. The coffee drinkers range in age from those who served in Vietnam and Korea to those who served in World War II.

Bud Garrett, the eighty-four-year-old retired postmaster, has a full head of bright white hair that swoops to the side of his forehead in an elegant wave. He wears a cream felt cowboy hat, Wrangler jeans, and one of three pale denim pearl-button snap shirts. When Bud got out of the service in 1945, one of his first jobs back home was helping to remodel the General Store, working from sunup to sundown for seventy-five cents an hour. "I got a quarter raise and I would've signed up at that point to work the rest of my life for a dollar," he said. "I thought that was big money."

Bud is six foot three, with long skinny grasshopper legs, and when he bends himself down onto the bench, his knees jut into the air high above his thighs. He thwaps his bony fingers at the front page of the *San Antonio Express-News* and winces at the headlines of debt and war. Bud is the lone Democrat in the group and he likes to wind up all the Republicans to his left and right. "George Bush has been rich all his life and that's all he knows," he cries. "He don't know who the little feller is!" For years he was met with eye-rolling jeers, but now, as the men admit that gas is high and the war goes on and on, they greet Bud's hectoring with weary fatigue. "Morris said a while back that he couldn't even remember who he voted for," Bud said. "Remember, hell! Ralph, you too!" The men don't like it much when Bud goes on about politics.

There are two aluminum chairs, paint-peeled from coffee drinkers settling back into them for decades now. Ralph, because of his long tenure at the store, has rightful claim to the left one, which offers a clear view up the center aisle out the front door. He sits with the polite stiffness of a man invited to his son-in-law's house for dinner, unsure how to hold himself now that he no longer finds himself at the head of the table. When Ralph is amused, he nods his head slowly in approval and lets his mouth slip into a smile. When he is annoyed, his face goes baggy with disapproval and he stares hard up that aisle, tearing and folding his empty styrofoam cup in on itself as he waits for the ridiculousness being inflicted upon him to pass.

Ralph's friend Ted sits in the chair next to him with his legs crossed, one tan Velcro-tabbed shoe bobbing up and down. Ralph has given most everyone in town a nickname, some of them inscrutable. ("But *why,* Ralph, do you call Melvin 'Tricky Bunny'?" I once asked him. "I guess he's just a tricky bunny is all," he said, shrugging his shoulders.) Long ago he christened Ted "Tennis Shoe Ted." Ted tried protesting for a while, claiming he didn't even own a pair of tennis shoes, but the name stuck. When Ralph met Tony, who moved to Utopia years ago after he married a local girl, he assumed the man's missing thumb was the result of a war injury in Vietnam and he took to calling Tony "Hero." When he found out that the man had in fact lost his thumb in a roping accident, Ralph rescinded the nickname and downgraded Tony to "Tiger."

Around 6:30, Sid waggles his fingers on his way out to open up the lumberyard and get a coffeepot going there. Albert, stuffing his pack of Red Man chew back into his jeans pocket, his Borden chocolate milk bottle a finger full of spit, lumbers off to meet his crew with a simple "yehhhhhp," and the superintendent, a large, good-natured man who leads with his generous belly, announces that it's his day to drive the school bus. As one shift of men take their leave, Henry or Baby Ray or Milton smoothly replaces them.

Milton, a sixty-eight-year-old retired carpenter with big saucer eyes behind thick glasses and a fading strawberry blond beard, brings a reliable coarseness to the group. He looks like a trim Santa Claus, if Santa wore plaid shirts and baseball caps and kept up a steady patter of cussing. One morning a cute little matchstick of a girl, a newcomer

Morris was trying out on the register, walked in the back door and up the center aisle. She wore a tight yellow T-shirt and a staggeringly tiny pair of shorts. The air went still as the men tried to look without looking. Milton broke the dumbstruck silence. "That girl ain't got enough ass on her to make a dying man a bowl of soup!" he declared.

Every morning save Sunday, the men sip from their cups of coffee, look at the floor, and laugh at one another. News of Ted leaving in a snit because Morris was out of the one-percent milk he liked bleeds into a story about the time a waitress at the café got him so cross-threaded that he banged out of the restuarant and refused to return for a year even though he'd left his favorite cap on the table. Meanwhile the store's wooden back door swings loudly open, smacking shut behind the bleary-eyed young and old men of Utopia, in boots and jeans and overalls, as they pass through for a pack of powdered donuts or a pecan roll and the day's first cup of coffee. "I tell everybody I should've bought stock in Folgers," Morris said. He inherited the coffee drinkers from Ralph's reign, and just as tradition demands that Ralph keep getting out of bed before dawn, it also means Morris must accept the old-timers' helping themselves to boxes of sugar cubes and swizzle sticks from the shelves when the supply in back runs low.

Ralph always perks up when Morris's thirteen-year-old daughter, Kassie Jo, her brown hair mussed and legs endless in long, yellow satin Utopia athletic shorts, drops by to check on her box of kittens and grab her book bag before the school bell.

"Mornin', pardner!"

"Hiya, sir!"

"You got a track meet this weekend, Kassadilla?"

"Yessir, it's going to be a tough one. See ya!"

Ralph used to have conversations like this with all the kids in town, who had it clocked that they could walk from school in a minute and a half flat for sandwiches and apples and sodas at lunchtime. When Ralph and his best friend, Kenneth, ran the place, all the upperclassmen would come by in the middle of the day, laying their relationship and family troubles out on the counter, hoping for some wise counsel before they shuffled back for afternoon classes. Now the kids eat in the cafeteria or get premade burritos at the gas station or panini sandwiches at the recently opened coffee house, which has WiFi, a drive-through, and a flattering write-up in *The New York Times* framed and hung on the wall. (The owners, a cheerful and hardworking middle-aged couple, are also newcomers. For a few months after their arrival, a casual rumor persisted in town that the man, because of his Italian last name, was a mobster lying low in witness protection.)

The coffee drinkers float from talk about the weather to town gossip to the routine foibles of the many newcomers who now populate their once insular community. They like to remind Ted that he, too, is and always will be a newcomer to Utopia. The accepted rule here is that if one of your grandparents was born in Utopia, only then can you claim it as your own. When the coffee drinkers call someone a newcomer, the word begins with a growl and trails off in a sigh. People fresh to town who wander into the store in the innocent search for milk or paper towels usually have the good sense to cling to the side aisles rather than submit themselves to the long scrutiny offered by that march down center. When Ralph doesn't recognize someone—and he is depressed by the number of strangers in town these days—he tucks his chin in rote acknowledgment of the customer nodding nervously at the gathered men. Then he shakes his head, groaning "foreigner" under his breath.

"Ralph just wants the newcomers to drive through town without stopping, throwing money out the window the whole way," says Ted, who moved from Port Lavaca in 1985. Well, Ralph likes Ted just fine, considers him to be one of his closest friends, in fact. But it is hard to name a problem in Utopia—the road construction, the drinking and the drugging, the loss of fellowship and of land that's been in families for generations—that the man doesn't blame on newcomers.

A lot of people here will tell you that the heart of Utopia beats loudest on Sunday mornings at the many churches. But I believe it's at the back of the General Store where you'll find its soul. The coffee drinkers,

Utopia's own Greek chorus, could tell me what life used to be like in Utopia and why they were scared to let go of that nostalgia. Of course, if a stranger is a rare sight at coffee, women are more like a myth, spoken of in hushed tones so as not to encourage their reappearance. When I told a woman in town that I was hoping to inflict myself on the men's early morning routine, she looked at me with a disconcerting mixture of suspicion and pity.

To help my chances of showing up without being told to turn right back around and head to the beauty shop if I was looking for chitchat, word was that I better first win over Ralph. His wife, Jane—a woman who can only be described as fine, as she is bright-eyed, slim-waisted, and always prettily attired—arranged our first meeting after she took pity on me sniffing around Utopia's tiny library, where she volunteers on Friday afternoons.

Jane grew up in Uvalde, and was on a date with another man when Ralph first met her in the 1950s. The one gentleman might have picked the eighteen-year-old girl up at her parents' home at the start of the evening, but it was Ralph who returned her. On the surface, Ralph is not much of a romantic. When reminded of his long-ago hot pursuit of another man's girl he gives a little snort. "Well, that's what you get for stealing," he said. On the rare occasions Ralph agrees to escort Jane to a town function, the couple take separate cars so she can linger afterward, visiting with her various friends, while Ralph escapes as quickly as possible to the easier and more reliable company of his dog, Fudge. "My friends call him the mythical husband because I like to visit and Ralph," said Jane with her popcorn burst of a laugh, whistling as she slid one of her palms quickly against the other, "he wants to get home."

As promised, Jane very efficiently arranged a meeting, saying her husband would be available on this particular afternoon at this appointed time. She'd be visiting with her ninety-nine-year-old mother at the nursing home in Uvalde that day, but she would check in with me later to make sure that her husband had been civil.

When I knocked on the door of the Boyce ranch, with American and Texan flags flying high at the foot of the long driveway, Ralph opened the door and, at once formal and awkward, invited me in.

Behind his glasses, Ralph's eyes are sharp and skeptical, and his coarse gray hair is brush-cut into his forehead's pointy cowlick. His skin is mottled and scabbed from little battles with melanoma. He keeps his eyeglass case tucked into his front shirt pocket, and stopped carrying a wallet the day he retired from the store. He never did take to wearing a cowboy hat. "After I got out of the war I bought myself a brand-new Stetson," he said. "Wore it to a dance at Garner Park, got it stolen out of the backseat of my car. That was it for me and cowboy hats." Like most of the old-timers in Utopia, he wears his age tremendously well, trim and fit from a lifetime of hard work.

Ralph's boxer sat outside the back sliding-glass door, gazing dopily up at his master. Ralph had surprised himself by welcoming another dog into his life. He'd sworn he'd never recover from having to put down his last one, Spunky. "But then my daughter, she lives in Canadia, and she called one day and said, 'The animal shelter has a boxer dog and if I don't take him they're going to put him down and would you like to have him?'" Ralph groaned. "So I went up there and got him."

He looked at Fudge through the window. "What do you think about that, pardner?" Ralph asked his dog, his gruff expression softening. Satisfied that his master was safe in his recliner, Fudge slumped down for a nap. Ralph exhaled as if the tenderness he felt for his dog exhausted him. "I always tell him that I hope I die before he does." Spunky died when he was ten years old. Fudge just turned nine.

Ralph and Jane keep pictures of their two daughters on the walls, and framed photos of their two grandbabies—"the engine and the caboose," he said proudly—and some of the local kids as well. He has a large gun closet in the living room—he also sleeps with a .22 under the bed, like most everybody else in town—and another cabinet for his oldest daughter's rodeo buckles. He runs about two hundred acres of land, flush with Axis deer, and he lets all the young boys in town come and shoot one for free if their daddies allow. There's leather sofas and an old-fashioned wood-framed TV in the living room corner, and his beige recliner is perfectly trained toward it, though Ralph gripes that the damn box is to blame for the lack of proper visiting between friends and neighbors these days.

I asked Ralph to tell me the story of his life in Utopia. He leaned back in his chair and described what it means to be an old-timer. Ralph grew up a half mile from where his recliner sits today. His father, a water-well driller, died when the boy was just two years old, leaving Ralph's mother, Ruth, alone with three young sons. She soon married the Methodist preacher, Chester Jackson, who stepped in as a devoted stepfather to Ralph and his brothers. Mr. Jackson ranched a hundred head of carefully bred cattle and kept a little dairy business on the side. As a child, Ralph would milk the cows twice a day and then peddle the raw milk from house to house. When he wasn't at school or milking or shucking pecans, he was palling around with his best friend, Kenneth, who lived just fifty yards down the street from him. Ralph figured the first television set came out when he and Ken were getting ready to graduate from high school, not that they saw one until years later. At eighteen years old, it was hard for the boys to imagine what a wider world might look like beyond Utopia's familiar views. "Leaving wasn't much of an option," he said.

But soon the Army came calling. At twenty years old, Ralph moved to Georgia for three months of basic training before deploying to Korea, where he spent two years alternately too cold or too hot, willing the days to blur by and the Army to set him free. "After Korea, I said that I was never going back around the hard road," said Ralph. "I was tired of running, and I wanted to go home."

When the boys got out of the service they returned to a town with few jobs available for ambitious men. Back then the average Utopian felt flush just two times a year—the hot seconds after selling their mohair and wool at market. When mohair started drifting out of fashion, those two reliable paydays went with it. I once asked a local how he made his living. "I don't," he dryly responded. When pressed, he said, "I piddle." Problem was, he said, that people weren't as good these days at living on a piddling salary. Somewhere along the way we'd made the mistake of believing we needed what we wanted.

After Ralph's stepfather droughted out of the cattle business during a brutal summer without rain, the man opened up a grocery. So when Ralph came home from Korea, he went to work as a butcher at Jackson's IGA Food Store. Kenneth was helping out his cousin J.R. down the street at Utopia's other grocery store. The boys would get together in the evening at the café, and Ralph told Kenneth that his stepdad was getting itchy to retire and they ought to consider the possibility of entering into a partnership. "Kenneth said, 'Well, we don't have no money, I don't know how we can do it,'" said Ralph. Mr. Jackson offered to shoulder the boys until they found their footing, and he lent them several thousand dollars with the agreement that they would pay it back with interest when they were able.

And so in April 1957, ignoring the town whispers that Kenneth was betraying family, the young men opened up the front door to the newly renamed Boyce and Davenport General Store. During their first week of operation, the young men wanted to imbue the place with a sense of dignity, so they wore black bow ties over crisp white cotton shirts and prim paper grocery caps. They were mercilessly teased, forced to politely endure all the wiseacres who reached over the counter and popped their ties. "If you're going to be in business in a small town you better have some broad shoulders," Ralph said. After a week of dressing up, they'd had enough of ties and settled on white aprons over pressed jeans and cowboy boots.

Kenneth was a genial man so loved and admired in Utopia that he is still called "Mayor" by most everyone. (Though he'll always be "Chief" to Ralph.) The two men complemented each other well—Kenneth the steady calm to Ralph's unpredictable storm. Ralph was always indefatigable when it came to work but given to short temper. The boys decided that for the sake of their young business Ralph ought to man the back of the store, handling the feed, fertilizer, and meat market, and Kenneth, sunny and unflappable, would run the front. So with one of his Lucky Strike cigarettes always burning in a nearby ashtray, Kenneth did all the bookwork and ordering and greeting of the customers. "When you walked into the store, Kenneth would greet you like you were the person he was hoping to see come through that door," said his wife, Joy, who took a summer job at the General Store working the cash register when she was just twenty-one years old. After a month of dates Ken put a ring on Joy's finger. Ralph stood up alongside the groom as his best man.

When Kenneth was in his early forties he was diagnosed with emphysema. His children, Kenneth Jr. and Jan, were just seven and four years old. For years he was in and out of hospitals, felled by multiple heart attacks. "Ralph came to the hospital just one time all those years Kenneth was in and we had to about put him down," said Joy. Ralph shoved his grief into more time at the store, working up to seventeen hours a day. Eventually Kenneth told his friend he wasn't ever going to get better and it wasn't fair for Ralph to be working so hard for the both of them. Ralph had no intention of staying in business without his best friend, so they worked out a deal to sell the store to Morris.

The day after the Boyce and Davenport changed hands, Ralph drove down in the morning with his grocer's apron still knotted at the waist. "It was delivery day," he remembered, "so I helped Morris put the groceries up and then I pitched in my apron and said, 'Well, there it is.'"

Kenneth died in 2001 at the age of sixty-eight. When asked what about his friend he most missed, Ralph opened and closed his mouth a few times, swallowing back a soggy bubble in the back of his throat. "I can't even describe," he finally said, looking off at his sleeping dog until he could trust his eyes to stop tearing.

When Kenneth died, the General Store shuttered for the day, as it used to any time a member of the Utopia community passed away. Ralph was a pallbearer at the funeral, though in the effusive gathering following the service he found himself unable to offer or accept any words of comfort. "He walked by and patted Kenneth Junior on the shoulder," said Joy, "and then he left." Ralph and Joy were never particularly close during all those years of the Boyce and Davenport. Neither of them was very good at sharing Kenneth. But since his friend's death Ralph has done his best to look after Joy, just like he promised he would. When she goes to visit her grandchildren in Fort Worth, it's Ralph who feeds her sheep.

The routine of early morning coffee started at the Boyce and Davenport, as Ralph and Kenneth were eager to lure in the ranchers so they could impress upon them the newest feeds and vaccinations before the sun rose. It wasn't long before the men in town started leaving their wives in bed, gathering in a half circle at the back of the store to share news of a sheep with a particularly bad case of sore mouth or the rising price of hay or the surprise bust-up of a marriage.

When I asked Ralph if I might join the men for coffee one day, he sat there dumbfounded a bit before saying, "Well . . . sure . . . you'd be welcome. They all might think it's a little different now, with you and all . . . being different." He scratched his forehead nervously. "A woman might pass through the store, but just to come and sit down and talk? Nope, that hasn't really happened much. But you just come and I'll see that they be nice."

The first morning I showed up for coffee, Morris looked at me like he didn't get the joke. I waved two sets of crossed fingers back at him and crept down the refrigerated foods aisle toward the coffeepots. The men all stared up at me a little blinky-eyed when I turned the corner into their den. Ralph, true to his word, broke the silence and jumped up from his chair to sling out an old stool from the meat market. I sat for a few minutes before risking to turn my back on them to pour myself some coffee, shakily tapping the instant creamer into my cup. Nobody did much talking. A few mornings later, I told the guys I'd seen a scorpion in the ranch house where I was staying and they laughed at my squirming. They started telling horrible stories about scorpions falling from the trees and biting people in the eyes. The morning after that, and every morning after, we talked about anything and everything, from the Iraq war to wild hogs, the only subject they could all ever agree on being that not one of them had any desire to ever set foot in New York City.

One of the network channels in Utopia inexplicably plays its New York affiliate's local news every night at ten o'clock. People in small-town America are used to getting their news and entertainment shoved at them through the lens of urban America, but nightly crime and weather reports for a faraway city are offensive. New York City—or their inflated idea of the city—is as easy to snub as a small town. On the surface, the respective lifestyles represent such inconceivable extremes. One of the old-timers told me he'd rather deal with a scorpion on his bed pillow than have to suffer through a day in Manhattan. They liked me well enough so they forgave me for calling New York home, reassuring one another that I wasn't really from the city since I didn't have a thick Scorsese movie accent. Each morning Ralph would point to the stool and tell me to go on, get up there and roost. He even gave me a nickname, Cricket, because he said I was always hopping everywhere.

Ralph takes his coffee in shifts. His first ends around six, when he goes home to feed Fudge. He'll return about thirty minutes later to enjoy another cup before quietly announcing that it's time to officially start his day. He'll return again after he goes for the mail at the post office, and this time Fudge will have accompanied him, happy to sit patiently outside in the back of Ralph's pickup while his master dawdles in the store. One morning, at the end of a shift, Ralph took a three-pack of Dial soap bars and a box of powdered laundry detergent off the shelf and held them to his side like a baby while he nodded good-bye to us lingerers.

"You going to bleach your shorts today?" asked one of the coffee drinkers. "Make 'em match your legs?"

Ralph wears his ball cap, a blue satin Bandera Rodeo jacket, and Wranglers when it's cool out, tissue-thin short-sleeved button-up shirts and khaki shorts during the long Texas summertime. The men all sputtered and shrieked the first time they heard that Ralph had gone and slid his legs into a pair of short pants. They were never supposed to know of his transgression. Ted had driven down to Ralph's house one day to pick up the keys and get instructions on feeding Fudge while Ralph and Jane were away visiting their daughter in Colorado. Turns out Ralph likes to wear shorts when he drives in the summer heat, and Ted, who already has one glass eye, nearly lost the sight in the other when he got a load of his friend's pale and wrinkly knees.

As the coffee drinkers explained, a man from these parts isn't considered dressed if he's not in his boots and britches, with a hat on his head and a pocketknife in his jeans. So Ralph couldn't have surprised Ted more if he'd shown up at the front door in a terrycloth bathrobe and just let the thing slide languidly to his feet in a soft heap. "He seen my legs, and I mean you couldn't have put it in the newspaper any quicker," said Ralph. "He must have drove a hundred miles an hour to get to town and tell everyone."

On this subject, even the most laconic of the group can be coaxed to contribute to the conversation, turning their mouths into their cups to hide their delighted grins, Hose letting loose with one of his infectious high-pitched giggles as the men start talking over one another.

"With them little legs, he look like a kildee bird standing on a watermelon rind!"

"You walk through prickly pear in shorts and you're going to get your legs all scratched up!"

"We need to get him out there and let him run that welding machine."

"Burn up the hair on them legs!"

"I run a chain saw in my shorts," Ralph calmly insisted.

John Hillis hooted. "Yeah, but hell, you're tough."

"If I knew for sure he had something on underneath," Milton leaned over and whispered, "I'd reach over and yank!"

Ralph, lacing his fingers and resting them in his lap, looking up at the paneled ceiling as if there might be more civilized company available to him in the cobwebs, is a man who can bear a good deal of teasing from his friends. "You'd be surprised how much cooler they are," he informed the coffee drinkers, who shook their heads in amused dismay.

Back when Ralph ran the store, if he'd ever shown up to work in a pair of shorts, he swears he'd have lost every last customer. That was before over half the store's business came from tourists and newcomers, strangers who themselves were likely showing off their knees. That was before a Wal-Mart and an H-E-B opened up fifty minutes away in larger towns and locals started abandoning the General Store to load up on cheaper supplies elsewhere.

"They should fly a Chinese flag in front of the Wal-Mart," Ralph grimly told the group.

"They changed the national bird, didn't they?" said Baby Ray, with a glint in his eye. "Instead of the bald eagle, it's a Wal-Mart bag. They're everywhere you look!"

Ralph nodded in agreement. "One in every tree, one on every fence."

Back when the General Store ruled, Ralph's customers wouldn't have stood for their grocer cutting up their Sunday meat in a pair of short pants. But when he retired in 1994, Ralph pulled off his leather-soled boots and slid his socks happily into a pair of black New Balance sneakers. Once Ted spread the news of his wearing shorts around the house, he figured he might as well embrace the scandal. So now, from May to October, Ralph torments the coffee drinkers with the sight of him humming to himself down the center aisle in a pair of tan shorts, the waistband pulled up high.

"You wear those to church?" one of the men asked Ralph, who stood there shamelessly holding his soap.

"Oh no," said Ralph. "But then I don't go to church."

An out-of-town evangelical preacher breezed into Utopia a few years back, his mouth watering when he discovered a nest of potential followers. He pounced on the coffee drinkers and started enthusiastically preaching the word of the Lord. "Now let me tell y'all about Jesus!" he began, his voice booming off the concrete floor. Now these are men who don't much like being lectured, especially by an outsider on a weekday morning when there's last night's Spurs game to discuss. Eventually a customer pulled the eager minister aside, warning him, "Feller, you got yourself the wrong crowd."

One morning a local preacher, a year into his three-year post in Utopia, showed up to coffee. The man had bounced among small-town Texas churches his whole preaching career and Utopia was his final post before retirement. He was the type of person suited to a life behind the pulpit, where he could talk for an hour to a captive audience without interruption, the Sunday parishioners good enough to smile at his windy jokes regardless of whether they occasionally fell flat.

The preacher's first mistake that morning was helping himself to one of the two aluminum chairs, a disruption to the routine's natural rhythms. He sat low in the seat, his rangy body slumped down so that his trousered legs stretched insouciantly across the floor. At one point he looked over his glasses at Ralph in his shorts and undulated his ropy arm out to point a finger at him.

"You know, I'm just like you, Ralph," he said cheerfully. That was his second mistake. Ralph stared straight ahead and uncrossed his legs, his hands starting to twist at his cup. "Yep, it's true," the preacher went on. "Somebody came to the door of my parsonage last week at about seven in the evening. So I go up there and answer the door in my T-shirt and bathing suit. That is the most comfortable thing in the world to wear, I swear. They said, 'Preacher, you goin' swimmin'?' Oh, I couldn't stop laughing, but what's a man to do in the Texas heat?"

Ralph started breathing a little hard through his nose. In the middle of the preacher's story he got out of his chair and nudged Milton to scoot over so he could join the men on the bench. Preacher kept on talking, about growing up on his father's small ranch up near Goliad, about grocery shopping in Goliad, about the cheese wheel at the old store in Goliad. Finally, he announced that what Morris really needed to do was put a round table here in the back of the Utopia General Store so the men could visit properly.

"I bet that's number one on his priorities," a coffee drinker said briskly into his cup.

"Though I'm afraid," the preacher continued, "he might put a picnic table in here and ain't none of us can lift our legs high enough to even get over the bench." He slapped his thigh and laughed loudly, and a few coffee drinkers nodded at him with pinched smiles. Ralph turned sideways and glared at Milton's shoulder.

Finally the preacher peeled himself out of his chair, tipping a rubbery finger from his forehead into the air at the fellows, and wandered up the center aisle. Ralph exhaled dramatically. "God, I thought he would never leave," he said. Just then the preacher made a lazy U up by the ladies' shampoo and returned to the group.

"I know you enjoy funny stories," he said to me. "Ask me why I'm limping?"

He proceeded to regale the crowd with a tale of waking with a start at three in the morning in desperate need of the bathroom, only to stub his toe on the old metal tub and topple in headfirst.

"That sounds like a personal problem to me," Ralph mumbled to himself, refusing to look back up from his lap until the preacher was clear out the front door. Milton shook his head, declaring the good preacher to be "one of these guys who walks in and the first time you see him you want to smack the hell out of him." His frank assessment might have startled some of the men, but everybody rumbled with laughter, Ralph loudest of all.

"I know I'm not supposed to be going on this way, but that's just the way I'm built, I guess," said Ralph. "Too old to change now. The only good thing is he don't come down here very often. Okay, doo-do-doo," he hummed to himself, gazing around the store. "I'm going to have a cucumber sandwich for lunch today so I'm going to get me some low-fat Miracle Whip. See you, Cricket! Behave yourself!"

Seeing the preacher so summarily dismissed, I realized again what great luck it was that these men had let me into their circle. My God, we had some laughs. Of course, there was a flip side to the coffee drinkers' tremendous appeal. Sandwiched in there with their wit and ruggedness and community devotion was a reflexive suspicion of anyone who didn't share their background. There is perhaps no comfort zone deeper and narrower than that of an old-timer in a small town. The possibility of varied experience—racial, religious, aesthetic, geographic—is too easily written off as evidence of weirdness or corruption. It's hard to admit curiosity about a world you've long since decided can't compare to home.

Sometimes our conversations came out in spits and dribs, the men insisting that nothing goes on in this town, you've haven't missed a thing, this is Utopia, girl, nothing here ever changes. One morning, while the men were watching a one-winged queen ant spiral in a slow, confused circle around the floor at their feet, Ralph broke the silence. "People always say nothing changes," he said with some exasperation. "Everything changes. You just don't always know it when it's happening." The guys harumphed. Milton picked up the drifting bug between his fingers and threw it over his shoulder onto the floor of the meat market. "Got to have a little seasoning in there," he told me with a wink.

THE CAFÉ

Most everyone eats at least one meal a day at the Lost Maples Café. They might grumble some about the quality of the food, or wince when their shirtsleeves stick to jelly stains on the table, but still they go. On Sunday mornings, people arrive in shifts set to church bells. First come the members of the Church of Christ, then it's a dead heat between the Baptists and the Methodists. The Living Waters congregation likes to worship long and hard, so the evangelicals have to take tables where they can find them. But no matter where everybody comes from, at lunchtime they crowd together into the café to celebrate cheeseburgers and buttermilk pie. Tacy Redden, who along with her husband, Rusty, owns the Lost Maples, remembered a New York food critic who some years ago breezed through the front door to sample some small-town fare. "Well, he didn't like it here," reported Tacy with a raspberry sound of dismissal. She liked to tell herself that his real grievance was with their lack of pasta on the menu.

In the evenings, business slows and the waitresses sit sideways at a table by the cash register, their blue-jeaned knees facing out to the dining room while they pull on Marlboro Reds and sip from cans of Coke and Red Flash. Sometimes they get to good-natured bitching, about bad tippers and being on their feet all day. They're receptacles for news of the town's various dramas and intrigues, so it's no wonder that they specialize in the collection and hasty distribution of good dirt. It is not unusual for a local to bang in the front door and pronounce, "Let's hear some gossip and slander!" A yellow warning sign stands on the front counter, by the glass canister of straws and the bowls of half-and-half tubs:

CAUTION
GOSSIP TABLE
LYING IS
NOT PERMITTED
AFTER
7:00 AM

When strangers come into the café everybody gives them a thorough once-over, the waitresses shamelessly speculating aloud to one another about who they are and where they come from. Customers here have been broken down by the ladies into four distinct groups: turtleheads, tourists, locals, and regulars.

The turtleheads, so called because of the plastic helmets the bicyclists wear like crowns, are the crowd who zoom through town on the weekends, slurping water from their plastic sport bottles. Utopians have a beef with turtleheads for a lot of reasons, not the least of which being their insistence on riding shoulder to shoulder on these dangerous roads. A trailer will come roaring around the bend and have to accordion in on itself trying to avoid a bicycle's back tire. Still, Utopians would probaby have a higher tolerance for these sunscreened out-of-towners if they would only rethink their attire. "Uh-oh, look at the pokey peter pants," one waitress said as a man in shiny red and yellow shorts walked up to the café's front door. "What is it with the damn spandex?" an old-timer agonized, shaking his head clear of the sight, glaring back down at his eggs.

Tourists are another breed altogether. They're easy to spot, in their slacks and tucked-in tropical-flowered buttoned shirts. From the first weekend of November through the first weekend of January, the earnest birders and leaf gazers are replaced by boisterous clumps of hunters swathed in camouflage. "They'll just be going to spend the afternoon in a box stand with doe piss all over them, and still they come in with their camouflage," smirked one man. "All of them, the wife, the kids, Grandma—their faces all painted up for the day."

A girl here knows what to expect when she waits on a local. Regulars are even better. She knows when to expect them. Regulars roll in for dinner at what the waitresses refer to as "dark thirty," half past whenever the sun has gone down. They stick to their preferred meals, a half plate of nachos, say, with heavy jalapenos, or two chicken enchiladas with chopped onions on the side. Sometimes the waitresses think that the regulars' orders should just go up on the chalkboard along with the daily special. The café might be offering carne asada, rice, beans, salad, and dessert for $5.50, but a customer like Terry Jo will always order the Terry Jo Special: a hamburger cut into four pieces with a toothpick in each quarter, french fries and onion rings on the side. Terry has been suffering bad from Alzheimer's for a while now, so it helps that the waitresses know what she likes to eat for dinner.

J. R. Davenport used to be one of six regulars who would gather at the café at ten every morning to sip slowly on coffee and visit with one another. Most of those men have passed on now, including J.R. He was such a fixture at the Lost Maples, his presence such a dependable pleasure, that Tacy had the wooden chair he always sat in bolted to the ceiling. She hung his coiled rope over the left chair back, his walking cane over the right, and slung two of his lucky horseshoes over the chair's bottom rung. "Reserved for J.R. + Cronies," the hand-markered sign on the cushioned seat reads. Some things in this world are sacred. J.R.'s place at the table is one of them.

CHAPTER 2

Proud Mother of a
U.S. Army Soldier

Kathy Wiekamp was one of the café's best waitresses, chatty and familiar, tossing back snappy one-liners as she tacked around the tables refilling coffee cups and plastic glasses of tea. She was cute enough to flirt with but too tough to ever give a hard time to. The older regulars teased and asked after her as if she were their own, and she did the same for any of the kids who came through the café door.

Ralph dubbed Kathy "Carrot Top" because of her bright red hair, which she wears straight to her shoulders, her bangs and large blue eyes giving her forty-five-year-old face a pleasing hint of girlish mischief. Women in Texas seem to fall into two categories: those who accessorize and those who do not. Kathy never did see the reason to fuss over an outfit. She wore the same T-shirts and jeans to work at the café as she did when she made dinner at home for all the men in her family. Kathy is ruggedly handsome, her creamy Irish face free of makeup and her long arms and legs bruised from helping her husband, Randy, net deer for his whitetail breeding business.

Life at the café was a family affair. Kathy's mother, Jackie, works in the back a few mornings a week. Throughout high school Kathy's four sons reported for duty, pocketing the minimum wage for a little extra gas and beer money. Jeff, Kathy's oldest, spent evenings and weekends washing dishes and prepping food. Everybody loved Jeff, even though he kept to himself, working with his head down, smiling at but rarely contributing to the waves of conversation bubbling over the hiss and pop of burgers and eggs on the grill. "We were always teasing him, poor thing," said Tacy. "Our big joke was when he made chicken salad sandwiches—we always have chicken salad on Saturdays—he would chop apples to put in the salad. Well, he would never peel off the Washington label, so whenever you bit into your sandwich you'd get a little bit of sticker in your mouth! And you knew that Jeff was back there daydreaming again."

The Wiekamp brothers were always quiet around adults. Jeff was shy and serious and handsome, with dark hair and high cheekbones and the sinewy limbs of a boy not completely grown into his body. Josh is two years younger than Jeff, Jared two years behind Josh, and, two years younger still, rounding out their tribe, is the bright-blue-eyed baby of the family, Joey. The boys traveled in a pack, always together, a clump of good-looking, bored, thick-lashed Irish Catholic brothers, and they were known to raise hell in and around town. "Why there wasn't a jail cell that said 'Wiekamps' I have no idea," Kathy told me, trying and failing to hide a grin, tickled by the memory of behavior that had both enraged and amused her when her sons were younger. "Why I didn't have a parking space with my name written on it so I could just pull up and get my kids at the jailhouse in Uvalde I have no idea. Because my kids were *awful.*"

Kathy is still discovering fresh details about the trouble her sons got into when they were teenagers. She found out recently that when she would leave them alone at the house in the afternoon to run errands,

Joey, the shrimp in a sea of testosterone, would inevitably end up tied to a chair or duct-taped to the back wall of a bedroom closet. Jeff would have been put in charge, left with a checklist of chores that needed doing before their mother returned. Instead he would threateningly line up knives on the kitchen counter, daring his brothers to disturb him, before swan-diving onto the sofa in front of the television. One afternoon Kathy came home to find a curious hole in her bathroom wall. The boys, after a quick glance to the counter to make sure Jeff had remembered to stash the steak knives, all shrugged, pleading ignorance, without taking their eyes off the television. They would rough one another up until there was blood and bruises and battered walls, but they would never rat a brother out.

Kathy recently found an old videotape tucked away on a back shelf that showed a ten-year-old Josh reaching into the refrigerator while Jared let the camera roll. Josh danced around on her TV screen, egging on his brothers to dare him to drink a beer. Kathy, choking on her afternoon glass of tea as she watched her little boy start glugging, called up her now grown son and announced to Josh that he was retroactively grounded.

The Wiekamp boys were restless. They drove their GMC trucks fast and stayed out late and were on intimate terms with the initials DWI. Kids tend to drink early and hard in Utopia, often on their parents' property. Every few years there will be a fatal drunk-driving accident and the community weeps together over the wretched loss. Despite the routine tragedies, the school had never organized any serious campaign against drinking and driving. The twenty-mile beer run to the beverage barns in nearby Sabinal or Tarpley remains a local teenage rite of passage.

If kids in Utopia liked to party, the Wiekamps were happy to play host. Every year Kathy and Randy left town for an annual deer association convention. Randy is small and wiry and stoic like his sons, with his own GMC truck and a similar taste for Miller Lite out of a bottle. "The boys are talkative if they're drunk," said Kathy. "Randy doesn't talk at all. We could go four hundred miles and he wouldn't say anything." When their parents went away for the weekend, the Wiekamp boys hosted all-night blowouts where girls from surrounding towns got smashed and ground their hips on top of Kathy's coffee table.

The brothers were the first in town to peroxide their hair blond—the only artificial color the school would let you walk through the doors with—and experiment with hair gel. They wore chains with paint-chipped dollar symbol medallions and their pants sagging low. Jeff tattooed WIEKAMP down his forearm and got a huge Celtic cross on his ropy left bicep. He bought a new truck and the brothers installed a powerful stereo system so they could drive down Main Street with the bass cranked so high that Eminem blasting from the speakers could shake a man's cowboy hat right off his head.

Nobody in the Wiekamp family had ever gone on to college, and Jeff didn't know the first thing about applying for financial aid. When he was in his senior year, Army recruiters dropped by on one of their frequent runs through town and delivered the usual brash and breathless pitch of courage and adventure. "You all live in a small town," the friendly man would tell the classroom full of kids who had complained of little else their entire lives. "Do you want to just end up like one of those guys who hangs around at the gas station after graduation? Who keeps showing up to the basketball games in his letter jacket? Who doesn't have anything to talk about with the kids who come home from college on Christmas break except for old times?"

Jeff enlisted not because he was hot to serve his country but because this was the only way he knew to leave Utopia. "He was getting out of here," said Kathy, whose younger brother and brother-in-law also enlisted at the time. She remembered the day not long after his high school graduation when the recruiter drove up to the house to escort Jeff to basic training. "I can see him walking down the driveway," she said. "He got in the car and didn't look back, didn't even tell his brothers bye. He was just going."

Josh was the next to fall into the Army's back-clapping embrace. His grades in high school were passing, but sitting at a desk left him feeling antsy. Josh told me he signed up because of pride in his big brother and because, in the wake of 9/11, he felt that his country was under attack. Kathy barked with laughter when she heard her son's

claims of inspiration. The truth, she guessed, was that her second oldest only signed up to save himself from her wrath one evening. Utopia's
constable had just busted Josh for driving drunken screwy louies in the
field across from Joy Davenport's house, shredding the grass and leaving deep tire tracks in the mud while the rest of town slept. When
Kathy got wind of what her son had done, she spent a long evening
fuming on the sofa waiting for Josh to return home so she could rip
him open.

"So he comes in and I told him to sit and I proceeded to start ream-
ing him one," said Kathy. "About three minutes into the conversation
he says," her voice slipping into an imitation of her son's soft slurry
purr, "'Mom, Mom, I need discipline, I think I'm going to join the
Army. I need discipline. I need direction in my life.'" Kathy laughed
loudly at the memory, brushing her bangs off her forehead in mock exasperation. "He's just bullshitting me 'cause he's trying to get out of
trouble, but then he ended up going ahead and joining anyways."

While Jeff was able to walk away from his family without looking
back, Josh was barely out the front door before he started planning for
his parents to visit him on base. "Josh does not like to leave home,"
said Kathy. "I can remember when he was in high school—he wouldn't
spend the night out. He just always wanted to be home. But then again
there was always the four of them. There was no need to ever leave."
The Christmas after Josh graduated from Utopia School, he found
himself on a plane heading over to Iraq as part of the first wave of Operation Iraqi Freedom, choking suddenly on all the anxiety and am-
bivalence that must rise in the throat of any young person suddenly
looking down upon a war zone. "Maybe staying in town working at
the café wouldn't have been so bad after all," Josh remembered thinking as he touched down in a country he hadn't before had any reason
to look for on a map.

Jared was a great athlete in school, a star on Utopia's basketball
team, and a diligent student whose sweetness and charisma effortlessly
charmed his teachers. His brothers had pegged him as the nerd in the
bunch, the first Wiekamp who would go on to college. They believed
the Army would have to wait two years for Joey before it hooked an-

other brother. But then Jared waffled his senior year, unsure what to do with himself, and Kathy finally lost her patience with all the hand wringing. "I said, 'I don't care what you do, but make a decision already,'" she said. "'Because if you want to go to college, I need to start learning about the financial aid stuff.'" So, the path well trod in front of him, Jared opted to follow his brothers into the Army. At Utopia's graduation ceremony, Jeff, in full dress uniform, presented Jared with an oversized check for $77,000 that his little brother could theoretically collect and use toward college after he completed his six-year Army commitment. Just before graduation, Jared had fallen in love with a sweet classmate named Meagen and the two teenagers married before he left for basic training. In their wedding photos, Jared's bride wore braces.

At Jared's modest wedding Jeff introduced his own new wife to his family. Ashley, a Korean American girl who was beautiful and wild, with long, thick hair and enough tattoos on her lithe body to rival any Wiekamp, had been stationed at Fort Campbell in Kentucky with Jeff. Ashley had been adopted by two Americans as a baby. Her mother had died when she was in the eighth grade and her relationship with her father was strained. Jeff and Ashley got married by the justice of the peace on base without telling Jeff's family or Ashley's father. She was thrilled to suddenly find herself welcomed into the Wiekamps' raucous fold. The honeymoon was brief. Within a few short months the young couple had to tell each other goodbye. Jeff was being sent to Afghanistan, Ashley to Iraq.

With her sons overseas, Kathy never turned off her cellphone. "I have three boys in the service," Kathy told everybody at the café, "and if one of them calls me from Iraq I'm answering the phone." She balanced orders of chicken fingers and chalupas on her arms with her phone pressed between ear and shoulder, shouting into the receiver for her children to speak up.

Every day Kathy showed up to work in a different patriotic shirt, like the white homemade sweatshirt that proclaimed I AM THE PROUD

MOTHER OF A U.S. ARMY SOLDIER from within a border of hand-stenciled chili peppers. She wore her heart-shaped flag earrings and eventually got her ears quadruple-pierced so she could wear red, white, and blue cubic zirconia studs. A cherished memory is the time her boys arranged to come home on leave at the same time. One by one they walked through the café's door, staggering out the surprise, and into her arms. They came dressed up in their uniforms because they knew how much it touched their mother to see them wearing their military finery.

One afternoon Jeff called Kathy at the café with news from Afghanistan: He had volunteered to be a crew chief. Jeff had trained to be a crew mechanic, working behind the wire on base, where Kathy wanted all her boys to remain. But now he told her that the Army was honoring his request and enrolling him in school to become a doorman. "And I thought, Oh, the Army is so fricking stupid," said Kathy. "They're sending him to school to learn how to open and close a fricking door. I kept telling everyone that. It was about a week before a customer was kind enough to tell me that he wasn't going to be a *doorman*. He was going to be a door *gunner*."

Sergeant Jeffery Wiekamp, having already completed a tour of duty in both Afghanistan and Iraq, was twenty-three years old, married to Ashley for less than a year, when he was sent back to Kunar Province in Afganistan as the chief of a six-man crew on a Chinook helicopter with the call sign Colossal 31. "He always wanted to fly," Kathy said, looking at pictures on her kitchen table of Jeff standing next to his helicopter in his flight gear, holding his headset microphone to his mouth, his blue eyes steady and alert. "He was so happy up there in the air."

Randy was at home one evening watching Fox News—the only network they could count on to run encouraging stories about America's fight against terror—when he noticed a blurb on the crawl. 10 AMERICAN SOLDIERS KILLED, HELICOPTER CRASH IN AFGHANISTAN. He didn't say anything to Kathy, not wanting to worry her unnecessarily, and when the phone didn't ring, he allowed himself to unclench. A few days later, in the cruel early hours of a Sunday morning, Kathy was woken up by a two A.M. phone call from the Uvalde County Sheriff's Department.

"I have some gentlemen who would like to speak with you," said the somber policeman, who asked for the best route to the Wiekamp ranch. Kathy curtly gave him some directions, instructing the man to turn right on her county road, wind up the hill, and look for the large fence festooned with yellow ribbons. When she hung up the phone she threw off the bedcovers, yanked on some clothes, and stomped across the house to Joey's bedroom, where her youngest son lay sleeping with his mouth open.

"I woke him up and just started screaming at him," said Kathy. "'What the hell did you do this time!?' It didn't even cross my mind that there could be another reason a policeman was coming to see me in the middle of the night. Never even occurred to me." When she saw headlights snaking up their long driveway, she pulled some sneakers over her bare feet and went outside to talk to the cops. "I walked outside, a man was standing in front of the headlights of his car, and he said, 'I'm from the United States Army.' I blacked out after he said that and started screaming and screaming, going to the ground. Then I started yelling about what the other men with him were wearing. If they were wearing camos, then my boy was just hurt. But if they were in dress greens I knew he was dead. I kept asking what they were wearing but then the chaplain came up and I saw the men in their dress greens and, well, that took care of that." One of her sons was dead, and she knew instinctively that it was Jeff.

The men started asking for Randy, taking a few steps toward the house. Kathy waved them back, warning the men that Jeff's black German shepherd, Riley, who they'd been taking care of while he was deployed, wouldn't let them pass. "If you think you all can get through my son's dog, then go for it, but I don't know what he'll do."

Kathy got to her feet, her legs like heavy, wet clay beneath her. She stumbled back into her house and took down from the wall her favorite picture of Jeff, preening and proud in his dress greens the day he graduated from basic training, and went to wake her husband. The two of them, poor Randy barely conscious, blinking and wiping his brow as he tried to absorb his wife's words, went back outside to listen to the men complete their terrible ritual. Kathy asked them all once more if they were absolutely sure her son was dead. They nodded sadly, and asked if she had any other questions. "Okay," Kathy said coldly, "tell me one reason why you had to ruin my life at two-thirty in the morning? My life is over, so why couldn't you have at least waited until the sun came up?"

After the men left, Kathy went to wake up Joey again, this time her voice a hoarse murmur rather than a holler. Joey called his girlfriend, who was at the house within the hour. She hugged Kathy and went to lie down with Joey behind his closed bedroom door.

Kathy had horrible hours of darkness to survive before dawn finally broke. She dragged the vacuum cleaner out of the closet and started furiously straightening up, telling her husband, "You know what it's going to be like in three or four hours when people find out. The town will show up." Years ago, they'd had a fire that blazed through one room. The house had been spared, but soot had gotten into everything. Friends told the family to bag up all of their belongings and drop them off at the General Store. Within days, everybody in town had carted home a bag at a time, and returned everything washed and neatly folded. If people rallied around their family like that after a simple house fire, then news of Jeff's death would have them all surging up the Wiekamp hill by sunrise.

Randy finally persuaded Kathy to stop with the dishes and come back to bed with him for a few minutes. She climbed in next to her husband, stared at the ceiling, and cried. When the sun finally made its meek appearance, Kathy called two of her brothers and her sister. She called Jared, who was stationed in Kentucky with his now pregnant wife. Josh was scheduled to be on a plane from Iraq, coming home from his fourth deployment to what was supposed to be a joyful celebration. He was the brother everyone worried would take the news of Jeff's death the hardest, and Kathy thought she could at least wait to tell him once he was safely back in the United States. She didn't know that his unit's departure had been delayed at the last minute and that he was still on the ground.

Ashley and Josh were deployed to the same base in Iraq, and would occasionally run into each other at the mess hall. So when Ashley, having just heard that her husband had been killed, was convinced by some worried girlfriends to go get something to eat, she assumed Josh was already on a plane home. When she bumped into him crossing the compound, Josh lit up at the sight of his sister-in-law, who was forced to choke out the news. Broken, they left Iraq together, Ashley having attached herself to Josh's unit and side.

Back at home, Kathy got out of bed and called the café. Rusty answered and Kathy brusquely spat out the news to her boss that Jeff had been killed in the line of duty. Rusty hung up and immediately mobilized Kathy's friends. Valerie and Rhonda, the coffee drinker Milton's daughter and daughter-in-law, rushed right over. Kathy crumpled at the sight of her friends in their SUVs, passenger seats loaded with still-warm casseroles. A couple of years earlier, Valerie and Rhonda had each lost a teenage child in a freak car accident just outside Utopia, the grief over which buckled the whole town. "They were the hardest for me to see," said Kathy, "because I thought it was bringing it all back for them. I now knew exactly what they had gone through." That afternoon Valerie pulled Kathy aside and looked at her with loving firmness. "It doesn't matter what you do," Valerie told her friend, "or how you do it. Don't worry about entertaining, don't worry about anything. Whatever you're doing at the moment to get through this is what you're supposed to do."

Every time a new set of friends poured in the front door, red-eyed, hands to their sagging mouths, they'd take Kathy by the shoulders. Everyone stared hard into her eyes and told her what a brave, honorable man Jeff had been. Kathy just kept saying thank you, thank you. "Thank you, but this sucks, this sucks, this sucks," said Kathy. "It got to be my favorite phrase. This sucks. That about summed it up."

She was worried about Randy, her quiet husband, who in the best of times disliked crowds and had long suggested that Utopia may have loved Kathy and the boys but it had little interest in him. All of Randy's adult life he'd worked brutal hours, leaving at six in the morning to go work on out-of-town ranches and not returning home until seven or eight o'clock in the evening. He always arrived late to the boys' ball games, and then he lingered on the sidelines away from the chatty clump of his wife and her friends on the bleachers. The only time he ever had conversations with people in town seemed to be when it was about the boys, and usually after they'd been screwing around and had pissed somebody off. So on this painful afternoon, Kathy was sure Randy would shrink from the nervous attentions and remembrances and slip out the door. She expected him to seek a private, sandy-eyed refuge on top of their hill and not come down again until the house was empty. "And I watched him," said Kathy, "and it was about an hour and a half and I think he finally realized, 'I can either embrace this or I can run.' I think it broke down a lot of barriers. It got to where he would hug people before they even went to hug on him."

The Wiekamps still hadn't been told why Jeff's Chinook had crashed, and the wait for his body to be returned home chewed at their nerves. Josh got a four-week leave from his unit, and later received approval to extend it for another two weeks. He said that he coped by staying drunk that whole time home, worrying Kathy when he insisted that it should have been him who died.

Joey only had a few weeks left of his senior year but he just quit going to school, sleeping in his dark cocoon of a room until late in the afternoon. His teachers passed him without forcing him to take his final exams, and his class came out on the school bus one afternoon to pay their respects. They presented him with a token of their united affection, a small cross on a delicate chain. Joey did attend the prom, even dancing awkwardly and posing for pictures after it was announced that he had been voted the senior class king. And on graduation day he walked across the portable stage set up under a basketball net to collect his diploma in front of the sniffling crowd.

All along Kathy was forced to endure terrible updates about Jeff's body. "Each time we got to a point where we were okay and handling things," she said, "I'd get the phone call that said, 'Okay, he's out of

Iraq and getting his autopsy,' and then, 'Okay, now he's coming home.' But I just thought, 'No, no, I'm not ready. I don't want him to come like this.'"

On May 18, 2006, a white-hot Texas morning, the entire Wiekamp family—Josh in full uniform, Jared kicking himself for forgetting an element of his dress greens, forced to settle instead on his fatigues—stood on the tarmac at the San Antonio airport watching soldiers unload Jeff's coffin from the plane. Inside, travelers lined up behind the windows and watched the military ceremony with their foreheads pressed to the glass. "Ashley was standing next to me," said Kathy, who before Jeff's death had only met her daughter-in-law that once at Jared's wedding. "I was fixing to lose it when she started to drop. I grabbed her and lifted her up and I said, I was kind of mean but I didn't know any other way to put starch back in her legs, so I said, 'Stand there and honor him. You *honor* him.'"

When the Wiekamps left the funeral home in Sabinal, beginning the twenty-mile procession back to Utopia, they were led by a string of police cars in front and one in the rear. "And we're all sitting in the limo going, 'Jeff would hate this, all these cop cars,'" Kathy said with a sad laugh.

When the limo rolled down Ranch-to-Market Road 187 into Utopia, every child in school, from pre-K through the twelfth grade, stood silently on the sides of the road holding up American flags. The notice board in the town square was wrapped in ribbons, its simple block letters promising WIEKAMP FAMILY YOU HAVE OUR PRAYERS AND SYMPATHY. Toddlers wearing nothing but bathing suits and Velcro-tabbed sneakers held their parents' hands and on whispered commands gave pudgy-fingered salutes. Tearful mothers of all the local young men and women who were stationed overseas in Iraq and Afghanistan held their breath as they watched the limo pass. And the dozens of old veterans who call Utopia home held their caps and cowboy hats to their hearts, their naked foreheads exposed to the merciless sun.

At the café, Tacy and Rusty hung up a framed picture of Jeffery on the wall next to J. R. Davenport's chair. He's posed in front of the flag, handsome in the uniform his mother always liked to see him wear. On

Jeffery's grave site, which Kathy keeps lovingly decorated with artificial gerber daisies and blue hydrangeas and a silver angel floating in the center of a rusted metal cross, someone placed a peeling laminated card bearing the Soldier's Creed on the mound of red dirt:

I WILL ALWAYS PLACE THE MISSION FIRST
I WILL NEVER ACCEPT DEFEAT
I WILL NEVER QUIT
I WILL NEVER LEAVE A FALLEN COMRADE

Kathy still doesn't know who put the card there, but the gesture gave her some real comfort, knowing that other people in town recognized her son's goodness and courage. But she still didn't know how he died.

Ashley lost her husband a month shy of what would have been their first wedding anniversary. She had her own favorite picture of Jeff, taken on their one trip together to visit Jeff's hometown. She had gotten lost in Utopia, confused about how to find her way back to her in-laws' ranch, and called Jeff on her cellphone. She asked that he come meet her at the school parking lot so that he could lead her back home. When Jeff arrived to the rescue, he leaned into the passenger window of his wife's truck, flexing his left bicep with a roguish grin. He wore a white tank top, and the Celtic cross tattooed on his arm shone from the flash of his bemused wife's camera.

The Saturday after the funeral, the brothers and Ashley drove to a tattoo parlor in Uvalde. Jeff had had WIEKAMP inked down his left forearm, so Josh got his brother's call sign, COLOSSAL 31, tattooed in the same place. Over his heart Josh got a replica of Jeff's cross, hung now with intricately detailed Kevlar and an image of his brother's dog tags. Above the cross, Josh asked the shop owner to tattoo IN LOVING MEMORY OF SGT. JEFFERY WIEKAMP—7 AUG. 1982–5 MAY 2006. Jared and Joey got the same tattoo, but when Ashley sat down in the chair for hers, she was inconsolable. There were signs that customers shouldn't drink during the procedure but the owner took pity and sent the boys to get the young widow a bottle of vodka.

Months later the Army finally gave the Wiekamps an official account of how Jeff had died. Originally, the family had been told they'd have an official explanation by June, but the meeting kept getting postponed. There were nine other families to meet with before the Army finally invited the Wiekamps to Fort Campbell, where Ashley was stationed. That September morning, after five minutes of listening to some men in uniform piece together what happened on that Afghan hillside, Ashley stood up and left the room. She was unable to listen to the banal circumstances of her husband's death spoken aloud.

The men painstakingly detailed their theory that Jeff's CH-47 Chinook had crashed when the pilot was attempting his first nighttime landing during what was supposed to be a routine evacuation. The pilot had mistaken some burning trash embers from a nearby garbage pile for enemy fire. After having been shot at just the previous day, he panicked and bucked his helicopter in the air. When he tried to land again, his rotor clipped a tree and snapped. The Chinook couldn't right itself, tumbling with its crew down the side of a mountain. Six aircrew members on board died, as well as four soldiers on the ground. The Wiekamps left Fort Campbell with shrunken hearts.

Kathy was in so much pain, going over and over her last conversation with Jeff in her head. He had called her on the phone while she was at work, and asked his mother to send another one of her elaborate care packages. "And then there was silence," she said. "He couldn't talk about certain things. You didn't know what to say. So I was like, 'Jeff, I'm here working, I got things to do.' And I cut the conversation short. But how was I to know?"

After his death, Kathy quit her job at the café. She didn't have any energy left for small talk. She threw herself instead into raising baby whitetail deer at home, bottle-feeding them in pens the people of Utopia helped her and Randy build on their twenty-one acres. "It gave me something to focus on and a reason to get out of bed, which I have to have," said Kathy. "Because, yes, there are moments when I think of just driving myself into a pole." She named all the gangly fawns, fuss-

ing over them and holding their wriggling bodies close and making sure
they grew up healthy and strong. When they were big enough they'd be
released onto hunting ranches to fend for themselves.

In the evenings, Kathy stopped watching even Fox News, unable to
hear reports of a war that showed no sign of ending when she still had
two boys in uniform. She read more romance novels and started playing games on the computer, anything that would keep her mind from
spinning. She lost whatever taste she had had for alcohol, nervous that
her emotions would creep scarily upon her if she were to relinquish any
shred of control. When friends told her they didn't know what to do or
say to ease her pain, Kathy told them to quit wondering. "You guys,
there's absolutely nothing you can say to make me feel better, and
there's nothing you could say to make me feel worse. Nothing is going
to make the pain go away."

Growing up, Kathy was the oldest of six siblings. She was eighteen
when her baby brother, Steven, a proud Army lifer who threatened to
go AWOL for Jeff's funeral, was born. Her job, from a young age, has
been to take care of everybody around her. But privately she wondered
if she'd ever stop feeling like bits of her would scatter if the slightest
breeze blew her way. Kathy had been the mother of four beautiful sons,
and now she felt her heart stop pumping whenever strangers asked her
how many children she had.

Now her remaining sons were once again scattered, Josh back to
Fort Carson in Colorado Springs and Jared to Fort Campbell in Kentucky. Joey, out of high school and unsure what to do with the rest of
his life, the Army no longer sounding like such a great deal, retreated
back into the bedroom his brothers used to lock him in as a boy.

ERMA'S BEAUTY SHOP

They call her Erma the Butcher. Because if she gets a head of long hair in her hands, she'll just start whacking. There used to be a man's ponytail nailed up on her shop's white walls, fair warning to the stragglyhaired who stopped in looking for a trim. You could sit down in front of one of her two cutting mirrors, side slots crowded with pictures of Utopia's babies and grandbabies, and pull tenderly at your ends, murmuring that all you wanted was a little taken off the bottom. But there is an inch and then there is an Erma inch. "When she cuts my hair," said one man, with a tremble in his voice, "she just peels it off."

Erma Schaefer has short, thick, permed strawberry-blond hair and peachy skin. She wears cosmetically tinted glasses and sherbet-colored smocks, tight blue jeans over her sturdy legs. Years ago Erma's mother paid for her daughter to attend a nine-month course at Audy and Joyce's Beauty College in San Antonio, and after Erma graduated she opened her shop. The business of beauty runs in the family. Her mother, a woman of much-admired sophistication, used to run the Charm Beauty Shop out of the building that's now home to the justice of the peace (who happens to be Erma's cousin by marriage). "The Chaaahm Beauty Shop," said Erma, drawling out the word with her pinky in the air. "That was so my mother. It couldn't have just been the Utopia Beauty Shop. It couldn't have been the Curl Up and Dye Shop."

The sign in the front curtained window of Erma's white trailer is always turned to OPEN, no matter if Erma is at home asleep in bed. The twenty-by-fifteen-foot trailer has a wooden ramp leading up to the screen door for all the grandmothers and great-grandmothers who are her main customers. The girls in town go to salons in larger towns or to the malls in San Antonio. "Any excuse to get out of Utopia," said Erma, who remembers well what it was like being a teenager in a small town.

She charges ten dollars for a haircut, fifteen for a shampoo and set, and fifty for a permanent. The last time she raised her prices was in 1999, after Erma told her customers that she could either charge more or shut down the shop. The brown wooden trailer on the other side of Main Street, with an American flag waving out front and BARBER SHOP scrawled hastily in black paint above the door, is cheaper. The man there, who drives the mail route in the mornings and opens up for business after lunch, charges only eight dollars for a trim. He caters to the men in town but is rumored to be something of a 9/11 conspiracy theorist and can be hard to pin down for an appointment, so a few of his clients have started drifting timidly over to Erma's.

"Some men are pretty shy when they come in that door," Erma said with her raspy laugh, thickened by a lifelong affair with Doral cigarettes. "It's like a ladies' restroom. They'll say, 'Is my wife in there?' before they admit they've come for themselves." The men slide in the door, bury their heads in one of the several copies of *Bassin'* magazine that Erma keeps on the rack, above the Schwan's food delivery catalog and the fraying hardbound copy of *Hairstyles for Real People* left over from 1982. When word gets out that a man had a meeting with the Butcher, he'll get some funny looks from the old-timers, who titter and tease, "Well, sister, did you get a manicure too?"

Erma has three turquoise and teal vinyl seats where women in loose blouses and slim-toed loafers sit cozily under old-fashioned dryers, the papery blue-veined skin between the hem of their pants and the top of their socks exposed. Meanwhile Erma holds court, laughing and cracking wise with her colleague, Rosella. On a Friday afternoon, the two talked about a particular breed of sensitive client, the man fretting over his bald spot. "I always just tell them, 'God gave men that aren't good-looking their hair,'" said Erma. Rosella, a finger tucked under the wet gray curls of her one o'clock, waved her scissors at her audience of two under the dryers. "Doesn't take much to puff up a man, does it, girls?" A Friday beauty appointment is something of a status symbol in town. "It means a woman has *standing,*" said one of her regulars, who herself has had the same Friday appointment for the last fifteen years.

When Erma was between clients, she rehashed some of the town news. "Did you hear about old R.C.?" she said, clucking in sympathy. "He showed up for Sunday school on a Saturday." Her white sneakers padding noiselessly on the linoleum floor, she busied herself tidying up the shop, then she slumped down on one of her cutting chairs and palmed the splayed spine of her Anita Shreve paperback. "Oh shoot," said Erma, looking over at the empty coffeepot resting unplugged on a side table by the dryers. "I never did get that coffee started for Lahoma and she'll be here any minute."

CHAPTER 3

The Land Tells You
What to Do

Colter Padgett and his best friend, Grant Potter, were getting out of town. It was Friday night and Colter sat idling in his old white Chevy Blazer outside his friend's trailer house. The driver's side looked like it was bleeding, painted a blotchy red from a crude repair job after a deer slammed broadside into him. Grant grew up down the road from the Padgetts and they'd spent weekends together like this all through high school. The boys didn't drink, and unless they wanted to kill another night in Colter's dank bedroom playing video games or watching one of his hundreds of DVDs, they fled to darkened movie theaters in distant towns. Grant waved goodbye to his mother, and Colter promised Mrs. Potter for the hundredth time that he'd watch for deer and mind the speed limit before he peeled out of the driveway. While most kids their age were idling driver's window to driver's window, clumped together in the parking lots at the Church of Christ or the shuttered water plant, these boys were busting out of Utopia in Colter's rattling car with the stereo cranked loud.

Grant, the first Utopia graduate ever accepted to an Ivy League school, was home from his fall semester of freshman year at Yale. Despite the months apart, he and Colter had fallen effortlessly back into the easy camaraderie of lifelong male friends. They avoided any topic of conversation that bore a wisp of intimacy, relying instead on inside jokes from their favorite TV show, *Scrubs,* and on gentle cracks about each other's looks and nonexistent luck with girls. When Colter teased Grant for looking like a hobbit, Grant shrugged good-naturedly. "I've got an enormously large head," he conceded, shifting to smile at me in the backseat. They had agreed to let me tag along with them on their last night together before Grant returned to school.

Grant is pale and stocky, with a short thick mop of ashy brown hair and an air about him of genuine humility. He is patient and earnest in ways teenagers by nature rarely are. He is beloved by most everyone in Utopia despite the fact that his academic dreams launched him far from his hometown and its proud ethos of manual labor. Grant's best friends in Utopia are Colter and Joey Wiekamp, young men opposite in every way, who themselves have zero interest in each other.

Everybody in town was a little nervous when Grant paddled away from their comfortable shores toward what they imagined to be the head-swirling waters of an elite northeastern university. But the boy slid gracefully into college life. A devout evangelical, he joined the Yale Students for Christ group and made fast friends with his suitemates— a Hindu prince, an African American son of a famous CBS newsman, and a Jewish Catholic boy from Connecticut who freelanced for *The New York Times* and was still collecting income from an Internet company he launched when he was ten years old. Grant was the only person he personally knew of at Yale who was almost entirely dependent on scholarships and financial aid. And sure, sometimes he wished for better clothes. Sometimes he had to silently wait out his friends' discussions about skiing in Aspen or summer escapes to Europe. But he didn't feel that not having money defined him any more than his new friends were defined by their history of privilege. Grant went to Yale knowing what kind of man he and his single mother and his math teacher back in Utopia expected him to be, and he was determined, desperate almost, not to disappoint anyone. Take for example the promise he once made his mother that he wouldn't drink until he was twenty-one years old. When Grant was invited to a college friend's house for his first Seder dinner, he called his mom, Susi, back in Texas and asked for permission to sip from the ritual wine. She told him of course, go enjoy yourself, but he ended up passing when the glass circled around his way. He wanted to keep his word. (When I told one of the coffee drinkers this story, he shook his head and wondered what kind of boy—he didn't care how "book-smart" Grant was—called up his mama asking for permission to drink.)

While Grant was away for fall semester, he and Colter relied on brisk IM sessions and text-message exchanges about random pop-culture minutiae. Colter was still pleased with the Christmas e-gram he had sent Grant while his friend was busy studying for his first pressure-cooker round of Yale finals. "It was called an ass-gram, actually," said Colter, grinning at me in the rearview mirror, "and the card was this big butt with legs talking. And my message was, 'Hey douchebag, happy Kwanzaa.'" He looked over at a patiently amused Grant in the passenger seat and started laughing hysterically. "I mean, how is that not awesome?"

Grant couldn't afford the trip home for Thanksgiving, so this Christmas marked his first return to Utopia. News of his earning a 3.7 GPA preceded his arrival. "It was a 3.67 actually," Grant said, with a sheepish smile. How, he marveled aloud, could a boy from the country, who missed the nightly spread of stars blanketing Utopia almost as much as he missed his friends and family, have gotten anything less than an A in astronomy? Grant wanted to go on to medical school to become a doctor for NASA and he didn't think that a B+ was going to help him get there. Somehow his love for science seemed to complement rather than conflict with his ardent passion for God. At a young age, Grant had learned to be comfortable with seeming contradictions.

While home on winter break, Grant stopped by the school one afternoon to say hello. His teachers teased him when he acted disappointed about his grades. They didn't understand the impossible standards the boy set for himself. But he was embarrassed to once again have the town marveling over his success, the way it had when he received a near perfect score on his SATs and when stories in the *San Antonio Express-News* celebrated his acceptance letters from MIT, Stanford, Harvard, and of course Yale. "He's an exceptionally bright young man," Utopia's superintendent bragged to me. "But I like to give him a hard time. 'What? You weren't smart enough to get into any Texas schools?'" Grant, uncomfortable with the attention, told everyone that he couldn't take credit for his brains. Intelligence was in many ways luck, he explained, or an inexplicable gift of both good genes and God's will.

Colter, outwardly unimpressed by his friend's series of remarkable achievements or his unimaginable new life at Yale, turned up the volume of the radio. "I'm going to college in September," he announced. "Or August. Whenever it starts, I don't remember. It's the University of Advancing Technology in Arizona. I saw an advertisement for it on TV—which is how I make most of my decisions, actually—and it looked pretty cool." Grant asked Colter if he'd yet been accepted to the program and he shrugged distractedly. "Mostly, yeah. I just have to fill out the scholarship stuff." Colter spoke with great confidence about his imminent future as a video-game designer. He outlined his fantasy of a future spent working on computers in a downtown air-conditioned office. For now Colter was working road construction earning $8.90 an hour as part of a crew that was adding five feet worth of bicycle lanes onto the roads in and out of Utopia. He drove a pilot car back and forth in slow circles for ten hours a day, going nowhere.

"You got to live in the city," he explained, eyeing me in the mirror once again. Colter is twenty-two years old and often assumed a tone of endearingly cocksure bluster when explaining his worldview. "Realistically, the one city that has a high chance of me living there is L.A., or somewhere at least in the Silicon Valley area. Of course I'd really like to move to Tokyo. Though I could end up moving to Connecticut or

New Hampshire. That's where EA Sports is, obviously. It just depends on what company I end up going with."

Colter had a habit of speaking definitively, with great authority, on all matters. But his theories on the world, however declarative, often finished with a question mark as he tried to gauge his listener's response. He'd wait a second or two without blinking and then sputter out a few quick beats of anxious laughter. "I was extremely timid and unconfident in high school," he told me in private. "So when I graduated I decided I needed to be completely different." Throughout his childhood in Utopia, Colter had found it impossible to connect with any young person other than Grant. Since graduation he'd decided to tell himself that perhaps his unpopularity had been his call all along. Maybe it was just that *he* didn't like many people. And so he patched together a new persona, relying on a handful of poses in town. He often looked bored and smug. When someone at the General Store or coffee shop did engage him in conversation, his face, despite himself, transformed into an expression of surprise or gratitude. Alone again, he leaned upon a blunt sarcasm that might be obnoxious were it not cut with such a polite eagerness to please.

People in Colter's life were used to his glib dismissal of Utopia. They rolled their eyes and wondered if that odd boy with the moussed hair might be adopted. Colter still lived with his parents and his sixteen-year-old sister, Alyssa, in a one-story house on sixty-seven acres just outside town. The rest of his family wanted only to live and die in Utopia. But Colter kept himself at a remove from town, announcing his otherness with hair products and vintage clothes he ordered off the Internet or found at the Goodwill store on weekend trips to San Antonio. He'd wear his sister's pink Crocs to the café, or a *SpongeBob Square-Pants* tie to Living Waters.

"I saw a gray Polo shirt that said UPS on it for only a dollar," he said, describing a recent shopping triumph. "When I got to the counter, it was half off. Fifty cents! I haven't worn it in a while because I can't wear a tie with it and I'm in a tie phase." He started explaining the rules of putting together a proper outfit to Grant, who was wearing old jeans and a frayed generic T-shirt. "If I was wearing brown shoes and a black belt, that would be atrocious," he lectured his friend. "I dressed horribly in high school," Colter continued with a wince. "Like a forty-year-old real estate agent—Hawaiian shirts and generic Dockers every day."

Colter is three years older than Grant. They've been friends ever since the Potters moved to Utopia, when Grant was in kindergarten. Susi Potter had decided on a whim that she wanted to give the country life a try. She caused quite a stir when she showed up in town, telling her new neighbors that she was raising her children as vegetarians, and that her husband planned on staying home taking care of Grant and his older brother while she drove back and forth to San Antonio for freelance IT work. When Susi and her husband split up, Grant's dad left town and quickly remarried. Susi took on a part-time bookkeeping job for a local rancher in addition to her freelance load. Susi was too proud to ask for help in tough times. But when she returned from work, there would often be sacks of groceries left anonymously for the family outside her front door.

Throughout Grant's childhood, they lived in an old trailer with only a hot plate for a stove and no reliable running water. They did their washing and some bathing in a creek two miles from their trailer or over at the Padgetts' house. Every weekend Susi would leave the boys with Lindy, Colter's mother, so she could work on her San Antonio clients' computer systems while their offices were closed. Lindy treated Grant and his older brother, Josh, as if they were her own. Josh and Colter were in the same class but never grew close, which was odd as Josh rivaled Colter in his obsession with breaking free of Utopia. Of course, Josh got his wish. When he graduated he accepted a full scholarship to Harding, a Christian liberal-arts university in Arkansas that was popular with Utopia graduates. Grant may have been the one who got into an Ivy League school, but he always insisted that of the two Potter boys, his older brother was the real brain in the family.

Colter's father, Clif, became a loose father figure for Grant. Clif is a fourth-generation Utopia rancher who, besides having the family house in town, runs six hundred acres just east of Utopia. He's a hard man, given to regular admissions that he sees no need in this life for friends unless they can offer him something of practical and immediate value. Colter's lack of athletic skills and physical toughness confused him. But something about Grant—a comet in the classroom and a basketball player who, while he'd be the first to admit he lacked any natural talent, would leave his heart on the court after every game—had him smitten. "Clif loves Grant beyond words," said Susi. "He considers Grant his son, and whenever I see him he'll always say, 'How's our boy?!' And what he'll do, when Colter will be standing right there, is say, 'Colter, why can't you be more like Grant?' Now, here's the funny thing: Colter has never resented Grant. Grant would be in kindergarten helping Colter with all his homework, and there was never any jealousy. From the beginning Colter just loved Grant and Grant loved him."

Susi believed that Grant would have floundered in a bigger school, without Utopia's doting teachers and small, close-knit classes. "When Grant was little he suffered from a form of aphasia," she said. "When he talked, he sounded like a stroke victim." Grant was unable to say his *r*'s until he was twelve years old. When the telephone would ring he'd stare at it, too scared to answer. Whenever Susi took him outside Utopia, he'd fold into himself, paralyzed into muteness by strangers and unfamiliar surroundings. "He was so shy that he would have just been lost and stuck in a corner by the kids at another school," said Susi. "But here they just embraced him." In the eighth grade Grant was cast as the lead in the small drama club's annual play and his role called for a British accent. Mrs. Potter fretted that her timid boy would freeze up on stage in front of the whole town, until she found recordings Grant had made of himself on her computer. He'd been practicing his lines aloud for hours a day, correcting and perfecting his pronunciation and accent after listening over and over to his taped voice. She credits that play, and the drama teacher's faith in Grant, for curing her son of his speech impediment.

Grant humbly took on the role of anchor in his class of nineteen. (His was a large class by Utopia's standards. Ralph's youngest daughter graduated in a class of seven girls, a curiosity that drew the attention of *The New York Times* and San Antonio radio stations. The girls' fathers, including Ralph, started worrying that all the media fuss would attract young men of ill repute to town.) By the time Grant was in the seventh grade, his teachers were gasping over the boy's unstoppable mind, marveling that he could solve complicated math problems that left them stumped. He single-handedly raised Utopia's rank in statewide testing scores. Soon enough a few teachers murmured to Susi that her son might benefit from a bigger school with better resources and a more advanced curriculum than little Utopia had to offer. Susi, who always made sure there was a fresh stack of library books on the nightstand and carted her boys all over Texas to museum exhibits and astronomy clubs and photography seminars, shushed them and insisted he was in the exact place he needed to be. "If you take care of his socialization," she assured them, "I'll take care of his education."

In his junior year of high school Grant was accepted to an elite summer program at Harvard University. When Susi told her son that there was simply no way she could afford the tuition, his class took it upon themselves to throw a bake sale to raise the money their friend needed. One weekend afternoon, they arranged their homemade brownies and cookies and cakes on card tables they'd set up on Main Street. At the end of the sale, Grant counted the day's money that he and his friends had stuffed into Ziploc bags. When his math teacher, who had helped organize the event, put her arm around his shoulders, he burst into tears and leaned into her embrace. Grant's class had raised, down to the exact dollar, the $2,123 he needed to go to Harvard. "He's got the figure written down because he's going to pay the town back ten times over," said Susi.

Grant was the editor in chief of Utopia's newspaper, a statewide academic-meet superstar, the homecoming king, and the senior class valedictorian. At graduation, he gave an emotional speech that celebrated every one of his fellow classmates, whom he'd come to view as family members, breaking down in tears at the end of the alphabet when he got to Joey. He wanted the Wiekamps to know what love and respect he felt for them during their time of loss. After the ceremony a shaky Grant surprised his mother by expressing a desire to stay in Utopia instead of heading to Yale in the fall as everyone expected of him.

"What would happen if I just didn't leave?" he asked. "If I just didn't go off and do all this. Why can't I just stay here?" Susi felt great sympathy for her son's conflicted heart. "This town is his family and he felt like he was leaving his family behind," she said. "And Colter! All throughout their childhood we would never go to the Dairy Queen in Sabinal without picking up Colter first. It would have been insulting if we hadn't, like we were leaving one brother on the couch and taking the other. I think it was hard for Grant to *want* to go to college."

But Susi had been preparing her boys their whole lives to leave Utopia, and she always warned them that she wouldn't let them settle on a Texas school. "You have to be far enough away that you can't run home every weekend," she said. "I always told my kids that when they turned eighteen, I was going to break their plates. So I told Grant, you have to leave Utopia. Then if you want to come back, you come back. But first you have to leave."

If Grant cherished life in Utopia—writing in his Yale application essay about "the same beloved friends who've known me since diapers, same loving community steadfastly believing that someday I'll walk the moon"—Colter had forever felt ignored or suffocated by his hometown. He didn't have such fond memories from high school. He had loved basketball just as much as Grant, but was so clumsy out there on the court that he was relegated to the dreary role of team manager. He went stag to his senior prom, standing awkwardly in the high school cafeteria that had been decorated to look like the setting for a Hawaiian luau. While his classmates gathered after the dance to drink and reminisce about their glory days, Colter went home early to watch a Spurs playoff game. The night ended with him bent over the toilet with a bad case of food poisoning, puking his heart out until the early morning.

Colter never could fit in with the more rugged boys in town, who loved to hunt and fish and comb the hills looking for Indian arrowheads on the weekends. "They called me Special Ed Padgett in school," said Colter, with a smirk that didn't quite sit easy on his face. His mother, Lindy, remembered the first time she realized how adrift her son was from the pack during a T-ball game with the other kindergarten boys.

"They put him in the very back left field," said Lindy.

"With the retards!" said Colter.

"But when he was out there he'd just watch the butterflies and pick grass and swing an imaginary bat."

"I didn't care about baseball," Colter interrupted.

"And finally the coach said, 'Okay, it's the last game. We're going to put Colter on the mound!' Anyways, it was so funny, everybody was laughing. All these other kids were so serious and of course the mothers are yelling for their kids. And Colter was just in his own world." She paused to tenderly imitate her son throwing a pitch with a rubbery arm, droopily swinging a bat, and running in a little circle, oblivious to the waiting parents in the stands or his peers staring after him impatiently. "He wasn't there on the field with the other kids," said Lindy. "He was just playing his own game."

During high school, Colter went twice a week to the worship services at Living Waters and spent Saturday nights with Grant at the church's popular youth-group meetings. While Grant's relationship with God was intimate and evolving, steeped in serious Bible study and questions of real-world practicality, Colter's faith was always more extreme and emotional. Upon graduation, he watched as his classmates went off to college or started working manual labor at their family businesses in town. He stumbled into a job at a tourist shop in Leakey, a town twenty minutes from Utopia, that was run by his youth group pastor's wife. She soon pulled him aside and told him about her invigorating experience at a tiny, two-year Christian school called the Texas Bible Institute, four hours from Utopia, seventy miles outside Houston. Unsure of his future, Colter accepted a full scholarship from Living Waters to attend TBI, a school where prospective students needed to testify to their born-again experience in order to attend. "It was the best option I had," he said. He figured that when he finished at TBI he could get a job as a youth pastor at an evangelical church like Living Waters.

But Colter was miserable at school, overwhelmed, he said, by the righteousness of his instructors and surprised by the wildness of some of his fellow students, like a classmate who dealt meth in between lectures on scripture. Colter tumbled into a deep depression, and he turned for the first time to drink. He stayed holed up alone in his room with a bottle of vodka for most of the first year. He was stunned to find himself just as alone and miserable at school as he'd been at home. Colter didn't tell anyone, not even Grant, about his escalating sense of isolation.

In the summer before his second year, Lindy was shopping at a Circuit City in New Braunfels with Colter's little sister when her body suddenly wilted to the store's hard linoleum floor. She started choking and convulsing and eventually stopped breathing. While Alyssa cried for help, confused and terrified that her mother was dying on the floor at her feet, a customer turned Lindy on her side and got her heart started while yelling for an ambulance. It was the first of countless seizures that would fell Lindy over the next couple of months as doctors struggled to find out what was wrong with her. "They'd say, 'Well, we just don't know, you're having little strokes,'" said Lindy. "But it felt like they were saying, 'Oh well, whatever happens, happens.'" Finally a doctor in Kerrville took her mini-seizures seriously, keeping her in the hospital until tests confirmed his dreaded suspicion. He diagnosed Lindy with an advanced brain tumor that had been eerily clever about disguising itself as harmless tissue.

Lindy, whom Ralph calls "Gabby" because the woman has no use for the word "stranger" and will sit down and chat with anyone, was instantly overwhelmed by the love and support of Utopia. The women in town took turns driving her back and forth to San Antonio for radiation treatments five times a week. Her best friend, Kim, watched over her like a wolf, making sure that Lindy remembered to eat and stay hydrated and alert somebody when she felt another seizure approaching. Despite Kim's well-intentioned barking that she should take care of herself, Lindy lost fifty pounds in a few short months. When she wasn't in the care of her friends she was often alone in her bedroom, her butterscotch-colored cat, whom she had found wild and half-starved in the bushes out at the Padgett ranch, lying on her chest with his paws protectively crossed over Lindy's heart.

Colter tried his best that hard summer after his mother's diagnosis, but he tended to treat the matter with a maddening fatalism. Lindy's enmeshed circle of friends, fiercely protective of her, were furious with him after he announced his intention to return to TBI for his final year. His mother had just been given a death sentence, they warned him. Clif was away from home two weeks every month, working on an oil rig off the Louisiana coastline, and he couldn't quit his job to take full-time care of his wife. Clif's company gave him health insurance that saved him from having to sell his ranch to pay Lindy's exploding medical bills. Her friends all loudly agreed that Alyssa was too young to deal with this situation alone. It was time, Lindy's protectors told everybody in town who would listen, for Colter to grow up and stop being so selfish and start taking care of his saint of a mother.

So when Colter completed his tenure at TBI, graduating with a certificate in Christian life studies, a degree meant to prepare a young person for the ministry, he moved back in with his family in Utopia. He'd long since realized that alcohol was feeding his depression, so he swore off liquor, living instead on a steady diet of distraction from movies and MySpace. Now that Grant had left for college, Colter's support circle was quickly shrinking to zero. But one day soon, he promised himself, it would be his turn to break free.

On a Friday night a few months after Grant had returned to Yale for his spring semester, I asked Colter if I could join him on one of his solo trips to the movies in Uvalde. We hadn't checked the listings, though, and when we pulled up to the theater, he realized he'd already seen all four movies playing. He offered to see any of them again, but he looked so beat up by a long week of waking up for work at 6:00 A.M. that we went instead to dinner at Applebee's.

Colter's back and shoulder muscles were blooming from the year of physical work. His face was scorched red except for the harsh outline of his sunglasses. "When I'm sixty or seventy I'll be worried about skin cancer," he said of his refusal to wear sunscreen. "I'll be married by then and I'll be able to see if she really loves me." He laughed harshly, then called himself an idiot under his breath.

Colter was still planning on leaving for college in the fall. He was adamant that his mother was doing better and it was time for him to strike out on his own. "I'll be running when August comes," he promised. "I'll jump on top of my car while it's rolling." But he didn't have any money saved up, and he was still paying off his own medical bills from when he'd broken his thumb playing basketball on the small stretch of asphalt behind the Baptist church with Grant. Colter knew his parents didn't have any money to give him for school, but he was determined not to let practical concerns dampen his enthusiasm that evening. A technical school in Arizona might sound awfully far away from Utopia, but that, Colter insisted, was the allure. He'd long since given up the idea of finding work as a pastor, and lately his relationship with Living Waters had cooled. Whatever passion he'd felt for the church he now directed toward the idea of pop culture as his savior. When he became a video-game designer, he figured his rejection of Utopia would be complete. "No one else has ever done it," he said. "Then when I see everybody back in town I can go, 'Screw you, I made something of myself.'" I asked Colter once who in Utopia he was so angry with, and he just shook his head. "Everybody who says I'm stupid for wanting something out of life other than to live there."

The next morning Alyssa's new puppy, Cinch, a six-week-old Great Pyrenees, rolled around on the grass outside the coffee shop Utopia Joe's, his short legs tumbling and spilling over one another as he nipped playfully at the back heels of a town cat. Colter and Alyssa had stopped for fruit smoothies before taking me on the thirty-minute ride out to the Padgett ranch. Alyssa, dirty blond hair pulled back into a high ponytail and bangs bobby-pinned away from her bright blue eyes and naturally scowling face, was dressed for a hard day of work, as usual. She wore a Utopia Horse Club T-shirt, already streaked with dust, and tight jeans, the side seams of the legs split open a few inches above her worn pink and chocolate brown cowboy boots. A rhinestone belt buckle, a prize from one of last summer's Monday night riding competitions, sat haughtily on her waist. She drove down Main Street, a few fingers cradling the bottom of the steering wheel, her left hand pushed into her jaw, with the breezy nonchalance a wealthy woman might show when giving a stranger a tour of her mansion. She'd nod and starfish her hand at anyone who passed. When one of the ladies in town signaled for her to stop so she could pull alongside and ask after Lindy, Alyssa politely nodded and said, "Yes, ma'am, yes, ma'am, she's doing real good today."

Colter kept his head down in the backseat, holding Cinch on his lap, tickling the dog's belly and wondering why such a dignified puppy dog didn't have a more regal name. "You should have been a Frederick," he told the panting animal, who licked Colter's chin and turned his stumpy legs around in circles on his lap.

Just south of town Alyssa turned off Main Street onto a gravel road that got less and less hospitable the farther we traveled. It's a long, lonely haul out to the Padgett ranch, fourteen hundred acres of rough land that's divided between Clif and his brother, a businessman who lives in Houston. Alyssa kept her '96 Ford truck, which her mother had passed down to her after the seizures got so bad the doctor told Lindy she should no longer trust herself behind the wheel, under twenty miles per hour, patiently navigating the bumps and crags of the unpaved road. Alyssa didn't have a driver's license but she had learned to drive when she was five years old, sitting on her daddy's lap while he worked the pedals. It was rare to meet a young person in town who didn't know how to drive. The country version of driver's ed, according to one of the coffee drinkers who had shot his first gun when he was four years old and was driving by the age of six, was simple: "Your dad put it in low granny"—Utopians' shorthand for low gear—"and stepped out so you could slide over and start driving while he was in the back of the truck pouring out feed for the cows or the goats."

Alyssa wanted to take over the Padgett ranch one day, and as far as Colter was concerned, it was hers. As we jumped and pitched in the truck, Cinch letting out a yelp whenever a hole got the best of the Ford's whimpering shocks, Alyssa said that when she was older she'd put together the money to fix this beat stretch of road. Back in the eighties the school decided to quit sending the bus out this far into the country, as it had done back when Clif was growing up. So before Colter started kindergarten, after years of Lindy swearing to her husband that the isolation of life out on the ranch was killing her, Clif finally agreed to move the family closer to town. But Alyssa swore she'd live out on the ranch again some day, after she graduates from college. She wanted to go to San Angelo State with her best friend, Katey, because the university has a rodeo program and she said the students were all country kids like her.

"Why don't you go to clown school instead?" Colter asked from the backseat. "You might be good at that."

"Your face!" said Alyssa, cranking up Merle Haggard's "I'm a Lonesome Fugitive" on the radio.

Colter howled in dismay. "This guy sings slower than the guys I work with talk," he said, burying his face in Cinch's neck. "And that's saying something."

This was already Colter's second trip out to the ranch that day. He'd woken up early to help his father burn trash and clear cedar. When Clif was offshore, Colter grudgingly hit the ranch on Saturday afternoons. He'd throw some protein pellets on the ground for the cows, and then race back into town, his tires shredding as he floored his way free of the land he was expected to assume control over one day. He might have to occasionally play the role of future rancher, but that didn't mean he had to dress the part. Where his sister proudly wore rhinestones and boots, Colter had on a Nintendo remote-control belt buckle that he'd found on the Internet for thirty dollars. Instead of a cowboy hat, a pastel blue Kangol. He wore a vintage Mister Rogers T-shirt with YOU'RE SPECIAL emblazoned across his chest, blue jeans cut off below the knees, and bright orange suede Puma sneakers that he'd found on sale at a San Antonio outlet store.

When they pulled up to the house, Clif looked up from sawing cedar, blinking in the fuzzy humid haze. His shapeless black cowboy hat looked like it was made of charred paper that would disintegrate if he were to ever remove it from his head. Clif wore a brown barn jacket without a shirt underneath, a slash of angry red skin around his neck where the two top snaps were undone. His thick, colorless mustache drooped over his upper lip. His glasses were filmy with grime, and when he squinted into the backseat at Colter his sweaty face took on the look of a tired walrus just out of the water. Clif never could understand what possessed his son to dress the way he did.

"Sad," he said, grimacing down at Colter's bare calves. "Now you're just looking to be stupid. There are snakes out here. I myself been struck three times. If you get a fang in one of them legs, that leg is never going to come back right." Colter scratched Cinch's wriggling belly and told the puppy he was a good boy. "You wear plaid and Wranglers," Colter said, his words muffled in the dog's fur. "And you're going to comment on what I'm wearing?"

"He's going to have to live somewhere else if he insists on dressing like that," Clif continued. "San Francisco, maybe?" He grinned harshly at me and waved his left hand, bright with bloody snags from a recent run-in with a chain saw.

"Dad, put your glove on!" said Alyssa. "It's freaking me out. There's blood everywhere."

"You're way too squeamish," laughed Clif, splaying his thumb and forefinger to show off his crusting wound. "Looks like I been playing with a crocodile," he said with admiration, before slipping on a white glove with the word "Pride," the name of his oil company. "Y'all get in my pickup real quick and we'll catch these cows. It'll only take about ten minutes."

Alyssa clambered into the bed of her father's truck and sat in the base of a spare tire. Colter, still holding Cinch to his chest, sat on the edge of the truck bed. Clif's black lab, Lucas, jumped with Clif into a front seat littered with sandwich wrappers and dirty tools. "Lucas left one of these beer cans in here," Clif said with a wink. He stroked his dog's neck, nodding at the smattering of crushed aluminum empties on the floor. A miniature plastic bucking bull bobbed up and down on the dashboard. Back when Clif was in school, in a graduating class of ten, he dreamed of riding bulls to glory. But Clif said that to be a professional rider, a man had to be short and stout, with a low center of gravity. "Grant has the perfect body for a bullrider," he said approvingly. Clif is six foot four, and his long limbs hang like the heavy branches of one of Utopia's massive live oaks. So instead of ever making it onto a professional circuit, Clif waited for the annual Utopia rodeo, where he joined a few other men dumb and nervy enough to sit at a poker table in the middle of the ring waiting for a bull to be set loose. The last man sitting at the table wins the pot. "Several years back, Clif went out and sat in that chair," one of the coffee drinkers told me. "He was the first one hit. That bull laid him out." "It takes a little guts to sit there," said Bud with admiration. "Go see his ranch and you'll find out how tough he is," added Hose, whose large ranch borders the Padgett land. "That's a bugger out there."

At the wheel, Clif slugged tea from a giant red plastic mug that he always kept on hand. "I sniff Dad's tea jug before I drink it," Alyssa once said. "I've tasted gin too often." His family hates it when Clif gets to drinking. They stomp and complain and eventually the whole town knows that he's hitting the hard stuff again. "Every once in a while this deal with Lindy will get to me and I get pissed off a little and slip," he said. "Makes the whole family mad and they throw my whiskey away."

Clif's father drank himself to death the year before Colter was born. Like most of the ranchers in town, Milton Padgett made a living on goats until the bottom fell out of the mohair market. He later opened his own bulldozer outfit. For fun, Clif's dad used to join Ralph on an annual fishing trip down below Laredo. "He was just as good a feller as you could meet," Ralph said of his old friend. "If he told you it was going to rain, you better get your slicker." When Clif's mother was diagnosed with multiple sclerosis, they watched her suffer for eight long years until she died when Clif was just seventeen. "I did a bunch of praying and she died anyways," said Clif. So he cursed God. "I think it's a weakness," he said. "I despise organized religion. I'm an agnostic.

If there is a God, he'd be out here talking to me. He wouldn't be in some goddang box in town."

Lindy's friends all grumble about her hard husband, about how he's away two weeks every month, and how when he's home he always seemed to makes things worse with his crude sarcasm. One morning at the coffee shop, Clif left Lindy and her best friend, Kim, at the table so he could go look at a bulldozer. " 'Bye Kim," he teasingly hissed to his wife's loyal guardian. "Sod off, Clif! Don't let the door smack you in the ass on the way out!" she barked back.

"Poor Cliffy," said Kim, her mouth curling in distaste. "I don't think there's anybody in his little world except him."

Lindy nodded wearily. "He's always telling me, 'You just don't know what I'm going through.' "

From a nearby table, the rancher Frankie Jones started clucking a little at his sausage biscuit, looking over at the two women.

"Do you want to add to this conversation?" asked Kim.

"Well," Frankie said, pushing back from his breakfast, "I was just going to tell you that he's going through the same thing you are. He just handles it in a different way. And his way may be worse. But whether it's right or wrong, as a man you're supposed to be the protector. And the reality of this thing is just beating him up, don't think it isn't. I saw Clif go through his mom dying and then lose his daddy that he worshipped, so don't think he isn't hurting, because he is."

Times are hard at the Padgett house, with everyone constantly retreating to their separate corners. When Clif started drinking, Lindy retaliated by pouring his alcohol down the sink. Colter warned his mother that she was only egging the man on worse. Usually Lindy ended up calling a friend to come pick her up. Colter shut himself in his room, cocooning himself in a virtual world on his computer. Alyssa would usually sit with her dad and watch television, the History Channel or professional bullriding, and she had enough sway over him that she could sometimes convince him to put his half-drunk beer back in the fridge.

"I'm probably not ever going to quit drinking," Clif said as he slowly drove his truck out to the field where his hungry herd of snorting cows waited. "I'm sure I'm an alcoholic by somebody's scale in the medical community. Bunch of idiots! But the working stiff, he gets off and has a six-pack."

"Or a twelve-pack or a twenty-four pack!" Colter called from the back of the truck.

"You come out here and cut cedar with me all day long," Clif continued, "and I don't care what, you're going to be hurting. You're going to be dehydrated and your muscles aren't going to work. You go home and have a couple beers and that hurt will go away. And then you have the rest of the six-pack to make sure you got there." I asked what brand of beer he favored and Clif, grimacing, looked at me with impatience. "I drink the national beer of Texas—Lone Star. Let's get serious!" With alcoholism running deep in his bloodline, Clif admitted it was probably a good thing that Colter didn't drink. "But when someone doesn't drink beer I kinda wonder about them," he said. "There's something different about that kid."

Clif parked in front of the gate that held the thirty-two cows that he was fattening up for market. Alyssa jumped down and shimmied the fifty-pound bag of feed off the truck bed. Colter remained where he sat, whispering of unknown adventures into Cinch's ear.

"You're the one supposed to be out here stringing feed," Clif grumbled at Colter.

"Alyssa told me to hold the puppy dog," said Colter.

"Oh, I can take care of the puppy dog real easy," Clif said with a low chuckle, laughing and swatting at Alyssa, who punched him hard on the arm.

After the cows had been fed, Clif leaned against his truck and wondered aloud when his son would straighten himself out. This relentless fantasy of Colter's to work a desk job, hunched over a keyboard in some lifeless cubicle in a strange city like Los Angeles, had him twisted.

"You're supposed to be running women and drinking beer and riding wild bulls," Clif told his son.

"A lover, a fighter, a wild bull rider!" Alyssa singsonged, kicking a heel into each boot to shake off the dirt.

"There's nothing else," said Clif, nodding approvingly at his daughter. "What kind of world do you think you're getting into on Rodeo Drive, or wherever it is you want to go?" He hit his hat against his thigh, sending dust flying. "Everybody's got enough nerve to sit in front of a computer. Very few got the nerve to sit on a bull."

While his son sat there, with a blank smile on his face, I suggested the possibility that Colter's vision of his future entailed a different kind of nerve. Maybe the boy wanted more of a creative life than a physical one.

"And I don't create anything?" Clif asked me angrily. "I've produced more hamburger than this yo-yo will ever produce. I can do without a video game, but I can't do without eating. That's a habit I got into, see, when I started living. Eating? I produce. I make this land produce. I'm proud of that. What's he going to produce?" he said, jerking his gnarled hand at Colter, who looked shielded up in some private world, impervious to his father's scathing assessment.

"Like I told you," Colter said calmly, "entertainment is where the money is."

"What do you think I do?" spat back Clif. "These calves here will try to go to the rodeo and become bucking bulls. You can sell them for ten thousand dollars! I got jeep people who come up here to drive on these rocks," he said, looking out at the jagged molars of hills that have been in his family for over a century. He knew every inch of this rough country from when as a child he and his friends would set hunting traps, skin coons and sell their pelts, and jimmy boulders free, marveling at the way they crashed through brush on their mad descent.

"I'm fifty-seven years old," Clif said, looking seriously at his son. "And you're already an invalid at twenty. Now your goal is to sit in a chair all day?" Clif looked back over at me and threw his hands up. "He's wasting his time! He should be offshore making three times as much money. Out there with the ex-convicts—people he can converse with."

"Trust me, there's plenty of ex-convicts where I'm working now," Colter said with a sigh.

"He's learning to cuss though," Clif said, with a cocky grin. "Guess I'm making progress. He's not up to truck driver yet but I'm working on it. Now I just got to teach him to drink whiskey."

"If I'm not working on the ranch or a roughneck," Colter said, ignoring his father, "my dad is never going to be satisfied or sentimental about anything I do."

Clif turned on his heels, taking in the land that spread out around them. "I love it here in Utopia," he said. "I was born and raised here. But I wanted to see the world—unlike Colter, who just don't want to do anything." By the time he was his son's age, Clif had already graduated from Sul Ross State University in Alpine, West Texas, and gone overseas to work in oil fields.

Clif swelled with pride when he talks about those youthful years of adventure. "I looked down the muzzles of machine guns in Malaysia," he said dramatically. "I nearly drowned my ass in Indonesia. I raced motorcycles in Singapore. And after a while I found out there wasn't any better place in the world than Utopia." He's sure that Colter will come around to his way of thinking eventually. "This land is inside of him, it's just not coming out yet," he said, his tone of voice suddenly teetering toward something like affection for his son. "But he's a tough kid, he's strong. He's got the willpower to go ahead and handle things. Like most people, he just doesn't understand yet that you do what you need to do. You've got to shove what you want to the side. The land tells you what to do." From behind him, Alyssa tugged on her father's arm and reminded him that the land was in her blood too.

Her stubborn insistence that she could take over the ranch one day bounced off Clif, landing on the hard ground with a thud. "This is not a woman's world," he told her. "Too much work. Takes too strong a will. Women don't have it. Girls always lose the land when the family gives it to them."

"Don't listen to a thing he says," Alyssa told me. "I'll be out here all summer helping out."

"You're a girl," he said, discussion over. "You're never going to be able to start a chain saw."

Alyssa pulled her fist up as if to hit him again. "Don't you have a special ed class to go to?" she asked.

Clif laughed and shook his head. "See what kind of mess I created?"

On the drive home, Colter and Alyssa said that their family was sitting on millions of dollars' worth of land. Recently, Clif was moping around the house, his emotions heightened by drink, and he started whining about how nobody in his life gave him the love and respect he deserved. "If y'all hate me so much," he told his smirking son, "I'll just sell the ranch and get the millions of dollars and spend it myself."

Colter pounced on him, warning Clif that this was a dangerous threat to carelessly throw down on their family room floor like a piece of meat. "Go ahead and sell it," he warned his father. "See if I care. If you said, 'I'll take away your PlayStation 2 if you don't do what I say,' that might be a legitimate threat. Take away my iPod and I might kill myself. But the ranch? If there was no ranch I wouldn't live my life any differently."

Clif was just letting the whiskey talk that night. The only time I ever heard him sincerely speculate about the possibility of shaving off a chunk of his land and selling it to the highest bidder was at the coffee shop one morning, when a few people were passing along news that Susi Potter might not be able to afford her modest portion of Grant's tuition costs for his sophomore year at Yale.

"Oh no," Clif told the room. "There's no way I'll allow that boy not to get to finish his time. Do you know how hard it is to get into that school? He's staying. We'll figure it out. We'll keep him there, no matter what. I don't care what I'd have to give up."

It's a hard thing to predict just who in Utopia will succumb to the allure of easy money, and how much it will take for them to sell out. On the ride home from the Padgett ranch that afternoon, Colter swore that he would always hang on to the family land. Despite the repulsion he felt for the ranch and the lifestyle it demanded, he said there was no amount of money that could ever persuade him to permanently amputate himself from these hills.

"I'd never sell the ranch, because of what it meant to my dad," he said firmly. "I hate the place and I'm never out there and sure, that's why we don't get along. But I do have a sense of loyalty. Besides," he said, echoing the same confused wonder of all the other holdouts in Utopia, "once I got the money what would I do with it? Absolutely nothing. When I look back at the end of my life, what am I going to think if I sold the ranch and squandered all the money? No, I'll just pay the taxes every year and let it sit." He looked up at his sister in the front seat. "Alyssa wants it anyways."

PICO GAS STATION

For the most part, Christi Thomas likes her job at Utopia's gas station just fine. She gets Mondays and Wednesdays off. She works with friends—Cody, a Utopia boy who dropped out of college, and P.J., a tall, intense girl with a taste for heavy black eyeliner and vampire novels. Christi leaves her daughter, Mackenzie, at home with her younger sister when she goes to work, but they visit her at the Pico gas station most afternoons. They spread Mackenzie's toys over the table facing the register while the sisters visit. And when Christi's husband, Ken, came home on a two-week leave from Iraq, her bosses let her paint Pico's two front windows to celebrate his brief return. WELCOME HOME SGT THOMAS! she scrawled in large, puffy letters surrounded by stars and bright yellow ribbons. WE MISSED ♥ YOU.

One evening shortly before closing time, I sat at the table and waited for Christi to lock up. The twenty-two-year-old cashier was friendly and relaxed with her stragglers. On her green cotton collared Pico shirt, which was long and baggy and, she complained, made her feel fat, Christi wore a small fluorescent button P.J. had given her. IF YOU DON'T LIKE MY ATTITUDE, QUIT TALKING TO ME, the pin read, though it was hard to picture anyone ever accusing this soft-natured girl with a butterfly tattoo on her shoulder of copping attitude. It was harder still to imagine her cutting a conversation short. The door jangled open and a shirtless man, who she later sighed was one of her relatives, bought a pack of Marlboros and a drumstick from the ice cream freezer. When he leaned in and purred that he knew where Christi could get some good shit if she was interested, she smiled brightly at him and pulled her dirty blond ponytail tight. "I've got a kid to take care of now," she told him firmly. "I can't be doing that."

Christi met her husband at a party in town when she was a senior in high school. He was from Canada, where he'd spent time in jail for a drug deal gone bad, and had been sent to live with a tolerant aunt and uncle. At the time, Ken was studying for his GED and waiting to join the Army. "If you're going to marry a guy from here," said Christi, "they're either going to stick around town working for the water wells or on a ranch or they're going to be military. Guys don't usually go far." The teenagers were married that September by Utopia's justice of the peace. Two weeks later Ken left Christi behind for basic training, and then kissed her goodbye again for a year in Korea.

"I stayed here, of course," said Christi, absently pulling on Ken's heavy basic-training graduation ring, which hung from a silver chain around her neck. "Lived at my mom and dad's. Worked at Pico all the time." The young couple wrote letters to each other, Ken revealing himself on paper to be wonderfully articulate with his feelings. But the distance was hard on them and they started discussing the possibility of a separation. "We just grew apart," she said. "It wasn't what I expected it to be. We thought we couldn't make it because it was just too hard." Christi grew fragile and depressed. A doctor diagnosed her as bipolar after she suffered a breakdown that resulted in a brief hospitalization.

After a long year, Ken finally came home and the couple fell back into each other's arms. They packed a few bags and moved into an efficiency apartment on base in Fort Knox, Kentucky. "I was ready to get out," Christi said about leaving Utopia. "I'd never been anywhere!" In Kentucky, she applied for a job at the local Wal-Mart but found out the day before the interview that she was pregnant. Then she got a call from home telling her that Jeff Wiekamp had been killed in action. She grew up with those boys. Josh Wiekamp had been her first love.

Eleven months after Mackenzie's birth, Ken left for Iraq. Christi and the baby moved back home to Utopia and to minimum wage at the gas station. Because Christi's family was terrified of her having another breakdown, the Army was given instructions not to contact her directly if her husband was ever wounded or killed. So when Ken was shot in the leg on a special mission, Christi's mother got the call. "Your husband's been shot," she told her daughter, after shaking Christi awake on the sofa, "but he's okay. It happened yesterday. This is the first that they've been able to get ahold of anybody. He'll be online in an hour." Over instant message, Ken explained that he had been on one of three American boats when they started taking enemy fire. The gunner from one of the other boats was shot and killed, so Ken jumped aboard to take over the gun. A bullet had nicked him in the leg, but he'd held firm to the trigger.

"He got sixteen confirmed kills that day," Christi said proudly. "He was pulling out the rest of his men from the water and they were telling him he's shot and he kept saying, 'No! I'm fine.' We always tease him and tell him he's too stupid to die." Ken was awarded the Silver Star after that mission. Christi got a new tattoo on her ankle—a Texas yellow rose with her husband's initials inside.

CHAPTER 4

Black in a White Town

Kelli Rhodes spent the summer before her junior year working the register at the General Store. Morris's niece Jamie Lynn, a tall, thick-boned blond classmate who wore shiny lip gloss and thick mascara, trained her on the tab system. Only tourists paid with cash. Locals charged everything to their store accounts. The two girls squeezed behind the same small counter on their shifts. Jamie chatted with all of the shoppers while Kelli carefully added up the charges that customers were supposed to pay in full at the end of each month. Around strangers, Kelli was always shy, smiling with tight, closed lips, her large, almond-shaped brown eyes soft and wary.

Morris said Kelli was one of his best employees because she showed up on time and was always thorough and polite. But the job forced the sixteen-year-old girl into intimate, regular interaction with a town she'd never felt comfortable enough in to claim as her own. She quit shortly after a customer, an annoying man Utopians tolerated only because his elderly parents were good and kind, plunked his drink down by the register and gave Kelli a squinty leer. "Yo, what's up, my nigger!" he cried with sneering exaggeration. Kelli turned to Jamie and whispered that her friend better take over before she flew over the counter and slapped that smirk off the man's face. Kelli went and busied herself in the back of the store. Her long tumble of dark curls shielded the hot flush radishing up her brown neck and cheeks as she ripped open a box of deliveries.

When I first met her, Kelli was the only black student enrolled in the entire Utopia School. She and her family had moved from Fort Worth when she was in the sixth grade, and by now she'd grown accustomed to the queasy-making reality that she was the first and only black friend most of her classmates had ever had. At school, when she heard younger kids in the halls casually slinging around the word "nigger" in their conversations with one another, she'd kneel down and look sternly into their eyes. "No, no, no, no. This word is bad!" she'd scold them, like a babysitter yanking a pair of kitchen scissors out of a child's hand. Those were scenes Kelli felt equipped to handle—important ones, even, for her and maybe even for the wide-eyed elementary schoolers she held gently by the shoulders. What cut deeper were the times when someone aimed their ugliness square in her direction, or when friends rolled their eyes and excitedly tattled to her about their parents' reflexive disdain for black people.

"One friend just loves to tell me that her parents are racist," said Kelli. "And I want to ask her, 'How is that supposed to make me feel when I go over to your house and your parents are smiling to my face? How do I know that they're not calling me a nigger behind my back?'" When Kelli spoke of being black in a rural Texas town, she sounded tired and resigned, cracking each side of her neck and jaw the way she did whenever she was tense. If her family had stayed in Fort Worth she would have attended a predominantly black public high school. Now she was ashamed to admit that she sometimes felt intimidated by large groups of black people when she went on day trips to San Antonio or Austin. She hated that she always seemed to have crushes on freckled country boys, worrying that they would never be attracted to "my big black ass." Kelli is a petite girl, five foot two, with a narrow waist and delicate shoulders that swim beneath the black leather motorcycle jacket she wears like a security blanket. In the summer the sun brings out red highlights in her long curly hair, which her mother trims just twice a year. When she turned sixteen, people in town, from the justice of the peace to her teachers at school, marveled over how Kelli was growing into a great beauty.

Of course, Kelli's friends never meant to hurt her feelings. And the fact was that all of their parents *were* always kind to her face. "They're nice people but they're racist," she decided. "Or is it that they're nice people *and* they're racist? All I know is they're not going to change just because I'm friends with their daughter. And I guess my friend doesn't know that it might not be a good thing to tell her one black friend that her parents hate black people."

Kelli lived in Utopia because her grandfather, who was white, grew up there. Ed Jones was born nine miles northwest of town on Spring Branch Creek in 1922. He spent his childhood in a three-room house, living on food that was raised and harvested on the family's twenty-acre ranch. Ed's great-grandfather was one of the early settlers in the Sabinal Canyon, and would garner a place in state history books as a heroic Texas Ranger who served as a courier during the siege of the Alamo. Ed himself would go on to a decorated military career in the United States Army Air Forces during World War II. He was captured by the Germans when his B-24 was shot down in southern Hungary. While his young wife, Beryl, Kelli's grandmother, soothed herself to sleep at night back in Texas, unsure if her groom was dead or alive, Ed lived on one boiled potato and a piece of brown bread a day at Nuremberg's Stalag for three months. In a journal entry called "Looking Back," Jones wrote about his POW experience:

> Barracks were old and filthy, most windows broken, no heat, no bathroom facilities of any kind. . . . Just about all thoughts were

about food. A number of times I would dream that I was in a small room that had a real tall table. When I would step back I could see a white coconut cake on the top, but it was so far back from the edge that it was impossible to reach.

When the war finally ended, Ed returned home forty pounds thinner to a hero's welcome in Utopia. He was discharged from the Army Air Forces and hatched a plan with his buddy, the coffee drinker Bud Garrett, to open up their own sandwich shop. They had three hundred dollars of mustering-out pay between them, and the boys knew that with the still unpaved road between Sabinal and Utopia finally under construction, there'd be plenty of hungry men looking for a cheap lunch. When they opened the J&G café, they served simple diner food to customers on four tables. They indulged in one streak of whimsy: Sitting atop each little table was a tiny pinball machine, and they had a jukebox that played 78s. "It was a nickel a lick," said Bud. "And those boys would wear out a record in a week's time." Bill Schaefer, whose justice of the peace office now sists next door to where the men once ran the old J&G, remembered as a teenager plunking in coin after coin to hear the latest Mills Brothers or Ink Spots records. The boy was teaching himself how to play the guitar, and back then the jukebox served as his best teacher.

Bud remembered those early days at the J&G as the perfect antidote for men just out of the service. "Ed didn't get much to eat in the war, and I was stationed in Alaska and got a lot of salmon to eat but very little meat," he told me with a laugh. "When we got in the café business we decided we'd eat steak every night, and we pretty well did." But after a couple of years the hours were killing them, opening up at four in the morning and not turning off the lights again until ten at night. So the J&G closed its doors. Ed would go on to spend the rest of his professional life as a salesman for Hormel, stationed out of Uvalde. When he retired, he and Beryl bought three acres of land five miles south of Utopia and built themselves a house from the ground up with their own hands. In his retirement, Ed was the county commissioner of Uvalde County for two terms, president of Utopia's Lions Club, and a revered member of Utopia's Church of Christ. Ed had clout in Utopia, and people looked up to him.

Ed and Beryl were mortified when their only daughter, Nancy, who had long since left Utopia and made a life for herself in Fort Worth, called home with news that she had fallen in love with a black man. She was thirty years old when she met Ron Rhodes in a chemistry class at the local community college. Ron, who was studying to be a registered nurse, was already twice divorced. Divorce alone was grounds for being kicked out of Utopia's Church of Christ. But it was the news that Ron was black that made Beryl break down in tears. Unwilling to ditch the man she loved just because her parents didn't approve, Nancy stayed with Ron. He got her a job cleaning floors in the hospital where he worked while she finished up her training to be a lab technician. When Nancy called home to announce that Ron had asked her to marry him, Ed pleaded with his daughter to hold off. "'If you'll wait a year, maybe I can accept this,' he said. I guess he was thinking maybe I would change my mind. And so we waited a year and they never would accept it. So we just went ahead and did it without their blessing."

Ron and Nancy got married in the small backyard of their Fort Worth home. Nancy wore a simple white dress and they passed around pieces of wedding cake to a few of their friends from work. When Ed found out that his daughter had gotten married against his wishes, he broke down in tears on the phone. But whatever confusion Ed and Beryl felt, hanging up in shock as if they had gotten news of a death, they were at least able to treat the births of their three grandchildren as celebrations. Eventually Beryl got up the courage to move the kids' school pictures from the bedroom out onto the living room shelf next to the old grainy photo of Ed's famous great-grandfather. And when Nancy worried about sending her son, Michael, whose grades were already starting to slip, off to a crumbling public middle school, Ed invited the boy to come live with his grandparents in the country. Students didn't have to pass through a metal detector to get into Utopia School. The halls were clean and safe, and teachers looked after their students like they were their own children. So Michael agreed, and became the twentieth member of Utopia's seventh-grade class.

Michael walked into that one-story school in sharp new clothes he'd persuaded his grandparents to buy him. He aimed for swagger. Michael talks with a slow Southern drawl, his words taking their sweet time getting from the back of his throat out into the world, and he spent those first few months slumped in the back row, coolly assessing his new surroundings. What was most startling, he said, was less how country all his peers were than how intimately close. Each class here bonded together like a surrogate family, with children who had grown up with one another since before they could walk and whose parents and grandparents had just as likely gone through Utopia School together. There simply weren't enough students to splinter off into cliques. In the cafeteria, there was a freshman table, a sophomore table, and so on. A rich kid in a polo shirt whose parents owned a big ranch sat next to the Mexican transfer student from Sabinal who sat next to the fat girl with good grades. And now, adding to the mix, was a boy from the city with a black father and his hat cocked sideways.

High school transfer students tend to endure a more rigorous hazing process. Michael was young enough for the circle open up, and he made friends he would grow to cherish. But he had to adopt a cavalier attitude when it came to matters of race. Just as the Mexican boys had to get used to their white friends regularly calling them "wetbacks" or "beaners" in the locker room, Michael had to learn to laugh at people he didn't always find funny. "To the upperclassmen, my nickname was 'black man,'" Michael said. "It wasn't derogatory. That's what they knew me by. My friend Christi, she works at the gas station now, would be like, 'What's up Blackie?' and I'd be like, 'Sup Cracker.' The teachers would freak out but I didn't care. We were just joking around. I was friends with everybody. I was their token black guy! The class clown. The laid-back guy who cracked jokes all day. People would mess around with me, and we'd exchange black jokes, and I'd be like, 'Hey, did you hear this one?' But, you know, after a while you get tired," he said, softly rubbing his smooth jawline. "And I'd think,

'Dude, shut the fuck up. You're about to get punched in the face right now.'" Despite his fast affection for his new friends, he confided in his mother that he expected to graduate from high school without ever having a girlfriend. "Ma," Michael told Nancy, his mellow mask cracking open for an instant, "none of the girls' parents are ever going to let them date me."

Back in Fort Worth the rest of the Rhodes family was fast coming undone. Ron and Nancy had been forced to file for bankruptcy when their home health-care business went bust and Ron, after suffering in silence for months, was diagnosed with Lyme disease. He was too ill to hold down steady nursing work any longer. Nancy, who is almost completely deaf, was wearing herself out driving sixty miles a day back and forth to her job at the Deaf Action Center, a nonprofit organization in Dallas. Worried over the increasingly erratic behavior of their oldest daughter, they had enrolled her in a summer program for at-risk kids. After dropping her off, they got a call that the counselors had caught Racheal flushing pot down the dormitory toilet.

So in 2001, two years after Michael had moved in with his grandparents, Nancy and Ron found themselves at a loss with their sixteen-year-old and worried over whether they could make their next house payment. Ed called to say that he had set up a refurbished trailer home on his property and suggested they join Michael in Utopia. When Ed passed away a couple of years later from an abdominal aneurysm at the age of eighty-four, Michael said that his grandfather was "the only man I ever met who I was sure was going on to heaven."

One afternoon Nancy and Ron sat together on the maroon leather couch in their trailer. Dust motes hovered in the sunbeam coming through the thin, candy-pink curtain that was knotted with a rubber band above their heads. Nancy doesn't have any close friends in town, so she looked delighted to have company. She jumped up and brought back plastic glasses of tea from the kitchen that spread water rings on the checkerboard coffee table. Nancy is fifty-five years old, ten years younger than Ron, and has a sweet vulnerability about her. She always wears an expression that seems at once eager and wistful. She reads lips, but when she doesn't catch everything in the conversation, she'll nod and smile anyway.

Nancy was four years old when she lost the majority of her hearing, a side effect of taking a new experimental antibiotic used to treat upper respiratory infections. Her father decided to keep her mainstreamed in the larger Uvalde public school near his Hormel office. Maybe in Utopia, the teachers and students would have rallied around Nancy. But at the larger school, her deafness became hers alone to manage. She was forced to learn to read lips quickly but whenever anyone turned away she felt plunged underwater. Because she was so young when she lost her hearing, her speech has a thick, marbled quality. Nancy's great regret in life is that she was never taught sign language, and thus lost the chance to feel at home either in the deaf or hearing world. "I still kind of wish that I'd been able to work with my condition instead of against it," she said sadly. Nancy grew up with an acute sense of isolation she's never been able to shake. When she takes her mother, Beryl, to her Friday afternoon hair appointments at Erma's, Nancy sits awkwardly on one of the dryer chairs with her hands tucked shyly between her legs as the boisterous conversation swirls around her.

Speaking about the adjustment of moving back to her old hometown as an adult, Nancy's smile drooped. "I'm not sure that this community was ready for an interracial couple," she said slowly, smoothing her gray-blond bob behind her ears. She believed that the respect and affection her father built up over a lifetime, over his ancestors' lifetimes, served as a buffer. "But Ron getting messed with has always been in the back of my mind," Nancy said, shaking her head. "It's just hard to believe that that is still out there."

Ron rubbed a palm over his close-cropped white hair and moved to the recliner. "Oh, I know it's out there," he said calmly. In Fort Worth, when Ron used to mow their front lawn, white men would slow down to an idle by his curb. "Hey, how much do you charge?" they shouted at him through the passenger-side window. "Twenty-five bucks," Ron would call back, his deep voice calm and dry. "And I get to sleep with the woman of the house!"

Michael once told me about the time his father accompanied the family to a Sunday church service. "My dad was sitting up further with my grandparents and my mom," Michael said. "I was in the back row with this old guy and he was just staring at my dad the whole time. He wasn't singing the hymns. Wasn't praying. He just sort of glared at the side of my dad's head." Afterward a prominent member of the board pulled Ed aside and warned his friend that if his son-in-law ever showed up again they'd be forced to boycott and take their membership elsewhere. Michael didn't sound particularly bothered sharing this story. "My dad takes that stuff with a grain of salt," he said. "He's an old man. He just chills. That's what I also learned. Don't let it bother you."

Ron leaned back in his recliner and smoothly tapped a pack of Newports on his leg. "I don't have any friends here," he said. "I don't really bother with anybody." He had no complaints with the people of Utopia, and as far as he knew nobody had a beef with him. People liked to gossip and speculate about Ron every once in a while. When word got out that Ron had quit delivering the *San Antonio Express-News* around town after having the job for just a few weeks, an old-timer rolled his eyes at me. "Apparently that was just too much work for him," he said, with a pious little shrug. But nobody knows that Ron retired early, or that he had Lyme disease, or that when the family found itself pressed for cash he picked up an overnight shift at a San Antonio hospital. They don't know, because they don't know him.

"I'm a minority here," Ron said. "The number of blacks in this community before me was zero. And people here can deal with me, what with all of us being so educated. But if I decide to bring my brother and my cousin and my nephew and all these other people down here, I think they'd feel threatened." Ron and Nancy had heard stories of Ku Klux Klan pockets in nearby larger towns like Hondo and Boerne, but they said they felt safe in Utopia. "Plus, if anybody comes out and burns a cross at my house, I'm going to shoot their ass," said Ron. "I'm going to shoot the cross down and shoot them and pull their masks down and take their pictures and put them on the Internet. I am not a pacifist."

Ron eased himself out of his chair and opened the screen door onto the trailer's cluttered wooden landing. He put his elbows on the rickety railing that overlooked his neighbors Tacy and Rusty Redden's large pen of goats in the distance, and lit his cigarette. Nancy looked at me and laughed nervously, pushing her thick glasses up her pale nose.

One Friday night toward the end of her junior year, Kelli sat cross-legged on her fuzzy *Star Wars* blanket. The guitarist Slash leered down at her from the poster she had taped to the ceiling above her sagging full-size bed. Kelli liked to joke with her mother that Slash was her real dad. "We look so much alike!" she said. "We have the same hair! We both love the guitar! Are you sure you didn't get knocked up back in the day at a Guns N' Roses show?" The walls of Kelli's room were covered with posters of bands like Green Day and Queen, concert stubs, and colored ink scrawls of Kurt Cobain and Patti Smith quotes. There was a tower of comic books and graphic novels in a plastic laundry basket, and the old television had a TiVo stuffed with episodes of science fiction shows.

Kelli didn't dress like the girls in town who shopped at city malls and favored the suburban preppy aesthetic of American Eagle and Abercrombie & Fitch. Kelli bought her clothes at JCPenney and wore concert T-shirts like they were her uniform. Around her neck hung a silver chain with a treble clef charm that Nancy had given her for her sixteenth birthday. Every night Kelli spent hours practicing on her guitar, which she'd named Francisco. "If Francisco was a man he'd be this beautiful Grecian god type with dark hair and eyes," she wrote lovingly on her MySpace blog. Kelli spent hours each day connecting with the world outside Utopia on the Internet, messaging her favorite bands and blogging about her frustrated life in Utopia. She worried that she would never fall in love or, worse, would shack up with the wrong man. She vowed that she'd never settle down before she made any of her own rock-and-roll dreams come true.

But first Kelli needed someone to teach her the guitar. She wanted to play the blues, to write songs like she heard on her father's Motown record collection. Ron had recently found someone on the Internet in Uvalde who was offering lessons, but the cost and the coordination of everyone's schedules became too big a hurdle. So for now Kelli was teaching herself to play by watching how-to DVDs and earnestly slogging through music books. "Jimi Hendrix taught himself to play," Kelli said with a shrug. "Why can't I?" Her classmates invited her to join them on the weekends at pasture or barn parties, but she said that wasn't a crowd she trusted well enough to get drunk with for the first time. Her only plan that weekend was to master the chorus of Creedence Clearwater Revival's "Have You Ever Seen the Rain?"

Kelli was twelve years old when she arrived in Utopia. She coped with the massive culture shock by feigning a blithe self-confidence. She'd been painfully shy in Fort Worth, preferring to creep by in the background without drawing attention to herself. But in Utopia there was no way of denying that she stood out, so it seemed wise to project a sense of breezy authority with the eleven other kids who were now her classmates. For the first few months in town Kelli made sure to use what she thought was the expected slang of a black girl from the city. "It was yo this and yo that," said Kelli, wincing at the memory. "I just wanted people to know I was black. I wanted to make it very clear that I was black and comfortable with that, regardless of where I was." Finally she turned to a reserved girl named Perla, who had a white father and a Mexican mother, and asked her what it was about Utopia she liked so much. Perla had never considered such a question before. Her father, a preacher in Sabinal for a tiny congregation that consisted exclusively of Perla's family members, always talked about how Utopia was the best place in the world to live and raise children. Perla had never looked for a reason to doubt him. "Don't you know that there's a world out there?" Kelli asked her with impatience.

Meanwhile, Kelli's older sister, Racheal, furious at her parents for yanking her out of a class of over four hundred students and tossing her into what felt like a ditch on a road to nowhere, was breaking down. She quit the volleyball team, telling her parents that only students with the right last names ever got any real playing time on the court. When two girls who'd been giving her a hard time for weeks yanked on her curls one morning between classes, hissing that she was nothing but a "nappy-headed nigger," Racheal fought back. She knocked one to the floor and started popping her over and over in the face. Kelli heard the fight from her classroom, but her teacher closed the door and refused to let the young girl, who'd started crying that her sister needed her help, join the fray.

The country just wasn't proving to be the tonic for Racheal's troubles. She fell in love with a local boy several years older and started running away from home. She fought so bitterly with her parents that they finally felt their only choice was to kick Racheal out of the house altogether, refusing even to let her first pack a bag of clothes. For months Racheal bounced between spare beds at her friends' and boyfriend's house. "She was basically homeless," said Nancy. "Walking the streets of Utopia." An out-of-town social worker was called in to check up on Michael and Kelli. In the middle of the school day, brother and sister were called out of class for a joint therapy session. "And this woman pulled out this instrument and asked us if we would like to beat on the drums to let out our feelings," Kelli remembered sourly. She was humiliated by Racheal's public unraveling and resented strangers' judgment. Suddenly she was no longer just the black girl in town. She was the black girl with the fucked-up family. She shut herself in her bedroom and started planning for the day she could leave this town behind.

After Racheal, Ron and Nancy assumed they'd seen the worst of family drama. But then Michael went and torpedoed their calm. Michael had a different relationship with Utopia than his big sister did. He was happy and popular, a starter on the basketball team. He wore knee socks in school colors on game days. He wanted to stay in Utopia after he graduated. On the weekends he went out with the rest of the team and got drunk with them at parties. Eventually he moseyed over to the small cluster who huddled in the corner, passing around a joint like it was a specially held secret. Drugs hadn't yet made much headway into Utopia School. Hanging with the pot smokers was enough to wreck someone's reputation.

The first time Michael got busted for marijuana was in the fall of his senior year, when he was pulled out of class into the parking lot. The superintendent wanted permission to let the DPS drug dogs, who made random sweeps of the school premises, search his car. Michael, confident that he hadn't been stupid enough to stash a bag in his glove compartment, gave them the go-ahead. He knew he was in trouble when the cops took out tweezers and a magnifying glass and held a stray stem and seed up to the light. There wasn't enough to charge him with possession, but Michael found himself slapped with a misdemeanor for paraphernalia. The school suspended him for two months and kicked him off the basketball team. His vision of his senior year was flushed. A few weeks later he heard that the constable had found an iced-down cooler of beer in the truck of a classmate from a prominent family while she was on the court during the homecoming basketball game. When the constable regretfully told the young woman he'd have to write her up, the school sent her home for two days and gave her a three-game suspension. Michael didn't want to see his friend get in any real trouble, but at home alone, itchy with boredom and loneliness, he couldn't help feeling shafted by the system he had come to believe had his back too.

All of a sudden the highlight of his senior year was cruising the school parking lot when he went to pick up Kelli each afternoon. She'd get in the passenger seat, clutching to her chest the homework assignments she dutifully collected for him, and close her eyes. Meanwhile, Michael would roll through the parking lot, joking around with his friends, grimacing a little as they cheerfully reported hallway gossip and news from the basketball team. When Michael completed his suspension, it was only a matter of weeks before the dogs hit his car again. He hadn't learned his lesson. This time the superintendent found two seeds and a stem and kicked the boy out of school for good. Michael was three credits away from graduating, so he took those by exam. He felt stung by friends who suddenly gave him a wide berth, warned by their parents to steer clear of damaged goods. And he was devastated when nobody invited him as their date so he could attend the senior prom. The school forbade him from walking across the stage with the rest of his classmates to collect his diploma. Three weeks after the ceremony, the superintendent handed the boy his cap and gown in case he wanted them as keepsakes.

Michael had always planned on attending the community college in Uvalde after graduation, but now he was staring at a felony charge after getting popped for the second misdemeanor. A military recruiter pulled him aside and promised he'd press the district attorney not to prosecute if Michael signed a contract with the Army. Michael had always dreamed of living up to his grandfather's legacy, so he reached out to the Air Force, but they weren't interested in a boy with his criminal history. "So it was either have a felony on my record or join the Army," said Michael. "I joined the Army."

Not long after the rest of his class tossed their graduation caps in the air, Michael left for basic training in Kansas. When he signed up, his recruiter had promised that there was only a 50 percent chance Michael would be sent to Iraq or Afghanistan. When he got to basic, he was told his chances were more like 95 pecent. Within months, the Army deployed Michael as a power generator mechanic to the same base as Jeff Wiekamp in Afghanistan.

Michael remembered the day he heard about his friend's death. "We were having a little Cinco de Mayo party after work and I got a few pieces of barbecue and went back to my room," he said. "I was talking to a friend from Utopia on MSN and he was like, 'Did you hear about the accident?' And I said, 'Yeah, I heard about those Haloes going down.' 'Well, Jeff was on one of them.' I told my sergeant that I knew Jeff from back home, that I'd gone to high school with him, and could I get an hour or two off of work so I could go to the memorial service." Michael cleared his throat a little remembering the afternoon. "I wanted to give him the final salute." When Nancy heard of Jeff's death she covered her face with her hands, sick with regret that she had let her son join the military in a time of war simply because he felt out of options at home.

Kelli's brother was twenty years old and overseas. Her sister was long gone, living in San Antonio with her Utopia boyfriend and their two-year-old daughter. Racheal was twenty-two years old, with another baby girl due in the spring, and her parents still disapproved so strongly of her boyfriend, who'd had his own brushes with the law, that he wasn't welcome in their home. ("Yeah, I mean I've had some problems with him," Racheal said of her daughter's father, "but I'm trying to get past that. He takes care of his kids, so what more can you ask for?") With both of her siblings scattered wide, the trailer house was finally quiet.

That evening, Nancy knocked on Kelli's door to tell us dinner was ready at Beryl's house across the yard. When she saw Kelli with the guitar in her lap, Nancy sat on the side of the bed and asked her daughter to play her a song. Kelli hated that her parents assumed she would share with them the music she wrote late at night, long after they had both gone to bed. She was making slow progress on the guitar, and was shy playing in front of anyone. Recently a teacher at school suggested that she consider taking lessons from the justice of the peace. Kelli knew the man, and he'd been a sturdy source of support to Ron and Nancy during Racheal and Michael's troubles. But he played old country and gospel standards at funerals and every third Friday at the Senior Center. Kelli didn't want to learn the guitar from someone in town with intimate knowledge of her family drama, who didn't even listen to the type of music she yearned to play.

Kelli usually refused her mother's plaintive requests. But she was proud of a new blues song she'd written over a long weekend called "Lost and Broken." It was the first song she felt brave enough to post a junky recording of on her MySpace page. So with nervous hives blooming up her neck, Kelli obliged her mother's pleas and started strumming her guitar and belting out the story of a woman yearning for her man. At the sound of his daughter's voice, Ron came in and leaned against her open bedroom door. Nancy placed her hands on Kelli's knees and stared intently at her face so she could feel the vibrations of the guitar strings and read her daughter's lips. When Kelli finished she grinned nervously as her parents started clapping.

"I was mad at Kelli once and I told her, 'That's it. No more rock concerts,' " Ron said with a laugh from the doorway. His black GO ARMY baseball cap was pulled low over his forehead. "And she said, 'Dad, I don't mess around with boys. I don't drink. I don't do dope.

That's all I want to do is go to concerts.'" Kelli shrugged, gingerly setting her guitar down and rolling off the bed to go help her mother with dinner.

The family walked across the yard to Beryl's white one-story house. Beryl was in the living room, sitting on the sofa watching *Jeopardy!* with her tiny legs tucked under her. Beryl's two small dogs, a fluffy gray mutt named Roxy and a tan chihuahua named Hazel, were sniffing around the peppermint candy dishes on the coffee table. Beryl was in the early stages of Alzheimer's and Nancy spent most of her time taking care of her. After Ed died, Beryl just seemed to fall in on herself. Today she was just a whisper of her former self, a baby bird with a permanent in a pale pink sweatshirt and slim trousers. The little loafers on her feet looked like shoes for a child. Beryl didn't hear well, though sometimes it seemed she'd simply decided to tune out her family. Whenever the conversation veered toward anything involving her late husband, she perked up. "We were just as happy as two cats on a hot rock," she told me with a smile as Kelli set the table.

At dinner Beryl went long stretches without contributing to the conversation, laughing and talking instead to her playful dogs as they circled around her feet. Nancy got cross once with her mother when she caught Beryl sneaking forkfuls of meat off her dinner plate and dropping them on the floor for Roxy and Hazel to scrap over. "Meat prices are so high, don't be giving that to the animals!" Nancy scolded. On this subject Beryl will not be bossed. "They're my dogs and I'll feed them whatever I want!" she barked back at her daughter. So while the animals eat hamburger off the floor, Beryl seems to subsist solely on large bowls of Blue Bell ice cream.

While Kelli dished up plates of fried chicken, sugared squash, and a broccoli and mayonnaise salad, Beryl showed me a small framed grocery receipt from July 8, 1942, that hung on her kitchen wall. Ed's mother used to own the General Store in town. This receipt was from their first sale. Beryl held the frame close to her glasses, her finger trembling as she tried to read the faded prices for a stamp, spinach, peas, Oxydol, candy, and some growing mash for chickens. The customer was one of the coffee drinkers' mothers. The total came to $2.36, minus $1.28 for the farm-raised eggs the woman had brought into the store to trade.

Ron sat at the head of the table, under a pastel painting of a white duck in a bonnet leading a train of ducklings, and sipped from his can of Diet Dr Pepper. He asked Kelli to tell everyone more about her plans to move to Austin after she graduated from high school. She'd been to the city twice for academic meets, and that spring Nancy would chaperone Kelli and Perla on their first trip to the city's annual SXSW music festival. As much as Nancy tried to support her daughter's passion for music, she hoped Kelli would apply to the University of Texas. Kelli's parents didn't have any money to help her pay for school, but if she would only get motivated she could start applying for scholarships and financial aid. Whenever her parents started talking about college, Kelli's mood darkened; she would duck her head and remind them that her goal wasn't to graduate from a four-year university but to kick-start her music career.

"Well, we'll move with you," Ron said, winking across the table at his daughter.

"Ha, ha," she said with a smirk. "Uh, no."

"She wants us on opposite ends of the world," laughed Ron. "But she'll miss us. She'll be coming home with her car full of clothes to wash." He reached out to tug on his daughter's arm but Kelli playfully brushed his hand aside.

"It's not like we have tight reins on you," Nancy reminded her daughter. "We really don't dictate what you do now. The thing with Kelli is," she said, looking over at me, "she's been so different from Racheal and Michael. She's more responsible and I trust her. I didn't have that confidence in the other two." She looked sternly at her baby girl. "So don't make me lose it." Beryl looked up from Hazel, whose front paws were dancing up her left calf. "Kelli is just a good kid," she said approvingly.

Outside, under a lone oak, Kelli leaned back in a metal chair and admired the new black flip-flops decorated with tiny skeleton heads that she'd found at the Wal-Mart in Uvalde for ten dollars. The conversation with her parents had annoyed her. She was tired of being expected to dutifully go on to college just because her sister and brother had never made it there. "Kelli's going to make something of herself," Racheal once boasted to me. "She's going to be the one of us who does," agreed Michael. Kelli cracked her neck and looked up at the pale yolk of sun smearing the horizon. "I wanted to be good for the longest time because I didn't want to disappoint my parents," she said. "And I didn't want them to have to go through any stress again. Now I don't really care about that anymore. I can't live my life making sure they're never nervous again. I have to do me.

"Look how pretty it is here," Kelli went on, marveling at the acres of untouched land that spread out before her. "It's weird for me to say that, isn't it? It's almost like I try not to let myself appreciate the beauty." She paused and picked at the blue nail polish on her right big toe. "But the quiet drives me crazy."

On nights like these, when Kelli had a hard time falling asleep, she comforted herself with noise, keeping her stereo or TV cranked loud in her little box of a bedroom. And she would remind herself, over and over, that her world would one day open up and reveal itself. "I'm getting out," she said. "I don't care what I have to do. I knew the moment that we moved here that when I left I was going to scream, 'Hallelujah.'"

A few weeks later, Kelli and Perla got tickets to see their favorite band, My Chemical Romance, at an arena show in San Antonio. Kelli had bought a ticket for Colter as well. She'd always seen him around town, and she talked with him the two times she'd attended the Living Waters Youth Group before deciding the evangelical crowd wasn't her scene. But Colter had started sending her messages on MySpace and they bonded over their love of emo bands and indie movies. And he had a driver's license. So when Kelli's father wasn't available to chauffeur, Colter was game to give Kelli and Perla a lift into the city. Kelli spent all of her meager savings on concerts, shining flares from the outside world that every few months offered an escape from her predictable life in Utopia.

The morning of the My Chemical Romance concert, Kelli arranged for everyone to meet in town at the Church of Christ just after dawn. The arena doors didn't open until that evening, but Kelli was intent on getting the barricade position, pushing herself to the front of the stage so she could thrash around right under the singer's nose. Kelli and Perla were skipping school to stand in line all day for the show, and Colter had lied to his boss on the road crew, saying that he needed the day off to take Lindy to a doctor's appointment. Colter's car was in the shop, so I offered to drive.

Kelli was the first one to show up at the church, kissing her father on his cheek before bounding out of his truck, promising to call when we made it to San Antonio. Colter pulled up next, extra gel in his hair, wearing aviator shades and a tight, pale blue T-shirt. While they waited for Perla, Colter's mother called him on his cellphone. Her voice bleated anxiously from his receiver. Colter had forgotten to lock the front gate when he left and some of the horses had gotten loose. He listened with his mouth in a tight line, murmuring back a few clipped one-word answers. When he hung up, he looked tense and distracted. "I screwed up again," Colter said. "Everyone's mad at me. As usual."

They waited nervously for Perla, whose mother had listened to her daughter's My Chemical Romance album for the first time a few nights before. Afterward she came into Perla's bedroom, warning her daughter that she could hear the voice of Satan in the band's lyrics. So when Perla's father finally pulled into the church parking lot, Kelli gave a little whoop. The three noisily clambered into my car, and as the Utopia School bus lumbered slowly by in the opposite direction, the girls squealed for me to floor it out of town.

In San Antonio, Kelli and Perla bonded fast and hard with the other teenagers in line, immediately trading cellphone numbers and MySpace addresses. Kelli's leather jacket blended easily into the sea of teenagers outfitted in similarly terse attire. The thrill of eating fast food, sitting cross-legged on the pavement in a circle with a group of friendly goth boys from Brownsville, talking about who there had ever seen the opening band, brought excited red hives to Kelli's neck. Perla, so quiet and reserved at school, hopped on one foot in circles with excitement.

Bursts of giggles popped out of her like hiccups. After flapping in place for a few seconds, she'd catch herself and apologize for her display. She'd sit still for a few minutes only to give herself over once more to nerves of excitement. Colter tried to play the elder statesman. He leaned back on his hands at the head of the line, holding fries in the air, explaining to anybody who would listen what differentiated emo from punk.

When the doors finally opened, Kelli and Perla waved back at me and ran inside for the floor. I had an assigned seat up in the bleachers with the rest of the squares carrying paperback books in their purses. Before Colter cleared security I tugged on his arm and asked him to promise to watch out for the girls. His face turned serious and seemed to swell with a sense of responsibility. "I'll make sure they stay safe," he said solemnly, and turned and followed them inside.

Halfway through the concert the lead singer called for a moment of silence, beseeching the crowd to take a moment to acknowledge and mourn the horror that had struck the Virginia Tech campus that afternoon. All those kids who'd been in line all day had no idea that across the country one broken boy had gone on a killing spree. Soon after, the band lunged into their moody anthem "Cancer," the singer dedicating the song to everyone whose lives and loved ones had been polluted by the disease. Down there in the pit, Colter shouted along with the lyrics.

When the show ended, Kelli called me on her cellphone and breathlessly announced that there was a chance they might be able to get on the tour bus and actually meet the band. I garumphed back to her that the past fifteen hours had been swell but if I didn't see them back at my car in the next thirty minutes they better hope there was room on the bus to get them back to Utopia. She said she couldn't hear me, pleading a bad connection, and hung up. But after I had spent just a few minutes alone in my car, feeling as crotchety as one of the coffee drinkers, the kids appeared in the headlights looking stunned and scared.

Colter had turned his phone back on outside the arena and there were panicked messages from home. Lindy had had another seizure. She had collapsed that day at the coffee shop, knocking her head on the door as she went down. EMS had rushed her to the Methodist Hospital in San Antonio. Colter got in the front seat and tried to keep his voice steady as he reported the news.

We drove there in silence, Colter looking out the window, his mouth hanging open. His sweat from the concert filled the car with a rank, heavy smell. He seemed bewildered by how quickly an evening of release had turned sour on him. Kelli and Perla sat muted and stiff in the backseat, willing themselves invisible. It was after midnight when we finally pulled up to the emergency room driveway. The girls stayed huddled wide-eyed in the backseat while Colter walked stiffly through the red neon-lit doors.

Inside, the bright waiting room was in a depressing state of chaos, with people moaning and yelling and nodding off in their seats. A nurse waved Colter back to Lindy's room. He hesitated and exhaled sharply before forcing himself over the threshold. Lindy's head was lolled to the side so she could get a better look at her roommate, who was shouting and waving his arm sloppily in the air. He was a young Mexican whose drinking partner that evening had gone and taken a baseball bat to his head. The towel on his pillow was spritzed with bright blood and the back of his hair was matted and crunchy. Buffered by drink, the man jabbered happily away at Lindy about how his friend had always been an asshole and he wasn't that surprised that the night had ended so poorly. Lindy nodded drowsily at her roommate, murmuring back a few bolstering words of encouragement. When she saw Colter she sat up slowly, her face suddenly filled with pleasure. She patted the side of her bed for her son to sit.

Lindy wore a thin hospital gown, and the skin on her back was clammy. When she gave Colter a hug, hanging like a rag around his neck, he patted her shoulders awkwardly. "Well, I had a little seizure this morning," she reported, "and I was going, 'Oh no, please make it go away, please make it go away.' As the day went on and on, the seizures got more intense. At first I wasn't telling anybody, and then the big one came. But you know what, I'm doing so good now." She patted Colter on the hand. "There are times when it's hard, but most of the time life is wonderful and we've got to go, and smile, and just go."

Colter stood and looked down at his feet, unsure of what was expected of him in this hospital room. When he asked his mother if she needed a drink of water, her roommate bellowed from across the room. "Well, I'll take another beer!"

Lindy laughed and wagged her finger with affectionate disapproval. "Now, now, I think you better lay down or, no, no," she said, her hands grasping in the air for the right expression. "Lay on? Lay off? Yes, lay off of the beer now." The man seemed so surprised to be treated with such tenderness that he looked like he might fall in love with Lindy by the end of the night. "This woman is keeping me from losing my mind!" he roared cheerfully.

Colter grimaced, disgusted by the whole scene. "Mom, where did you pick this guy up?" he said under his breath, as her roommate continued to rant good-naturedly in the background.

"Colter, this man is in pain and needs help," Lindy said, shushing him.

"He's nothing but a damn drunk," said Colter, crumpling into the metal guest chair.

"Hey, damn drunks need love and affection too. Maybe there's a little something I said that will make him—that will bring a smile to his face. You know how I always have some chuckles . . ." Her voice trailed off dreamily as she pinched at the threadbare sheet covering her legs. Colter looked longingly out the door of his mother's room, where a sign pointed toward the nearest exit.

Kelli and Perla were still waiting alone outside in the car, fielding phone calls from their anxious parents, who were wondering if Lindy was all right and when the girls could be expected home. Colter realized he should stay the night at the hospital with his mother, but first we took him to a nearby Whataburger so he could get a meal to tide him over until the morning. As we idled in the drive-through, Colter tried for glibness, as if there was nothing desperate or moving about his circumstances. But when Kelli told him how sorry she was, he looked terrified for a second that he might start crying right there in the car. Back at the emergency room entrance, Colter took his time unbuckling his seatbelt, said good night in a flat voice, and trudged back through the automatic doors, one hand gripping a paper sack of hamburgers.

Kelli and Perla started talking in a rush as soon as we pulled back onto the highway. The night had held too much. They had seesawed from the wild joy of seeing their favorite band to the anxiety of watching a boy fight back his tears after seeing his cancer-stricken mother sagging in her hospital bed. On the drive home, half-listening to the radio rehash the horrid details of the Virginia Tech massacre, the girls sat upright, taking mouse-sized bites of their hamburgers, shreds of iceberg lettuce clinging sadly to their black T-shirts. Perla soon fell asleep, her head slumped over to the side. Kelli gazed somberly out the window as we whizzed past moonlit fields. Every few minutes she'd murmur for me to slow down when she spotted the glinting eyes of deer on the sides of the road ahead.

EMS

When someone in Utopia is in trouble, they don't call 911, or "9-1-somethin'-somethin'," as one of the coffee drinkers said in all earnestness. They call a local number that rings on the fire phone at the back of the General Store and at the home of John and Judy Hillis. The Hillises were founding members of Utopia's EMS, and they've spent much of their adult lives being woken up in the middle of the night by friends and neighbors in need.

John and Judy started going together in the seventh grade. John was a basketball star and quarterback of Utopia's football team. (The year after he graduated in 1960, Utopia gave up its tiny football program for good.) Judy was a basketball and volleyball star. They married in 1961. Ten years later, they formed the EMS. Prior to that, all Utopia had by way of emergency response was Lon Rushing's hearse at his Uvalde funeral parlor. "Heart attack? They called the hearse," said Judy. "Going into labor? Hearse. Back in the day you either dealt with emergencies at home or threw someone in Lon's hearse and rushed them to Hondo or Uvalde and waited for a doctor to show up the next morning."

So Judy, along with her husband, John, and a few other locals, went and got their EMT certificates. Judy's first official transport was her daddy. When her mother called one night with news that he'd suffered a heart attack, Judy and John rushed him to Hondo in their tan wood-paneled station wagon. Utopia didn't get an ambulance until 1976; Judy's father, after suffering another heart attack, was the first transport in the ambulance as well. Three decades later, Utopia's EMS has two ambulances, one full-time paid employee, and three local volunteer-based crews that rotate on-call evening shifts.

Judy showed me around the unassuming EMS shed, which sat off the center of the town square. They'd just bought a new ambulance for $183,000, with the help of grants, a modest county subsidy, local donations, and the annual EMS fund-raising barbecue at the Utopia rodeo. Judy introduced me to the bookkeeper, an older woman in high-waisted jeans and glasses who held a red binder to her blouse. "I don't do computers," she said, showing off her penciled rows detailing every EMS expenditure. "I started with this red book and I don't see a reason to change. I buy a hundred sheets of paper for a dollar and a half."

Judy is sixty-seven years old and doesn't get paid for EMS work. When she is out in the field feeding her goats, she keeps her cellphone on her in case an emergency call comes through that needs dispatching. When she and John go for supper at the café, they put their EMS walkie-talkie by the salt and pepper shakers and turn the volume up high. Judy is tired, but unwilling just yet to leave the department in the hands of others. "John and I are the only originals left," she said. "I don't mean to criticize anybody, but nobody else remembers what it was like before Utopia had EMS."

In her thirty-five years of service, Judy has seen every kind of physical trauma imaginable. She is unflappable at the scenes of accidents, but the aftermath of all that trauma has left her raw and always on the verge of tears. She still can't talk about that afternoon back in 2002 when she got a call that four local kids had been in a car wreck without crying. "I came over here to drive the second ambulance," she remembered. "When I got almost halfway there, Bobby Mauldin called and said, 'Just cancel the other ambulance because the other two were DOA.'" Judy said the loss of those kids marked the only time in John's decades of service that her husband attended what EMT workers call "a critical incident stress debriefing."

John stopped by the shed on his lunch break. His tan forearms and Wranglers were streaked with grease. John welds all day so he can keep up their eight-hundred-acre ranch, which lies about twelve miles east of town out on Seco Road. He took off his cowboy hat to mop his forehead with his handkerchief. John is sixty-six years old and has been threatening for a while now that he was fixing to quit EMS. But just like his wife, he didn't have retirement in him. John said the only surefire way to get him to walk was to force him to accept the twenty-five dollars EMS crew members are now paid whenever they make a run. Taking the money would be an insult to him. "I guess you could say I'm hardheaded," he said with a sigh. "But I started out one way and I'm going to go out that way." He had to get back to work and nodded goodbye, with a quick hand on the shoulder of his wife.

Judy took a tissue out of her jeans pocket and dabbed at her enormous blue eyes. Her husband's stubborn pride had gone and gotten her emotional again. "John really would quit before taking the money," she said. "There are some in town who want to start charging people out the gazoo. But we did not set this up that way. We set it up to be a service to the community. I know times change, but . . ." A garbled voice started bleating from the direction of her waistband. Judy blew her nose briskly, cleared her throat, and turned up her walkie-talkie.

CHAPTER 5

Black Is Black and
White Is White

Kelli's brother, Michael, was amazed to see how joining the Army seemed to reboot his reputation. Before I met him in person, Michael sent me a message on MySpace from Afghanistan warning me how easy it was to gain a bad image in Utopia. "U gotta watch out in a small town like that," he wrote. "Once you get a 'label' the whole 1,000 people think of you as that label. I was the town pot-head druggie who got kicked outta school, but since i joined the Army im the towns new american hero. Well i only have a few more weeks of this deployment and then should be home soon. im sure we're bound to run into each other at the store or cafe or something."

When Kelli and her family picked Michael up at the airport in San Antonio, he came down the escalator into the baggage claim area grinning like a little boy. Racheal, seven months pregnant, holding her young daughter's hand, broke down in tears when she saw her brother in his fatigues.

The Army paid Michael close to a thousand dollars a month in Afghanistan. When he'd saved enough money, he gave it to his mom with instructions to buy a used car he'd seen online. Before his bags were on the ground in Utopia, he jumped into the powder-blue Mitsubishi Eclipse parked on the lawn outside the trailer and sped into town to show off his new ride. That first night in Utopia, Michael logged close to a hundred miles cruising up and down the half-mile stretch of Main Street, swinging into the parking lots of the gas station and the bank, idling out front of the café. He ran a tender hand over the rear bumper, murmuring to himself that he ought to take a Q-tip to scrape clean the crevices around the car's emblem.

In high school, Michael used to cruise Main in his dad's old truck every afternoon, raising a hand to any driver he would pass. The road wave is about as trusted a tradition as there is in a small town like Utopia. Some drivers chuck their chins in the air. Some raise their hands like a cupped paw. The truly laconic lift an index finger an inch off the steering wheel. But unless it was one of Michael's school friends driving the other way, he was usually met with blank stares. After he got caught with drugs, Michael became invisible on Main Street. But here now, home from Afghanistan, he felt seen for the first time as worthy of his grandfather's legacy.

Three nights into his leave, three nights into feeling treated like a boy in uniform held proud and tight by his hometown, an EMS siren hollered down Main Street, coming for him. Michael had been driving home to get a change of clothes before going out for another long night with his friends. Eager to test out his new car's engine, he revved the speedometer up to eighty miles per hour, and then a deer flashed into his path. He swerved to protect his car from the impact and rolled three times before crashing into Ralph's fence. When Kelli and her parents arrived at the scene, they found Michael sitting in the back of the ambulance as EMS tended to a gash on his leg and checked his eyes for slivers of glass. His nervous family shuffled around outside the ambulance, pacing back and forth. Nancy's guts twisted as she looked over at the smoking car. Soon Ralph pulled up, his sleepy face pickled. The boom of the crash had woken him and he looked coolly upon the damage. "Who's going to fix my fence?" he demanded of Nancy and Ron, without even a glance over at the boy in the ambulance. "He didn't even ask if Michael was all right," Kelli said, "if he was dead or anything."

The next morning at the General Store, Ralph relayed the details of the accident to the coffee drinkers. "I think that boy was smoking more of that wacky tobacky," Ralph said, his voice crabby with fatigue. "Blamed it on a deer. One of those 'phantom bucks,' you know! More like wacky tobacky if you ask me. I told 'em he's going to help repair that fence."

"That boy ain't in prison yet?" Milton said with disgust.

Small towns pride themselves on coming together in a crisis. The only time I ever heard an approving word spoken about New York City was when a woman told me she thought she recognized the camaraderie and fierce spirit New Yorkers displayed after 9/11. And it was true that Utopia always had your back—as long as it considered you one of its own. Michael should have fit their narrow rules of belonging. His grandfather was born in Utopia and buried in the Waresville Cemetery. But still the coffee drinkers didn't claim him the way they did any of the Wiekamp boys, whose parents and grandparents, incidentally, hailed from South Dakota. When people here spoke about the "true Utopia," they often looked past those on the margins like Michael or Colter or even Nancy. It is natural, sometimes even a source of appeal, to feel anonymous in a city like New York. In a town as small as Utopia, such invisibility or outright dismissal felt like a slap of rejection.

Having coffee with the old-timers was sometimes like getting together with relatives for Thanksgiving. There would be a general glow of warmth and tenderness in the room, the conversation upbeat, and suddenly talk skittered in a direction that revealed something disturbing about these people you otherwise so greatly admired. It was hard to know when a benign story would wash out into an ugly ending. Wetbacks, beaners, towelheads, gooks, niggers, sand niggers, ragheads—slurs got tossed around with thoughtless abandon at the back of the store. Everybody told me not to take them so seriously. The men would argue that a term like "nigger" was just a harmless word, a descriptor even, and nobody in their right mind ought to take any offense.

"When I say 'nigger' I don't mean it as loaded," argued John. "If somebody else does, that's their problem."

"They call you a cracker!" Milton told him.

"In my eyes everybody was created equal," said John. "But they're still a nigger. And I'm still a white man."

"Honky!" Ralph clarified, pointing a finger at John.

Early on, when I first started joining the guys, they were laughing about a prank they had long ago played on Ralph. The man loves his vegetable garden. Once during a cold snap he left the coffee circle early, saying he had to get home to visit with his tomato plants. "I'm gonna go out and sit and look at my tomaters and cry," he said. "Because I know they're going to freeze."

"Talk to 'em," said Bud encouragingly. "You talk to 'em, go out there and talk to 'em."

Ralph shook his head. "I done talked to 'em. I give 'em a little pep talk just yesterday. 'Get with it or you're going to die!'"

A few years back, Ted and the late J. D. Snider—"that man would turn on you faster than a javelina," Ted said with amused affection—decided to gag their friend. The men bought a bunch of asparagus at the General Store and, giggling like schoolboys, stuck a few wobbly spears in Ralph's garden. The next morning Ralph rushed outside thinking his crop had sprung early. When he reached down to examine the asparagus, those stray spears plunked pathetically to the ground and he realized he'd been had. "But I knew who done it," he told me, "when I turned the corner and there was one of them culprits' nigger shooters . . ." I spat up some coffee. Ralph looked startled by the interruption. "What?" he said. "That's just their name."

I started breaking down the term's multiple offenses, and everybody just laughed at me. Baby Ray, who is always smiling, drinking his coffee from a mug he brings from home that reads, I'M RETIRED . . . OR

DID MY PERMANENT GRIN GIVE THAT AWAY?, believed my outrage stemmed from an acute case of political correctness. "It's not meant as anything intended against race," he said, his voice soothing and conciliatory. "It's just what they've always been called." He suggested, with a smirk that was not meant to be unkind, that Ralph ought to from here on out refer to slingshots as "African American rocket launchers" when in my presence. We went downhill from there. My huffy indignation fanned the flames of the men's baffled amusement. After we'd go at it, women who'd heard the ruckus while doing their shopping would find me later in town and pull me aside, swearing that the old-timers really weren't that bad and that shocking me had become a sport for them. "They're just trying to make you fall off your stool," one woman told me, her eyes worried that I was getting an unfair impression of her hometown. I just needed to learn how to take a joke, people seemed to agree.

"Utopia isn't racist like it used to be," the café owner, Tacy Redden, told me one afternoon after the dinner rush. "Not like it used to be. My grandpa was bad. He was racist against Jews, against Catholics, against anything. I mean *anything*. If you were out of his family, he was against you. Mother had a boyfriend come pick her up one day and he ran him off because he drove a Japanese car." Tacy smiled and waved goodbye to a Mexican ranchhand who was one of her regulars. She pointed after him as evidence of Utopia's progressiveness. "See? Good people is good people. There's not a lot of black people here, but we have some Hispanics. I don't think race is an issue at all anymore. In fact I think we make it too much of an issue today, but that's just my two cents. The old coffee drinkers who've all died off now, they would say ugly things about people who walked in here. My grandfather? It was an issue. But you know he fought in World War I, and those men were just different."

Nobody in town ever wanted to admit that he or she might still have a complicated relationship with race. Morris pointed to his close friend, a young Mexican construction worker everyone called Li'l Johnny, who came by every morning to joke around by the front register before heading to work. Morris would jovially declare to me that their friendship was proof positive that racism was dead down at the store. In private I once asked Johnny if he ever got tired of all the Mexican jokes. He shrugged agreeably.

"If Morris ever gives me a hard time, I just tell him he looks like a manatee," he said. Morris is a tall man, with the slowly blooming neck of a former high school athletic star. He has small eyes, close-cropped graying hair, and a coarse scrub of mustache. When Li'l Johnny compared him to a manatee, Morris laughed. Neither saw any reason to differentiate between blasting someone's roots, let alone their legitimacy in this country, and the more specific insult of calling someone out for having a fat neck.

One morning Ralph asked the coffee drinkers for their opinion on the recent developments in the national news story about some Duke University lacrosse players who had been acquitted, after a bloodletting of suspicion, of raping an African American stripper in North Carolina. "They done said that they're not going to press charges against the girl," Ralph said disapprovingly. "I think the whole thing was brought on by a district attorney trying to advance himself. He had to have that black vote."

I got myself a second cup of coffee, mumbling about how those rich white college boys were probably going to end up all right in the end.

"You're prejudiced," Milton declared of me.

"You've got her there," said Ralph.

"I don't care how rich they are," said Milton. "It ain't right. I feel like that girl should pay."

"Well, something happened," said Ralph. "There's a little clog in the churn here somewhere that I can't figure out."

The conversation seemed bound for a ditch, so I changed the subect to Ralph's plans for the weekend. He announced he was taking Jane to their usual Friday night dinner at a Mexican restaurant in Hondo. Milton groaned. I asked Milton if he'd eaten there, and he folded his arms over his chest. "I can't eat Mexican food!" he said. Seeing everyone's perplexed expressions, he looked around at us like we were idiots. "I'm prejudiced against Mexicans and niggers!" he reminded everyone. The man claimed, with what can only be described as pride, that he had never eaten so much as a burrito in his whole long life.

The superintendent moved a few inches away from Milton on the bench and looked him over with a cocked eyebrow. "That's kinda weird," he said. Milton shrugged. "I spent all these years cultivating myself and I'm not ready to change now," he said. "I've got too much time invested in being prejudiced. It's too late for change. When I eat out I either want a steak or seafood." He paused for a moment. "It might sound funny, but I like Chopsticks in San Antonio," he said, rubbing his hands together happily. "It's a Chinese restaurant, but they got good crabs and shrimp." I poked my finger into Milton's arm and pointed out the irony that he would eat at a Chinese restaurant but drew the line at enchiladas. Milton glared angrily at me as if I had called his very patriotism into question. "I don't eat Chinese food!" he said. "It's just crabs and shrimp. That's all I put on my plate."

It can be exhausting listening to men stubbornly deny the power of words while simultaneously insisting that they themselves didn't see the world in terms of race. That's why the bald honesty of a man like Milton was sometimes a relief. That man can't speak frankly enough on the subject.

Morris, hearing the rising voices back by his coffeepots, sauntered up and tried to play the diplomat. "We got plenty of white trash nowadays too!" he said.

"I tell you I'm prejudiced to anybody who listens to that rap music," Milton continued, before going on to bemoan that his own grandson Cody had gone and taken a liking to hip-hop.

Milton is a man with strong opinions on just about every subject. He pined for the days when men in trucks wouldn't think twice about bullying bicyclists back onto the shoulder, reminding them of who was the boss of the road. "That bunch of idiots," he said one morning about his two-wheeled nemeses. "When we was kids, we would have took a damn antenna off a vehicle and whipped their asses in them little spandex."

Once, during a lively conversation about politics up by the cash register, a twenty-seven-year-old newcomer from Tucson muscled his way into the discussion. He'd moved to Utopia in search of a more righteous community—by which, he explained in short order, he meant less overrun with illegal immigrants—to raise his family. He went on for a while, pissing and moaning to me about the decaying moral values of our heathen generation. Milton looked at him with one side of his face curled in suspicion. After listening to the newcomer dump on the priggish sensitivity of liberals, Milton finally interrupted. "So I guess you think old Bush is the greatest thing since apple jelly?" he asked the young man. "That's the sorriest son of a bitch to shit between two shoes." The newcomer stopped for a second, surprised to have lost his audience, and tried to regroup. He turned the subject to the Iraq war and made an amateur's mistake of quoting Milton scripture to defend Bush's decision to invade.

"There's a verse in the Bible," he began smugly, before Milton cut him off with a growl.

"I'll piss on that book and the goat it rode in on too," said Milton.

The newcomer's jaw tightened angrily but he pressed on. "Well, there's a verse that tells you who is going to come back and who the devil is going to come back as," he said.

Milton waved a hand in the air in disgust. "You read the Bible but you only read what you want," he said with fierce finality. Bored with the whole conversation, unsure even of who this fellow was he was talking to, Milton turned around and headed back to the coffeepots. The newcomer stared after him as if he'd been slapped. One of the coffee drinkers told me once in private that Milton could sometimes be a little much, and that I shouldn't make the mistake of thinking that he spoke for the lot of them. "He's just so *radical*," said the coffee drinker.

Every morning, Milton sat beneath a plaque honoring the local Boy Scouts in Troop 283. Milton once saw me looking at the engraved names of the twelve kids. "This one here got killed five years ago," he said, pointing to the silver slip of metal bearing the name of his grandson. Dustin died in that car accident back in 2002, when he was a sophomore in high school, along with his freshman cousin Kimber, Milton's granddaughter. The kids were driving home from an orthodontist appointment in Uvalde that afternoon when the driver, Chance, Morris's trusted second, reached for his drink on the floor of the passenger seat and the SUV, on account of poor design, spun off the road and rolled.

"I lost two of 'em at one time," said Milton, looking at the plaque. "Yeah," he said, coughing. "It was a big deal in town." His eyes started watering and he put a hand on the wall as if to steady himself. "So, I wonder if the rain is going to hold up . . . ," he said.

At the dreadful site of the accident, eight miles outside of Utopia, Milton built a beautiful wooden memorial in honor of his much-beloved grandchildren. MY SPECIAL ANGELS, the sign read. LOVE YOU, POP.

"You don't know how to cook?" said Bud, staring at me with his white eyebrows shot halfway up his tall forehead. There are some things in life Bud just cannot fathom. He once described an extravagantly wealthy woman who lived on a large ranch just outside of town as amiable enough but terribly eccentric. "She's one of these people," he whispered to me, in a tone that promised scandal, "who don't like meat in their hamburgers."

"You don't even know how to make backstrap and gravy?" said John, grinning at me.

"You do make red beans, don'tcha?" said Bud. He cocked his thumb in my direction and spoke to the coffee drinkers. "I think she lives around too many fast-food places."

I argued that I lived quite well at home in New York with a drawer full of Thai restaurant take-out menus.

"Let's work on that word 'tie,'" said Bud. "What is this word?" When I clarified that I was talking about food from Thailand, he smacked his chest and wheezed. "Good God!"

"What about biscuits?" asked kindhearted Hose, who must have thought he was providing me with a way to turn this conversation around. I just needed to assure the men that I at least knew how to make a simple pan of biscuits.

Seeing my sheepish expression, Bud looked playfully aghast. "Oh no, you'll never make it down here if you can't make biscuits."

"You stay around here and we'll have you bakin' biscuits in no time," assured Hose. "It's not very complicated now. Two cups of flour, two spoons of baking powder, and a little grease and salt." Hose's wife died a few years back, so he'd been cooking for himself awhile now.

"The first thing we got to teach this girl is how to butcher a goat," sighed John, taking a bite of honey bun.

"They holler a bit in the end," warned Bud as the men started snickering.

"You've got to cut the throat," said John. "Then just let him bleed out."

When the coffee drinkers asked me about my life in New York, they'd often listen with befuddled expressions as I explained to them that I lived in Brooklyn but commuted in to my office in Manhattan on the subway and that yes, sometimes the trains were rather crowded and occasionally one had to deal with ugly smells and inelegant manners. "You're a people person," Hose concluded, in a generous attempt to understand why anyone would ever choose a life in the big city over a small town like Utopia. "I'm the other way. I don't like to be around people. I like to be in the background." Country living may have the city beat in multiple ways, but I told them I'd gladly be subjected to public transportation before having to slit an animal's throat while keeping my ears open for its death rattle.

"I don't know about that one," said Bud. "Life on the subway must be like going to Mexico. You might be killed or stabbed anytime you go for a ride."

A few mornings later I rounded the aisle to find Ralph in a scrapping mood. I had barely taken a seat before he pounced and asked about a news story he had seen about a power outage in New York City. "And I'm wondering how you would have felt being up there in that blackout in the subway standing up aside some great fat nigger woman smelling her armpits?" he said, his words dashing out of his mouth in such a rush it was almost like he had no control over them.

I sputtered a little, not used to this kind of ugliness from Ralph, and pressed my fingers into the space between my eyebrows. Some of the men laughed, so Ralph kept on chewing. "How would you have liked it up there then? They always stink," he said knowingly, looking down the bench and nodding at his friends. "They got a smell all their own."

"Ralph, how would you know what black people smell like?" I asked him.

He paused for a second. "We used to have a grocery driver," he said dopily. "Remember how he used to smell?" he asked Tony, who shook his head, unwilling to get roped into Ralph's argument. Some of the guys hooted a bit, either from surprise at their friend's audacity or at the simple fun of seeing me so easily wound up.

"Make sure you put this in your book there," said Ray, covering his eyes.

"Just make sure you make clear that Ralph said it," Hose said quietly, giving me a sweet smile. "What are you going to call this book anyways—*Pure Bull*?" he said. "You'll have to put it in the comics section."

"Black is black, white is white," continued Ralph, who seemed to know his case was slumping but was going to go down swinging.

Several weeks earlier Ralph had come into the store in a mournful mood. He'd been following the news of radio host Don Imus, who was in trouble for dismissing members of the Rutgers women's basketball team as nothing but a bunch of "nappy-headed hos." Ralph surprised everyone by announcing that he thought Imus should burn for his disgraceful words. "Did you see them girls interviewed?" he asked the group. "The most well-spoken, ambitious bunch of ladies you ever did see. And you know what got to me? They weren't angry. They were *disappointed*. There's no place in society for that man after what he said. He ought to be ashamed."

Ralph expressed such real empathy that morning for those young women that to hear him now blather on about black people and their smell was depressing.

"What happened to the man who was so outraged by Don Imus?" I wondered.

"He was wrong," Ralph said, his voice taking on a tight defensiveness. "What he said was so totally uncalled for. It wasn't funny. It was just cruel. He meant it. I didn't. I was just stirring you up." Ralph looked around at the rest of the coffee drinkers for some reinforcement. "She needed stirring up this morning," he said, gesturing over at me.

Looking uncomfortable, Ralph announced that he'd better get going. His wife, Jane, would be home soon from Uvalde, where she'd been visiting with her mother, who had recently celebrated her hundredth birthday. He wanted to greet Jane with a proper meal when she arrived later. "I got my turkey fried and my green beans snapped so when my old girl comes in all I'll have to do is bake the potatoes," he said. He waved goodbye and gave me an embarrassed little shrug before disappearing out the front door. On my own way out of the store later, Morris laughed off the morning's conversation. "That's just Ralph," he said. "If a black guy walked in here today he'd shake hands with him and invite him for dinner."

The next morning the coffee drinkers forgot that I was heading out of town for a few days on a previously planned trip. After I failed to show at the store, a rumor raced through their ranks that I was boycotting. When I rounded the aisle a few mornings later, they looked genuinely pleased to see me. Everybody teased me for taking Ralph so seriously and was glad that I wasn't bearing anyone a grudge. When Ralph arrived on his second shift, he slipped in through the back door, grimacing when he caught my eye. He ducked as if I might greet him with a left hook. He didn't sit in his usual seat, instead positioning himself at the end of the bench next to the superintendent. I thought everybody seemed in fine enough spirits and that whatever tension had swirled around the coffeepots a few days earlier had been taken out with the trash. But Ralph seemed uncomfortable, especially when people started in on me about some imagined aspect of my life in New York. "That's okay, that's okay," Ralph mumbled to himself when one of the coffee drinkers got to needling me. "Even though you don't know what you're talking about, you can still yank her chain. It keeps her on her toes."

After an hour or so of visiting I said goodbye to the men, promising that I'd see them again the following morning. "Oh yep, Cricket, hey there," Ralph said, following me out of view of the rest of the men. He stood there for a second looking unmoored in the refrigerated foods aisle, his arms hanging down at his sides. "I was just pulling your chain the other morning," he said. And then, I think to both of our surprise, his face flushed pink and his mouth started trembling a little. "Because you judge somebody by their actions, not their color," he said as a tear snaked down his sagging cheek. How very badly I believed in him as that little line of tearful saliva hung there between Ralph's wobbly lips. I'd come to understand that if I was going to hang with the coffee drinkers, I was going to hear things that messed with my otherwise rosy picture of them. I would sometimes be uncomfortable. But here in front of me was a man badly wanting to make things right. So I threw my arms around Ralph and told him that I believed him to be a fine man. I probably excused him too easily, but I did so gratefully.

"Okay, all right," he said awkwardly after a second, patting my shoulders. "Like I said, I was just messing with your mind," he said, disentangling himself from our clumsy embrace. "Carry on, carry on."

He never mentioned the episode again, though weeks later he winced when I shared with the group a terrible dream I'd had the night before: I was standing up in front of the Living Waters congregation when I said something that greatly offended the exuberant group of worshippers. Ralph shook his head in empathy. "We're all known for our stupid statements," said Ralph. "They don't seem to go away. Just hang out there like a cloud."

Away from the jocularity of the coffee drinkers, I once asked Ralph what he thought about the brushfire of enthusiasm that seemed to be igniting the country for the charismatic Illinois senator Barack Obama. "I think he's too young and inexperienced," Ralph said softly. "But I don't know." He paused, fingering the arms of his recliner in his family room. "See, I've never been around black people. I know nothing at all about 'em. Even in the Army we were segregated. I was in Georgia, and when we went to Korea there was none in my unit." He took a breath, spooked, it seemed, by his meandering train of thought, and circled back around to his easier concern about Obama's experience level.

In that brief moment, Ralph didn't ape and bluster, dismissing the man as a nigger before denying that the word has a loaded history that continues to make it a bludgeon in the present. Ralph said that he was clueless when it came to black people, and that this cluelessness made him uncomfortable. That's about as honest and direct an admission of ignorance as there ever was—which doesn't make Ralph any less good and complicated a man. And which also doesn't excuse him for the fact that on the night of Michael's accident he should have asked after Kelli's brother, a boy sitting miserably next to his crumple of a car, before bothering the family about his damn fence.

THE MERCANTILE CO. MEAT PLANT

It's hard to pick a prouder moment in Utopia's history than when the Beef Industry Council rolled into town to shoot a national commercial. In 1989 the council ran an ad campaign that made cute plays on the names of some select American towns. (Besides Utopia, other honored communities included Manhattan, Montana; Luck, Wisconsin; and Yale, Washington.) It was a big deal when snappily dressed executives from Ketcham Advertising—"I think they were from New York because they were a little snooty," remembered one Utopian—swooshed down Main Street. "Utopia does exist," the narrator purred in the finished product, as the picture cut to shots of locals in their Sunday finest leaving the Methodist church and playing the fiddle at a country dance under twinkling white lights down at the park. "I've eaten there. And if you ever reach Utopia, take my advice. Order the hamburger."

Luis Santillano was barely two years old when he appeared for a couple of seconds in that beef commercial, standing in a pasture wearing a pearl-button snap shirt tucked into little belted blue jeans. The money Luis earned for that blink of airtime sat in the bank, accumulating interest until he turned eighteen years old and could use the savings for college. But when Luis, or Big Lu, as he is now known to his friends in town, graduated from high school, he put the nearly $15,000 toward a brand-new black Dodge Ram Mega Cab truck. He'd always wanted a new truck. Instead of going on to college, or joining the Army like his best friend, Michael Rhodes, he went to work full-time with his parents, José and Rosie, at the Utopia meat market.

Now twenty years old, Big Lu, his body a series of stacked spheres—pumpkin-round cheeks, a long barrel of a torso, and slightly bowed legs—lived up to his nickname. At work he wore a backward baseball hat over his shaggy black hair, a long white shirt jacket with pockets, and jeans tucked lazily into a pair of boots he got in Mexico in trade for a couple of cowhides. He kept a pen in his front pocket, and when I surprised him one afternoon at work he clicked the top over and over until he was freed from my presence. Luis has two younger siblings, Junior, recently graduated and considering a stab at the junior college, and Lupita, a sophomore and star writer for the school newspaper. So far neither of his siblings has expressed much interest in joining the family business.

Luis leaned against the small brick building with the hand-painted sign. "My dad owns the place," he said, "he and the Reddens," speaking of Rusty and Tacy, who along with the café ran their own private goat ranch. Suddenly, Luis's father, a sweet-tempered man with a gentle, amused voice, appeared from around the corner. "Rusty is the owner," José cheerfully corrected his son. "Still owns it. I don't own it, I'm just here to work." José put an arm around his boy and started, in his thick accent, describing the market's beginnings. "We first started building in November 1982, built the floors. But the water well over there we did in

1980. I put in the concrete. We open up here September 1983 at one o'clock. It was a Tuesday, the twenty-third. The twenty-third at one o'clock. At one o'clock we got the doctor and the inspectors. We open up at one o'clock." He paused to laugh about the hazards of working with meat all day. "I used to eat steak in the morning and steak in the evening and steak for lunch, and you know what happened? Cholesterol went up about to three thousand! I had to quit. Now we eat cereal in the morning."

Luis still lives at home with his parents, in a modest house a rib's toss from the meat market. Seems like he's been passing back and forth on the well-worn path between the two forever. "He started working here when he was this little," José said, his hand tapping lightly above his knee. "Maybe when he was six years old. But then he cut his finger . . ."

"I was at least eight," said Luis.

"No, no," continued José, "I put him cutting stew meat and he was cutting meat and, I don't know, he cut his finger—"

"Right down to the bone, right on the joint," said Luis, holding up the scar to the sunlight.

"—and I said no more until he grows up."

Luis went back to work when he was twelve years old, passing his afternoons on the kill floor, where he herded goats and cows up a chute before knocking them unconscious, and butchering in the processing room. Luis admitted that when Rosie took one of the baby animals home to raise up big and fat in their backyard, he left its killing up to the Santillanos' other worker. Luis can't thunk an animal on the head once he's given it a name. But for the most part he is stoic about the primal nature of his work. It pays well—his father gave him close to $1,400 last month—and he gets to work with the people he trusts most in this world. But if Luis ever strikes it rich again, like he did at the age of two, he is going to buy himself a few acres and start running his own little goat ranch. Somewhere where nobody would ever wonder who was the real man in charge.

CHAPTER 6

They Call It
Situational Awareness

That spring, while Josh Wiekamp was home on leave from Iraq, I called him up and asked if he would meet me for lunch. His little brother, Joey, had spent the past couple of months dodging me around town, polite but unwilling to engage. His friends laughed and told me that Joey half-suspected me of being a narc. Jared lived with his wife on base in Kentucky. If I wanted to talk to one of Jeff's brothers, Josh was my only hope. But people warned me that of all the Wiekamp boys, Josh had taken Jeff's death the hardest, and that talking about his brother would probably be too painful. So it was a surprise when he called me back late one evening and told me to meet him in town the next day at the bank. His instructions were to look for his tan GMC

Duramax diesel; though as it turned out his truck was the only vehicle in the parking lot.

Josh wore an old camouflage baseball cap and jeans, his henley sleeves pushed up to his elbows. His tan forearms were nicked with small scars from burning cedar and taking lighters to the skin back in high school. He rubbed one of the pale crescent-shaped scars and chuckled softly. "Doing another stupid thing," he said. "Back in the day, I was a little punk. You just get bored in this town, I guess."

Josh's handsome face was puffy from celebrating a rare week away from war. The night before he had gone with his family to the bowling alley in Uvalde and afterward they'd stayed up late, drinking and playing cards. This morning Kathy was busy preparing a large barbecue at which Josh's friends and family would give him a proper goodbye on his last night home. Tomorrow he would return to his base in Colorado Springs, and from there he would fly back to Iraq for another tour of duty.

The Army had given Josh the option of sitting out this next deployment. "The general came by and asked him how he was doing," Kathy explained. "Told him he didn't have to go. Well, (A) all of his men are going, and (B) he said, 'I'm not going to use Jeff as an excuse.' We never talked about it again." Kathy sighed with a mixture of pride and exasperation. "If Josh would've stayed home and the guy who took his place got killed—see, things like this Josh couldn't handle. Once he was going to volunteer so that his buddy whose wife was pregnant didn't have to go. I was mad about that and I did tell him, 'No, I'd rather you didn't.' But he said, 'Mom, I don't have a brand-new baby.'"

Josh drove us twenty minutes out of Utopia to a roadside café where we could talk without forcing everyone at the surrounding tables to pretend they weren't listening in on the conversation. On the ride we talked about his truck, which was so dear to the young man's heart that when he bought her back in 2003 he christened her Allison. Everyone called her Allison too, and joked that she was the first real love of his life. Today poor Allison was missing a front headlight because of a mudding accident. The kids in town found it hilarious that I had never heard of mudding, a favorite pastime of country boys, who drove their four-wheel-drive trucks into man-made mud pits and then ground the gears trying to haul their asses out. Joey had been mudding in the Wiekamp pit when he got stuck. So Josh backed Allison in to pull his brother out, and his truck slid down the slope of the hill into a stump that snapped her light off. "I was pissed," said Josh, with his endearing little grunt of a laugh. When he laughed it was a quick and quiet burst, as if it surprised him to be happy. In the sun visor, Josh had tucked a few pictures of the four Wiekamp brothers. In every picture of the boys, all of them are grinning with their arms slung happily around one another. And at least one of them is giving the camera the finger.

Josh pulled his truck into the gravel parking lot of a small restaurant whose kitchen was run out of an old fireworks stand. He ordered a sausage wrap, wouldn't accept my offer to pay, and sat down at a picnic table in view of Allison. His faded black metal bracelet chuffed on the table. He saw me looking at his wrist and positioned the bracelet so I could read it. SERGEANT JEFFERY WIEKAMP, KABUL AFGHANISTAN. He wore the bracelet on the arm with the tattoo of his brother's call sign. He looked down at Jeff's bracelet and his face sagged. Jeff had been gone for almost a year.

"I'm just trying to get by, I guess," he said, without waiting for the question he knew was coming. Josh still didn't know where to funnel his anger over the loss of his brother. "For a while I was pissed at the Army," he said softly. "If Jeff hadn't signed up, he wouldn't have been over there." He cleared his throat and shook his head. "I don't know. I don't know. He could've died here in a car crash. And if he had not been in the military and he had died I wouldn't have anything to blame." Josh spoke about his brother in as few words as possible. When a question pushed him too close to his pool of grief—"Was Jeff a good guy?" for instance—he'd flinch. He'd look at me, and jerk his head no, as if warning and pleading with me to move on.

Whenever a motorcycle growled up the hill or the bell on the door of the market behind us jangled, Josh tensed up and darted a look over his shoulder. When I told him he seemed jittery he laughed again, one sharp chuckle coughed up from deep inside his chest. "They call it 'situational awareness,'" he said, with just a hint of a sneer creeping into his voice. "I've been in convoys where we've been shot at or had IEDs go off." Josh spoke about Iraq in brief, vague bursts, light on detail and never going near the hard truth of his Special Forces missions. He'd rather talk about his friends in his unit and how they passed their free time, rewatching bootleg comedies like *Grandma's Boy* and *The Wedding Crashers,* working out in the gym, playing video games, or checking MySpace for breezy dispatches from home. They worked hard to get their hands on alcohol. On base he taped three pictures of Jeff above his bed. His favorite was of the four Wiekamp boys at the end of a long night in Utopia bunched together in an ATV buggy. Josh and Jared stood up in the back with their arms around Jared's grinning wife. Jeff is in the front happily slugging on a beer and Joey is at the wheel giving the camera the bird. Josh would do about anything for another night like that, huddled in an affectionate scrum with his favorite people in the world.

Josh was grateful to the people of Utopia who sandwiched his family with long rows of salutes as they drove Jeff down Main Street to the cemetery. He'd heard of funerals for fallen soldiers that were disrupted by protesters. Josh said he had no stomach for Americans who questioned the decision to go to war in the first place. It was hard for him to allow that anyone who wanted the troops out of Iraq also had genuine respect for the soldiers. "I can understand that they don't want us getting killed," he said, struggling for words. "I know everybody has a right to their own opinion, but when someone goes overseas to defend your country and dies and they come back and you sit there and bad-mouth them or their cause—it just seems like you have your free speech, but that subject? Just leave it alone."

Josh's military training had taught him not to question orders, so explaining his thoughts on the war was difficult. "I don't know if we did anything to provoke 9/11 but they attacked us. I mean, maybe the war shouldn't have been drawn out as long as it's been. Maybe we should have just gone in there and done something to show them, you know, mess with us again, we will do something. But when I was over there in Operation Iraqi Freedom 1, when we first invaded Iraq, the locals wanted us there. I know that now there's many people who don't agree with why we're there. But the best thing I can say is that I don't know. Maybe we need to be over there? I don't really understand completely myself."

All he knew for certain was that he was tired and that he only seemed able to take a full breath when he came home to Utopia. But then it'd get knocked right out of him again when a reminder of Jeff caught him like a blow to the kidneys. "Some days I'll go into town to get supplies for the house or just to get a soda and somebody stops and asks me how I'm doing when I hadn't really thought about it at all that day," he said. "I understand. It kind of bothers me sometimes, but when I'm away there's some days when I would like someone to ask me how I'm doing but no one fucking cares."

After lunch, Josh drove back to town, over sharply curving hills bordered by steep rocky cliffs, until the road eventually leveled out into a glorious golden straightaway home. The afternoon sun shimmered over grassy fields, the big sky above was scattered with puffs of cloud. Josh drove with his right forearm braced atop the steering wheel, raising a few fingers whenever he passed a truck headed in the opposite direction. He seemed to relax now that he was back behind the wheel, driving fast with the windows down.

He had one more night in Utopia, the hometown he was once so ready to leave behind, and was looking forward to drinking the day away. "I drink a lot," he said. People in his life had started wondering if maybe he drank a little too much. Josh shrugged. "Well, maybe I do," he allowed. "I don't try to fight people. I just like to drink. I like to be with everybody. I think I'm a good drunk." He paused to bite on his fingernails. Back in high school he'd been popped a few times for an MIP (minor in possession). "Even Mr. Dean wrote me a ticket once," he said, referring to the town constable, who was known to give the local kids a pass. Kathy never gave Josh much of a hard time about his drinking. These precious nights on his family ranch were his one chance to scab over some of the stress and fatigue of his deployments, and she felt that her son had earned the right to relax.

Unless the Army stop-lossed him, Josh would be eligible to get out of the military in 2009. He wasn't sure if he'd reenlist once his contract ran out. Sometimes a person could start to think of active duty like a prison term. You counted the days until you were free, only to then realize you were no longer built for the civilian world. I asked Josh to describe what he'd like his life to look like down the road. He thought hard for a few seconds, then shook his head with a little laugh. "I want to live in Texas," he finally said. "I want to live in a small town, where I know everything that's around. If there's any dangers, I would know about it." He waved at the land that seemed to wrap itself around us. "I guess you can say, you kind of know what to expect from day to day life in a small town. There's not a whole lot of surprises. Well, there are, but . . ." His thought trailed off sadly, and he was quiet for a few minutes.

"In a small town, people take care of each other," he said at last. "When I was driving home from Colorado there was a snowstorm in New Mexico and this guy had wrecked in a ditch and his trailer had turned over. He was all right. But I came up on the wreck and saw that nine cars had passed by and nobody had stopped to help. And while I was stopped there, six or seven cars drove by and didn't even care. They looked and drove by. I just thought that was kind of weird." Josh shook his head and chewed some more at the nails on his left hand. "I mean, there's an attitude in the big city I don't really like. I'll hold the door open for people and they won't say nothing. At a cash register, I'll say, 'Yes sir, no sir' to the cashier and they just look at me blank or don't look at me at all and are just like, 'Here's your change, buddy.'"

Josh came to the Y in the road, where there now stood scores of small billboards advertising various bed-and-breakfasts and real estate businesses. He bore gently to the left, along the fork that would lead him straight down Main Street. Josh nodded appreciatively at the view, where the only thing that blocked the expanse of sky was a trail of telephone wires. Josh pulled back into the bank parking lot and shifted Allison into neutral.

He started chuckling and pointed across the street where a truck had just peeled into the gas station, the engine rumbling loud enough for the whole town to hear. "There's my little brother over there," Josh said. "He's cruisin'." Josh sighed with affection. "Joey's probably bored. He's wild." Joey noticed Josh's truck in the bank parking lot and drove across the street, pulling his GMC alongside his brother's. Their five-year-old cousin, Morgan, was sitting next to Joey in the passenger seat. She had her knees curled up into her chest and she gave Josh a big, goofy grin, her mouth full of gum.

"Hi, Morgan!" Josh called to the pink-cheeked girl, who proceeded to carefully unwrap a stick of gum and proudly pass it out the open window as an offering for her older cousin. Joey had a Marlboro hanging out of his mouth and I asked if I might bum one. Without a word, he offered me two, passing the cigarettes to Morgan and gently motioning for her to go on and reach them out the window into Josh's outstretched hand. Then she slowly took two pieces of gum out of her pack and one by one gave them to Josh to pass along to me as well.

Josh said that he ought to be getting home to his family. His time in Utopia was running out. He was due back on base in less than twenty-four hours. "Tomorrow I'll double-check all my gear and straighten up my barracks room so everything is good to go," he said. He'd be in Iraq by the end of the week. "I'm just going over there to try to do my best," he said, his voice soft and sad.

Kathy shushed her excited pack of dogs inside her back gate. The beautiful white-and-gray blue heeler, Cooper, jumped up and down, while Kathy held back Jeff's dog, Riley, a black shepherd with one blue eye and one brown, by his collar. A colorless chihuahua named Pebbles hobbled in circles around Kathy's feet, hacking like a sick cat. "She's always like that," Kathy said with gruff affection. "She broke her leg and I spent three hundred dollars to fix it and it didn't get fixed. She's just like forever old and I've said, 'Is she in pain?' and the vet said no. I can't kill her just because she's annoying."

When Pebbles was born, she came out tiny and blue and barely breathing. Kathy wrapped the trembling dog in a towel and rubbed her down and eventually got out an old baby nebulizer from the cupboard to try and suck some of the gunk from the puppy's lungs. Every time she was convinced that Pebbles was dead, the dog would let out a little puff of air. "So I just dried on her like a mother licking her," Kathy said. "I laid down on the bed and I put her on my chest and I pulled the covers over us because she was so cold. And eventually she was fine." Kathy rolled her eyes and shook her fist at the wheezing dog at her feet. Pebbles stared back up at her and coughed unapologetically like an old man unwilling to give up his cigars.

Kathy wore blue jeans, a faded white T-shirt that said MY SON IS A PARATROOPER across the chest, and her American flag earrings. Behind her, at the top of the Wiekamps' caliche driveway, Jeff's blue truck sat parked by the gate. "It was hard in the beginning to get in it because of the smell," said Kathy. "You could still smell Jeff." She sighed and said that the truck would probably stay parked in that same spot forever. "We'll let it turn to rust," she said, before turning and briskly waving her arm for me to follow her into the house.

In the darkened family room, two cats fought on the shag carpet, rolling around in a tight circle while they hissed at each other. The TV was on mute, Rod Stewart was singing on the radio, and Kathy's romance novel, *Pirate's Promises,* was pancaked on the recliner. In the corner by the window her two iguanas, Yoshi and Iggy, dozed in their cage. A large basket of men's socks and underwear lay toppled to the side on the beige sectional sofa, which had throw pillows decorated with the heads of whitetail bucks.

Looming over everything was the wall Kathy had decorated in honor of all her family members serving in the military. There were framed photographs of Jeff, Josh, and Jared as well as Kathy's brother, Steven, dressed in uniform at their basic training graduations. She'd framed and hung up her sons' certificates of enlistment. There was a framed poster of the famous shot of the men planting the flag on Iwo Jima. After Jeff's death, one of Kathy's friends sent his photograph to the woman behind Project Compassion, a nonprofit organization that commissioned paintings of American men and women who died in active service after 9/11. A few months later the friend, nervous that she might be overstepping, presented Kathy with a large portrait of Jeff posed in front of the American flag. The painting was now the centerpiece of the wall.

Kathy took down a photo of Jeff and Ashley and tenderly wiped the dust off the glass. The young couple, standing in front of their barracks, grinned into the camera. Jeff had his arms wrapped so tightly around Ashley that one of her legs hovered off the ground. After Jeff's death Kathy had made it her mission to make sure the girl continued to feel like a part of their family. "I tell her every once in a while that I think she's Jeff's gift to us," Kathy said. Ashley recently called Randy on the phone in tears, asking him if he would consider walking her down the aisle if she ever ended up getting married again. Randy said he'd be honored. Kathy grabbed the phone from her husband and told the twenty-three-year-old girl that they both fully expected to be grandparents to Ashley's kids one day.

But Ashley seemed to give up on life after Jeff's death. "The Army prescribed some pills for her and she stopped dreaming and then the next morning she didn't know anything for about two hours after she woke up," said Kathy, describing those hard first few months of pain. "Then on the weekends she didn't take the pills—she just drank. I mean one continuous drink. But she's doing a hundred times better in these last couple months." Kathy announced that Ashley had been stop-lossed. I figured this was bad news. But Kathy said her daughter-in-law had been fighting for the chance to redeploy to Iraq. "See, she wasn't supposed to come home when Jeff died," she said, her voice flat and matter-of-fact. "In the beginning she was going back to take as many out with her until she got killed. The last time I talked to her she says she feels she has unfinished business. She even tried to be a crew chief. They won't let her, though. The Army is smart in some ways." Kathy shrugged and hung the picture of the kids back up on the wall.

Kathy took down the certificate of appreciation the Army recruiter who enlisted Jeff presented her with at his funeral. After news of her son's death, Kathy asked her brother to track down his recruiter. She wanted her brother to assure the man that she bore him no ill will. Jeff's recruiter had been transferred from Uvalde County to New York, but he arranged to come back to Texas to honor the boy. "He just handed me the certificate of appreciation real quietly off to the side," said Kathy. She shrugged and returned the certificate to its place of honor on her wall. "Three, two, one boys in the Army," she said with some pride in her voice. "The kids made their own decisions. I really don't think I did anything special other than supporting them." Above her head hung a small wooden wreath with painted sunflowers and a fat bumblebee flying over a banner that read BEE HAPPY. Kathy kept an American flag tucked behind the frantically smiling bee.

Kathy took me into the dining room so she could show me the slim wooden bookshelf that held her most precious memories of her oldest son. On one shelf she had arranged his various certificates of military distinction, his Army Commendation, and his Bronze Star medals. In between his various military honors were little homemade Christmas ornaments Jeff had brought home from school when he was a boy. On the bottom shelf stood the bright yellow plastic daiquiri cup and frosted beer glass that Jeff and Ashley had kept as souvenirs from their honeymoon Carnival cruise. Jeff's first baby blanket, a nubby pale blue and white throw Kathy had bought for him in Mexico, lay folded beneath his Tony the Tiger soccer ball.

On the top shelf, next to three of Jeff's childhood stuffed animals, there was a San Antonio Spurs championship ring nestled in the velvet pocket of its box. "I'm a big, big, big Spurs fan," she said. A few months after Jeff died, somebody in town—she still doesn't know who, and it's killing her that she hasn't ferreted out the identity of her benefactor—gave her four tickets to a playoffs game. "Well, which ones do Randy and I pick to go to the game?" Kathy said. "I have three sons and they were all home. Joshua had already planned a party at the house to watch the game. So we ended up taking Jared and Meagen. And we went, but you know, you sat there, you watched the game. As big of a fan as I am, I watched all these people clapping and cheering and pissing and moaning and I'm looking at 'em going, 'Why? It's a fricking basketball game.'"

These days when Kathy caught herself having a good time, she was stunned to the point of self-loathing that she'd let herself slip momentarily away from her grief. "The biggest thing to deal with is the guilt," she said. "I remember one time, see, I preach don't drink and drive. Well, Joshua was at a barbecue at his friend's house in Colorado and he was drinking and he usually sleeps in his truck or sleeps on the floor and doesn't go anywhere when he gets like that. But he called me up and said he got picked up for DUI. The lawyer asked him, 'Well, what was going on?' He gave him a little background about Jeff and said he was at this party and he'd started having a good time and then he felt guilty. As soon as he felt guilty he had to get away, and that's what he did. He got in his truck and left." She paused, and for a second she looked on the verge of tears. "See, nobody has told us what to do with the guilt."

Kathy waved me back deeper into her house, down a hall that was lined with framed collages of photographs of her four sons. "You really can't get any single shots of the boys because they were always to-gether," she said. The wall of the back guest bedroom was tacked with another American flag and a red and yellow Screaming Eagles flag from Jeff's unit. Kathy had wanted to freshen up the paint, but because Jeff's own fingers had hung up the flags, she was determined to leave them forever undisturbed.

Joey's bedroom was across the hall with the door closed. He'd been picking up some manual labor work in the daytime and helping Randy with the deer. But he had been struck low for several months after Jeff's death, sleeping in until the early afternoons. His girlfriend's father worked in the oil industry and offered to help Joey find a job working as a roughneck out in the fields. But Kathy said that she couldn't han-dle her youngest son leaving home just yet. "Each one of my kids, when they turned eighteen and graduated, I told 'em to pack their shit and get out. Because kids at eighteen think they know everything. They get smart-assy. But with Joey, I couldn't do that. I just couldn't have him gone. He's the baby. I don't think he wanted to leave, and I don't think my psyche could have taken him leaving."

Kathy went back into her kitchen and filled two plastic glasses with tea and some crushed ice. She plopped two straws into the glasses and sat down at the wooden table, whose top could be removed to reveal a poker board underneath. An aluminum pie plate full of cat food sat in the middle of the table and every now and then one of the cats would hop up and start crunching. Kathy threatened to throttle the animals while running a hand tenderly over their backs. When Josh described his mother to me, he laughed and said, "My mom's like, I don't want to say loud, but . . ." Kathy is not a woman of few words or faint opinions. After raising four boys, there wasn't a swear word, a dirty joke, or a raunchy movie that could make her blush. Threaten anyone she loved and she would go down swinging to protect them. But when I asked her if she was angry at anyone about the death of her son, she sat there stunned for several seconds.

"I have tried not to be," she finally said. "It . . . it . . . it is pointless for me. I'll get bitter about something that I can't then change. It was an accident and yes, it pisses me off." Kathy had tried telling herself that Muslims in general weren't to blame for Jeff's death. But she wasn't surprised when Randy confessed to her that he could no longer bear to go to his regular gas station in Hondo because it was owned by a Muslim family. She understood his anger and suspicion. She was angry too. When friends sent her propaganda emails excoriating Muslims and second-guessing Barack Obama's religious background, she forwarded them along to me. Women like Cindy Sheehan, who was also grieving the loss of her son, raised her hackles as well. Kathy thought a critical voice like Sheehan's undercut their children's legacy of service. In her mind, the woman's method of working through her grief, of getting through the moment, wasn't acceptable.

Placing her palms flat on her kitchen table, Kathy confessed that at times she had felt an uneasy flash of anger toward Jeff. The words seemed to startle her and she let out a gasp. But if Jeff had stayed behind the wire like she always told him to, if he hadn't been so intent on making crew chief, if he'd lobbied harder to get transferred to his brother's unit. There were so many ifs that might have saved her son from being aboard that doomed helicopter when it went down. If only he was still alive and if only he was coming home to her and if only she could put fresh sheets on his bed and wash his socks and make him his favorite dinner.

Life had knocked her to her knees by forcing her to get by in a world without her oldest son. But then she said her church had further failed her by letting her flounder alone. "My son died almost a year and a half ago and I have yet to have a priest call me," she said. "There were three priests that I had at the church and they have all let me down. They never called me when Jeff died. They didn't call me to ask if I was having a crisis of faith. Joey's an altar boy! Never called me. The ladies at the church were great. The congregation was great. But the priest never called me. They have no idea whether I blame God, nothing."

After Jeff's funeral, where the mourners at the Catholic church spilled in sad ribbons out of the wooden doors, Kathy tried returning the following Sunday. But sitting there next to Randy in the crisp quiet was too hard. "Going to church was a big family thing for me and the kids always knew that," she said. "When the kids came home for Christmas, Mom always wanted to go to church. You know, dress in your uniform, big thing for me." She cleared her throat and gave a weak smile. "My family is no longer whole. So going to church and sitting there was too hard. I'd start to think. The drive over to church I'm thinking. Now I read, watch TV, play on the computer, three or four things at a time so I always keep myself busy. I sleep with the TV on. I can't just lay in the quiet and listen and go to sleep."

That December, Kathy became a grandmother for the first time. Jared and Meagen welcomed Taylor Scott—his middle name in honor of his uncle Jeffery Scott—into the world. The baby felt like a Christmas present for a hurting family. When Meagen went into labor Kathy planned to fly to Kentucky to be with the young couple, but then her father had a stroke. She stayed in Utopia to help her dad, secretly thankful for an excuse to avoid the celebration at the hospital. "I couldn't do it," said Kathy. "Because she had her baby and I didn't."

Taylor was born with a harelip that a routine surgery would correct. Because of Taylor's condition, Jared got to sit out his scheduled deployment. But he'd since gotten new orders and would be leaving shortly for Iraq. Kathy went to the refrigerator and brought back a picture of her little grandson. "See, this is what he looks like now," she said proudly. Soon after his birth Meagen brought Taylor to Utopia to introduce him to her hometown friends and family. "When she first showed up it took me a little bit," Kathy admitted. "We were just afraid to love somebody else. You should see Randy with him, though. When he gets ahold of that little boy he just won't let him go."

Kathy was trying her best to live with her sadness. "I'm at the point where I'll always be," she figured. "It's gotten better. Better than I ever thought it was going to be. But there's that knowledge that at any point in time I could dissolve into nothing. And I won't let myself do that." She sat up straighter in her chair. "My thing now is projects. I redid the carpets. I redid my bedroom. I repainted the bedroom three different colors. I'm doing puzzles, you know, flattening them and putting them up on the walls."

But however distracted she kept herself, she lived in constant fear of the next loss. When Meagen was visiting, the phone company called the Wiekamp house one night in response to the young woman's question about her broken cellphone. "She gave them the house number to call, but I didn't know that," said Kathy. "So the phone rang. This was like ten after ten and I had gone to bed. I picked the phone up, and there was a man on the line saying Meagen's name. I hung up the phone and came out of the bedroom and stood there trying not to scream." She paused to catch her breath. "I don't like the phone to ring at night."

Kathy's brother Steven was getting ready to return to Iraq the following month. Josh was already back in Iraq. Jared would deploy in February.

WARESVILLE CEMETERY

Back before the golf course opened, before men started zipping around the grass in their little carts, anyone who turned off RM 187 onto Cemetery Road was going to the cemetery. Sid Chaney, who lives across the street, was at a Cemetery Association meeting one evening when the president walked up to him and said, "I don't have time for this anymore, Sid—you're the new president." Twenty-three years later Sid was at another meeting when he realized he no longer had time for the job. He saw his friend O'Neil Stout standing with his back to the group, so he announced, "All in favor of O'Neil?" When O'Neil turned around he discovered that he'd just been elected the new president. Even though he's been relieved of his official duties, Sid still likes to give tours of the cemetery to anyone interested in Utopia's past.

One Sunday afternoon, after a morning of chasing rabbits with his beagles, Sid sat on a low stone wall inside the cemetery, squinting up into the sunlight. He told me in his soft honeyed drawl that he and his wife, Jacque Lou, would be celebrating their twenty-fifth wedding anniversary in a few months. They would tape up notices of their anniversary party at the General Store and the post office, inviting the town to join them for an afternoon of cake and punch at the community center. On their first date, Sid took Jacque Lou to a John Wayne movie in Uvalde. He thought they'd had a pleasant enough evening, but then she went and moved to Del Rio. "I guess John Wayne turned her off," Sid said, grinning a little up into the bright sky. Seven years later Sid saw her on the street in Uvalde and they fell in love.

Sid, who is almost sixty years old, can tell you about pretty much everything that has ever happened in Utopia, though he would deny such a wealth of knowledge. He can tell you how all the men in town used to follow baseball—and how in 1951 his family, crowded around the white radio on top of the piano, cheered when Bobby Thomson of the New York Giants hit a home run and dashed the Brooklyn Dodgers' pennant hopes. He can describe Utopia's centennial celebration in 1952, when cases of "sody water" sold for just fifty cents. ("Jacque Lou went to the stock show yesterday in San Antonio and paid three-fifty for a bottle of water," he said as he delicately pressed his pocketknife under his thumbnail. "Now that's outrageous.") And Sid can paint vivid pictures of how everyone buried in the cemetery ended up there. Bertha Gibson died of screwworms, J. D. Walker was struck by lightning, and then there was Robert Kincheloe, whose tombstone rested here, if not his body; long ago he raced across the border after some Mexicans who had stolen his cattle and was never heard from again.

At one point during the tour Sid steered us slowly over to Mattie Davenport's grave. "Mattie was married to Jesse Davenport," Sid said, "and Jesse had a little blue Studebaker truck. Now, ma'am, the place by the Lost Maples Café used to be an Exxon gas station. We used to come there every Sunday morning to buy our paper. And one day as we came into town, we saw this little blue Studebaker truck coming up the road. We met Ward Clayton at the station and he said, 'Bad about old Jess, isn't it?' And we said, 'What happened? What's wrong?' 'Well, he died last night.' He died Saturday, and by paper time on Sunday, Mattie had already sold his pickup truck.

"There are no more Davenports in the canyon," Sid continued quietly. "Well, no, there's Joy, but she married a Davenport. Just like the Fenleys. There's no more Fenleys. Over these mountains is the Seco Valley, and the whole Seco Valley was Millers at one time. And there are no more Millers over there. Here," he said, gesturing to a tombstone, "is a Miz Tampke. I collect things, ma'am. I've got a 1943 telephone book and a 1947 telephone book and one from 1949. Back then there were thirteen Tampkes. Now there's two or three. That's sad to me. I don't have children, my brother John Dale doesn't have children, and neither does my cousin Charles. When we die there won't be any more Chaneys here. It's amazing how families disappear."

After Sid graduated from high school he went to the junior college in Uvalde, majoring, he said, in draft evasion. He flunked. "When I was in Vietnam, there was a boy there named Michael J. McDermott. And he and I equally hated the Army. Michael's *fah-thuh,*" said Sid, imitating the julep tongue of his new friend from South Carolina, "owned the *Charleston Times.* And Michael would record me telling stories and he sent them to his *fah-thuh,* who wanted me to come work for him after the war. And all I would have to do is go fishing and go hunting and stuff like that and write articles in the paper. That would have been pretty good. But it never entered my mind." Sid paused and nodded down at more tombstones. "Now this is my father and this is my mother. This is my father's parents here. And this is my nephew. My brother is here somewhere," he said, his blue eyes sweeping the grass. "Oh, there he is."

After an afternoon of listening to Sid tell stories, it seemed an awful shame that he didn't take that job writing for the paper. "But I didn't want to go to South Carolina," he said. "I didn't want to go anywhere. I just wanted to come home. Nowadays people are so mobile. You're from

Brooklyn and you're here in Utopia, Texas. But I never did have the urge to go to Brooklyn."

At the end of the tour, Sid closed the gate behind him and put a few fingers to his cap, bidding goodbye to O'Neil and his wife, Rita, who were spending their Sunday afternoon raking the leaves of the cemetery grounds.

CHAPTER 7

Happy Birthday

Within days of his long-announced departure date, Colter finally admitted to himself that he wouldn't be leaving Utopia for Arizona after all. On a Saturday afternoon in June, he sat at his computer, underneath a stolen NO DUMPING UNDER PENALTY OF THE LAW sign, the one adornment on his colorless bedroom walls.

Colter's room was dark and cramped, sealed off from the outside world by tamped-shut hunter-green venetian blinds. The air smelled of dried sweat from the clumps of work clothes. On the floor were tall stacks of DVDs that Colter had inhaled and were now gathering dust. In the corner sat the PlayStation 3 that he bought for six hundred dollars, kicking himself after he found out a week later that the price would soon drop a couple hundred dollars.

Looking around his small room, Colter explained that staying in Utopia really was the best possible decision for the coming year. "I had to check my motives for leaving," he said. "Plus, you know, I'm having a great time by myself. I guess a few weeks ago I just realized, 'Enh, it's actually not that bad in Utopia and I like my job so I can stand this for a little while longer,'" he said with a tinny tone of brightness, as he rattled the empty Dr Pepper can on his desk. His road crew manager had just promised him a small raise, increasing his salary from $8.90 to nearly $10 an hour.

"No way am I staying here for the rest of my life, and I don't want to make a career out of the job I have right now. But hey! I don't really need to get out of here that bad." He pushed a dirty sock farther under his desk with his foot. "Leaving now just seems like a bad idea, it wasn't to further my education, it was just to get the hell out of Utopia. And eventually one day it just hit me: You got to learn to be happy in the situation you're in, even if it's not perfect." His voice had taken on the aggressive zeal of a salesman who hated the product he was charged with pushing. Exhausted, his pitch dribbled to a finish. "And so I guess I'll just go to school in San Antonio next year and I'll stay living here with my parents because, I mean, whatever . . ." He was unsure if he even still wanted to be a video-game designer. "My life will be something with computers and technology. Maybe it will be something in film. Something with entertainment, because everything else I hate. Maybe I'll do special effects?"

Colter keeps a box in his bedroom closet with tokens of all the dreams he's deferred or dismissed. He saved the Bible and the new student name tag that he was given when he first got to the Texas Bible Institute, back when he had latched onto the idea of a future in ministry. And now, shoved into the same box, lay a folded-up map of Arizona and his acceptance letter to Tempe's University of Advancing Technology. "The box represents who I could've been," he said with a cavalier shrug. "Those were the only two big points in my life. You know, I could've gone this direction and who knows what might have happened. It's strange to think about how different my life could have been. But then I'm like, it doesn't really even matter. Things change and maybe I made a mistake, and maybe I didn't."

Colter's mother, Lindy, wearing a white flannel nightgown with faded pink cottage roses, appeared in the doorway and waved a wobbly hello. She reached to pat Colter's shoulders, but he ducked around her into the cluttered family room. She followed behind, pointing at photographs of her mother as Colter complained that we were late for the movies. Colter's and Clif's work boots were in a pile by a sofa that was covered in towels and one of the family dogs. Lindy's favorite cat lay curled on the dining room table, next to a large Ziploc bag holding Lindy's bottles of pills. Colter grimly stood with his arms lank by his side as Lindy hugged him goodbye. He half-heartedly assured her that he'd finally get to scrubbing the dirty concrete floor when he returned. Lindy, standing under an old framed painting of a horse, stared after her son with a look of confused affection on her face.

Outside in the driveway, Colter cut a strange figure beneath the basketball net with the Texas flag backboard. His face was a shiny, peeling red from long days paving roads. He wore jeans and a button-down shirt with an orange and brown striped tie knotted loosely at his neck. Sweating already in the summer humidity, Colter clutched a vintage wool sweater with leather arm patches that he'd recently bought on eBay for thirty dollars. The purchase had thrilled him until he remembered that Texas weather doesn't provide much of an opportunity for wool. Worse, the sweater was dry clean only. There's no such luxury in Utopia, though people with a taste for delicate fabrics can drop their clothes off in a bundle at the feed store. The owners took a load into a Uvalde dry cleaner once a week.

Surrounded on all sides by fence, Colter fiddled in his back jeans pocket for his wallet. He ignored the dozen or so goats snuffling around his feet, nosing and kicking at the overturned molasses buckets scattered in the driveway. When the animals looked up at Colter, they all wore the same dazed and desperate expression. *How did we end up here,* they seemed to be asking, *and how can we make a run for it?* Colter's escape route was eighty miles northeast to a new, badly reviewed comedy at a Kerrville movie theater. He'd made the same long drive the previous evening while the rest of Utopia was gathered down at the park for the annual ranch rodeo.

The rodeo is a beloved tradition in town, dating back as long as anyone could remember. It provided people in the Hill Country with about as fine an opportunity for old-fashioned visiting as existed today. After an evening of grinning and groaning over bucking broncs and calf ropers, everyone lugged coolers of beer into the outdoor dance hall under the pecan trees. One of the women in town usually brought a canister of cornmeal from her kitchen pantry tucked under her arm to shake on the slab of dance floor so their boots wouldn't stick during the two-step. A country band played old George Strait and Hank Williams standards on a small stage, and the boisterous clusters of friends and neighbors migrated back and forth between the picnic tables and the dance floor. Folks slipped twenties to the band so they'd keep playing long after their set had finished. This was Utopia's biggest party of the year and everybody wanted a chance to linger late into the evening.

At last night's rodeo, Lindy had made the rounds of the various picnic tables, her voice quivery from all the excitement. She'd been too weak to attend the previous year's rodeo and dance, and she told everyone there wasn't anything that could force her to miss out on another party. She barely sat down all evening, having more dance partners than she could count. Even Clif shepherded her around the dance floor a few times, his face flushed and boyish out there under the twinkling lights. Alyssa stayed entwined with her new boyfriend, a local boy who had dropped out of high school and was working building septic tanks in town.

Colter spent that Friday night home alone, playing on the computer and watching TV. So he'd felt stir-crazy enough to flirt with the idea of attending Saturday evening's rodeo. Colter figured he could take a separate car from his family and sit high up in the metal bleachers alone, with a look of studied detachment on his face. "I went through my mind and thought of eighteen different reasons to go," he said. "'Hey, it's fun! Hey, you can see a lot of people! Hey, you can go to the dance.'

Well wait, I hate country music. And then it was like, 'Hey, you can go to the movies by yourself!' Sold." So while everybody else in town converged in the park on a breezy afternoon for the annual EMS supper of beans, potato salad, brisket, and chunks of *cabrito* carved fresh off a spit-roasted goat, Colter drove as fast as he could to see a horror movie.

Less than twelve hours later, he was perfectly happy to be back on the road making the same long trip. "It's no big deal," he said. "Mostly I go to the movies by myself—usually twice a weekend. Most people think it's sad when you say you're a loner. But I don't really need somebody to hang out with." Colter's cellphone rang and his face lit up at the sight of his best friend's name. Grant had returned to Texas for the summer, but he'd gotten a plum internship working as a patient transporter in the radiology department at a San Antonio hospital. Colter answered the phone and asked his friend when they'd next see each other. On the other end Grant sighed that he was staring down another week of long hours at the hospital. "How many hours do you work a day?" Colter asked with a baiting tone. "Yeah, well, I work twelve. Booyah! And I don't sit in air-conditioning all day."

He hung up the phone and rolled his eyes condescendingly. "As of three weeks ago Grant is no longer allowed to ride with me in the car because apparently I'm a dangerous driver. His mom saw me going like seventy-five miles per hour down a road and she decided I was unsafe. I'm like, 'Grant, you're fricking eighteen years old, get a little bit of cojones!' And he's just like, 'I need to respect her.'" Colter smiled patiently, as if his friend would never grow up. "Grant just doesn't like to stand up to anybody. He just draws his hand and walks away. On graduation night I was like, 'Let's go to the movies!' and Grant called his mom and she was like, 'No, there's drunk drivers just looking to kill you out on the road.' 'Grant, just tell her you're going!' And he was like, 'I can't, I have to respect her.' All right, go and have fun with your mom."

Every time Colter went to Kerrville he made a halfway pit stop in Bandera, at the Sonic drive-in. He balked, though, on this trip, speeding up as we passed the bright yellow fifties-style sign. "There's a girl there who's madly in love with me," he said. A waitress—or carhop, as Sonic still liked to call its girls—had strutted up to Colter's Chevy Blazer on a recent Sonic run and enthusiastically introduced herself. She wore dark lipstick and her nails were painted black. She worked hard to engage him in conversation about her favorite bands. Colter, mystified by this pretty girl's attentions, could only mumble back a few wooden words before grabbing his food and shifting the Chevy into reverse.

"She just flirts with me hardcore every time," he said, his voice cocky now that we were safely past the restaurant. "The other day Grant said he refused to talk to me until I asked her out. I was like, 'Grant, you're really one to talk!' I'm still unsure about it, though. Maybe it'll just blow over and I'll never see her again. That'd be great." I pointed out that a girlfriend might help ease some of Colter's loneliness, but the idea of putting forth effort to make a connection with a stranger in a strange town made him squirm. "It's the more reasonable choice to stay single," he said. "I still want to get out of Utopia one day, and the less attached I am the better."

The next morning Clif, Lindy, and Alyssa ate breakfast together at the coffee shop. Lindy, who was trying to spread jam on her bread with a shaking hand, seemed anxious for Clif to leave so she could eat in peace. When I asked the family about Colter's decision to stick around town for another year, Clif laughed sharply. "Too lazy," he said, in a sneering voice. "I told you he wouldn't get to anything."

Lindy winced at her husband's harsh words, flicking her fingers at him as if she could shoo him elsewhere. "I think Colter's just kind of scared," Lindy said, ignoring her husband. Clif looked over at me and sat up straighter. "He never was like me," he said. "I take off down the road just to see what's on the other end."

"Also his job is going so good," Lindy said encouragingly. "He hates to give it up right now."

His family had long ago stopped taking Colter seriously when he spoke about wanting to leave Utopia. "I just don't think that's truly how he feels," said Clif. "He's really happier here. I think he's intimidated by the city."

Lindy nodded along. "I think once he thought about what moving would really entail, that he wouldn't be with his family, he realized what he'd be giving up." Clif laughed into his hand and Lindy glared at him. "*Anyways,*" she said, "I think when it got right down to it, he's scared. But I hope he does go off and do something else."

Lindy knew that Colter leaned on her failing health as an excuse for digging deeper into his rut. Despite his claims otherwise, she said that she badly hoped her son would muster up the courage to pursue his dreams one day. "I actually asked him to go," she said. "I asked him to go out there in the real world and see what it's like."

"Asked him?" Clif snorted. "You kicked him out."

Lindy blanched, shooting Clif a wounded look. Alyssa, whose main contribution to the conversation so far was some eye rolling from across the table, punched her father's arm. "Stop," she said fiercely. "You're making Mom feel bad. Mom, he's being a jerk, don't listen to him."

Lindy curled her lip once more at Clif and took a tiny bite of her toast. "You know what, I'm not ready for him to go either," she admitted. "And I know that's not a good thing."

Clif stood up, scraping his chair loudly under the table. "It kind of seems like Colter is turning on to the physical world a little bit," he said hopefully. "He's getting big shoulders. I think he'll come around at least some to the rough manly outdoors."

"He loves his job now," Lindy said again. "But you know, if Colter doesn't fit in here, that's fine with me. He's his person and I'm glad for that. I am so glad that he dresses kind of funny and stuff." She stopped herself and shook her head impatiently. "And I don't think it's 'funny' either. Just different. And I'm glad. I'm so glad because I don't want him to be somebody else. I don't want him to be just like Clif." She grimaced at her looming husband in his barn jacket and dirty jeans. "Thank God he's not like him."

Clif laughed loudly. "See what kind of world I live in? She's not kidding." He said goodbye to his family. He was going home to dig some post holes for a new fence. On his way out the door, I reminded him that some people do leave Utopia, and one day Colter might very well surprise him and do the same. Just look at Grant. "I know, I know," he said, waving me off.

"I'll still be here, Dad!" cried Alyssa.

"Oh joy," Clif grumbled to himself, giving his daughter an affectionate wink as she slipped past him out the front door. Left alone, Lindy looked exhausted by the state of her family. "My cancer is kind of one of those things that's scary for all of us," she said. "But you know what?" She forced out a carefree laugh. "I'm going so good. I can have these little seizures, but maybe they're just flashbacks." Lindy crossed her eyes and stuck out her tongue, then collapsed into giggles.

Later that day at the coffee shop, there was a joyful reunion between Grant and his former math teacher Miss Clark. When Grant told his favorite high school teacher that he had finished his freshman year with a 3.7, though he had been forced to drop one of his math classes, she wagged her finger affectionately over his sheepish expression. His mother, Susi, rubbed Grant's arm and tried to explain his disappointment. "I can understand his expectations, because he worked really, really hard and he wanted a 4.0," she said, blowing on the steam rising from her pot of green tea. "People misunderstand Grant and think he's being hard on himself."

"Oh, I am!" Grant said with a chuckle.

"No, you're not," interrupted Susi. "Because the way I see it is you want things right. If he was was adding 4 plus 4 and it was equaling 8.125, that wouldn't be right. So of course he would be unhappy with an A minus."

A long-haired out-of-towner who was passing through on his meandering way out to Marfa in West Texas asked Susi if the dark red Toyota Prius out front was hers. She nodded excitedly and the two launched into a spirited conversation about gas mileage.

Grant leaned over and admitted that Colter's decision to remain in Utopia for the time being had surprised him. While he'd been away at Yale, Grant had offered to help his friend with any school and financial-aid applications, but Colter had always assured him he had everything under control.

Susi, after waving goodbye to her new friend, threw her hands up in the air. "We've offered to let Colter stay at the house in San Antonio and go to UT. But he said, 'No, no, no, I'm going to Arizona.'"

"I think one day he will move to San Antonio," Grant said hopefully.

"No way," said Susi.

On this subject, though, Grant would not allow for anything less than guarded optimism. "I think he would," he insisted, "but you would have to keep telling him to go, go, go."

Susi remembered a time back when Grant and Colter were little. The two families were enjoying a summer day out at the Padgett ranch. There is a beautiful spring-fed pool carved into the base of one of the hills, where the water collects into a basin of clear turquoise blue. All the other kids were shrieking with joy as they practiced cannonballing into the water. But Colter could only teeter up toward the edge, his back hunched over as he peered timidly into the unknown. "He's standing there, literally not knowing how to jump in that pool and have fun!" said Susi. "And the look on his face, oh! how he wanted to get in there. So I reached up and said, 'Hey Colter!' and just pushed him. And once he got in the water he was fine. So I think if someone had their hand on his back . . ." Her wistful train of thought was interrupted as more locals petered in for lunch, letting out delighted hollers when they laid their eyes upon Grant.

After a series of warm embraces and humble reports from Yale, Susi and Grant said goodbye. Grant was due back at the hospital in the morning and it was time for them to get on the road to San Antonio. "He got to watch a bone marrow transplant the other day," said Susi, beaming up at Grant, who was clearing their plates from the table. "He gets to watch a kidney transplant next week."

That evening I passed Colter's construction crew stationed near the Y on the north end of town. Colter stood off to the side of the rest of the group, kicking the silver post of a YIELD sign. He wore a fluorescent lime-green vest over an old T-shirt, grime-covered jeans, and a baseball hat. He caught my eye as I drove by and gave a rueful smile. He stuck up both of his thumbs as if to say he was all good, though he could have just as easily been trying to hitch a ride out of town.

"Whenever I see him standing by the road," Susi once told me, "I cry after I pass him."

Every third weekend in October, all of Utopia turns out for the annual Fall Festival parade. Up until a few years ago, the event was known as the Halloween parade. But then Living Waters was formed, and the strident preacher, who had long since left town, decided it was improper for Utopians to celebrate a holiday of dark forces. And so, succumbing to the vocal minority, Utopians agreed with snorting resentment to rename one of their favorite annual traditions.

The morning of the parade, Lindy walked slowly up to the coffee shop, holding her arms limply out in front of her. She looked unsteady on her thin legs, like a swaying dandelion puff bracing for the next stiff breeze. She made her halting way over to her regular table and wilted into a chair. At this early hour, it was already bright and warm outside, but Lindy wore an old navy parka and jeans, rubbing her dry hands together. She seemed uncharacteristically crabby. "I'm dopey, I'm mopey, I don't like it," she explained.

Lindy's best friend, Kim, gave her a frown from across the table. Lindy had been having mini-seizures for a few days and Kim had been urging her to stop being so wishy-washy and get to the hospital already. Lindy held up her index finger to silence her friend. She wasn't checking into any hospital today. She wouldn't miss another Fall Festival. Lindy tried to explain how much the celebration meant to her, but she had trouble finding the words. She jerked to a stop midsentence several times and closed her eyes as her mind idled in neutral. She obstinately shook her head, beating her fists in the air like a stubborn child. "My body is trying to have a seizure," she said, "but I won't let it." Forcing a smile onto her face, she turned her head to the side and pretended to spit in the air. "That's what I say to you seizures!" she said. "I spit on you. I won't allow you to take this from me."

The people of Utopia had asked Lindy to lead the parade that afternoon, appointing her the Fall Festival's first official grand marshal. As the waitress placed Lindy's plate of toast and jam in front of her, Lindy started to tear up describing the honor. "I feel as if they had picked me to be the queen of England," she said. "I've been too sick to go to the parade the last two years, and, let's be honest, I don't know if I'll be here next year. But today I get to sit up high and wave at every single person in this town that has done so much for me already."

Several hours later, people set up their folding chairs on either side of Main Street or sat dangling their legs off the open beds of their parked trucks. A horn tootled on the north end of town and a shiny cherry-red restored Buick convertible purred into gear. Lindy perched on the top of the white leather backseat. She wore a gleaming yellow satin cape lined with burgundy velvet that hung on her like a listless sail and a black T-shirt with the word *Queen* written in girly cursive script over her chest. She held a gold metal scepter in her right hand and a glittering silver tiara sat at a cocked angle over her straw cowboy hat. As the car made its first pass through town, Lindy smiled brightly and waved her cupped hand, blowing happy kisses every time someone from the side of the road yelled her name. "I love you!" she'd call out to anyone in her line of vision, even if she couldn't remember their name. "Oh, look who it is! I love you! I love you!"

Behind Lindy followed a train of elaborately decorated floats representing each grade of students at Utopia School. The younger children whooped and hollered for their waving friends and families, who tossed candy at the slowly passing floats. The girls gave practiced beauty queen waves. The boys shot finger guns at the crowd. The juniors and seniors pretended to be above the afternoon's excitement. They rode by with studiously bored looks on their faces. Occasionally they'd shift discreetly to sneak pieces of thrown candy from the floor to their mouths. The parade was a chance for local mothers' competitive streaks to run amok. Every year they tried to outdo one another in the grandness of their float's theme and execution. The top honor this year would go to the eighth grade class, whose scene of a Roman bacchanalia, complete with a working fountain and papier-mâché pig turning on a spit, bested the kindergarten's child brides and grooms waving from their wedding-themed float.

Utopia is so small that the parade had to make a U-turn when it reached the Church of Christ. "We're the only town in all of America where the parade heads down Main Street and then circles back to make another pass," a local joked to me on the sidelines. "One just won't do it."

The coffee drinker John Hillis pulled up the rear of the parade driving a town ambulance. After he made his final pass, everyone folded up their chairs and snapped shut their tailgates and made their way over to the school for the carnival. There was a cakewalk set up in the school courtyard, a cotton candy maker, and a mini bucking bronc machine, on which one brave boy looked about to burst into tears as he willed the ride to end. Off to the side, a horse trailer had been decorated to look like a jail, from inside of which children squealed in excitement while they waited for their parents to pay their bail. Kelli and Perla sat next to the water balloon dartboard and recorded guesses of how many pieces were piled inside a giant plastic jug of candy. Kelli's parents made a hasty loop around the carnival, Nancy holding her granddaughter Blossom's hand and carrying her sleeping baby granddaughter, Scarlett Rain. A country song belched out of a crackling stereo speaker, clashing with the lilt of carousel music. Ron looked ready to go home.

Inside the cafeteria, people gathered for supper. Five dollars for a styrofoam tray with brisket, a scoop of potato salad, beans, pickle slices, onions, and a piece of white bread. Alyssa and her boyfriend took dinner tickets. Both of them wore pink pearl-button shirts over clean jeans and dirty boots. After standing in the same cafeteria line the Utopia students waited in every weekday noon hour, the townspeople young and old squeezed themselves onto the benches. They sucked sauce from their fingers and visited with their neighbors under the lunchroom's fluorescent lights. Many sat next to the same friends they had sat with decades earlier when they were students in school. Lindy quietly ate her supper as her friends talked loudly over one another. Her tiara drooped forward into her eyes, and when people tapped her on the shoulder she blew them air kisses and extended a hand.

The junior class started setting up their cakes on card tables arranged on the cafeteria's small stage. It was tradition for the juniors to sell their specially decorated cakes in a spirited auction. The money raised got socked away into a fund that would pay for the weeklong trip the seniors took every year before graduation. For many Utopia students the senior trip marked their first time traveling on an airplane. While one junior auctioned off a round cake his mother had decorated to look like a cheeseburger, and another clapped her hands in delight when a family member bought her chocolate ganache for a stunning one thousand dollars, Lindy left the cafeteria. She looked pale and woozy. Her left hand trailed along the tile wall of the hallway for balance as she made her way toward fresh air. When people stopped her to coo over her performance as grand marshal, she grabbed their arms sloppily and agreed to pose for pictures despite the fact that she looked ready to jellyfish onto the floor. When one of her friends found her slumped over, John Hillis was told to get the ambulance ready for another drive down Main Street. With the carnival still in full swing, John loaded Lindy into the back, and Colter, who was watching television at home, was alerted to follow them into San Antonio.

The next morning, Colter and Alyssa took a break from the hospital to go to a nearby mall while their mother, weak from severe dehydration, rested. Alyssa pleaded with her big brother to buy her a new outfit from Aéropostale and he handed over his credit card. She threw her arms gratefully around him and his face scrunched up in disgust. Then he paid for Alyssa to have her hair trimmed and blown out before finally insisting that it was his turn to treat himself. He led us straight to a shoe store playing loud techno music on the speakers. He removed his dirty socks and old sneakers and slid his blistered feet into a pair of white fake-leather loafers that were on sale for forty-five dollars. He slapped his credit card down at the register and fumbled for his ringing cellphone. He looked at his screen and his face fell. Lindy was awake and wondering where her children were. It was time to go back to her bedside.

In the parking lot at the hospital, Colter and Alyssa turned quiet, and their shoulders sagged with every ding in the rising elevator. Alyssa wrinkled her nose and stuck out her tongue, complaining that the hospital always reeked of the same sour smell of bats. Colter exhaled loudly, wondering when his sister had last smelled bats. When they nervously poked their heads into Lindy's hospital room, they found their mother dozing again. One of her legs, its foot swimming in a baggy terrycloth sock, lolled off the side of the bed. Lindy was still wearing her *Queen* T-shirt from yesterday's parade with a pair of black-and-white pajama pants that had a row of small red cotton pom-poms hanging from the ankles. Her tiara lay upside down on the side table.

"Wake up, Mommy!" Alyssa said, hopping onto the end of the bed. Lindy started awake and let out a hoarse cheer, beckoning both of her children to come and give her proper hugs. She ignored her cellphone's ringtone of Rod Stewart's "Da Ya Think I'm Sexy" dangling in the air, guessing that it was another one of her worried friends from Utopia calling to check in. Colter went into the bathroom to change into his fresh new clothes. He'd spent the night sleeping on the spare bed in Lindy's room.

Alyssa yanked on her mother's foot. "Mommy, it's Colter's birthday!" she whispered frantically. Lindy smacked her forehead. Colter came out of the bathroom, smoothing his new T-shirt over his long torso and adjusting the way his jeans fell around his new shoes.

"What's that you're wearing, Colter?" Lindy said to her son. "Come here and let me see."

With a suspicious look on his face, Colter edged toward Lindy. When he was within arm's length, she grabbed him and pulled him down to her, giving him three loud kisses on both cheeks before she started singing, her hands waving in the air like a conductor.

"Happy birthday to you, happy birthday to you, happy birthday, dear . . ." The room went quiet. Lindy wasn't pausing for effect. She snapped her fingers, searching her head for the name of her son. Alyssa yelled, "Colter!" and Lindy laughed about the holes in her brain.

Alyssa groaned and flounced onto the spare bed. "I reminded him of his own birthday," she said with a disapproving tone.

Lindy grinned sheepishly at her son. "I remembered your birthday earlier."

Colter shot her a skeptical look.

"I did!" she said defensively. "But I've been snoozing a little bit, so when you walked in I forgot. So let's see, you're twenty years old now? No, no," she laughed, "I know that you're twenty-five."

Colter exhaled impatiently.

"No, I'm just jacking with you!" Lindy said with a wink, blowing a kiss at her son.

Colter rolled his eyes, sliding his back slowly down the wall of the hospital room until he was balancing in an awkward squat. "I'm twenty-two years old," he said, though the conversation had already moved beyond him.

THE NEW GYM

In the mid-1990s, the global water giant Perrier bought out Utopia Spring Water, which for several years had supplied bottled water from local artesian wells to the Texas market. The new owners kept the plant open for a couple of years, and then, as everyone guessed had been their plan all along, they shuttered operations and in a gesture of magnanimity donated the empty factory to the school. One of the wealthier newcomers in town, a retired CEO from Houston who was fast buying up every available plot of land, snatched up the lot from the school. Today a small colloidal silver company and a local electrician paid the man rent for two small office spaces. Otherwise the former plant sat empty, the parking lot used only by kids gathering on weekend nights looking for action.

The school voted to put the money from the sale toward building a new and modern gym to replace the cramped original, which lacked air-conditioning. So the coffee drinker John Hillis and his son Duane and teenage grandson Michael, who had just graduated from high school and had been a star on the basketball team like the men in his family before him, started to work on the structure. In 2005, the new gym finally opened and now served as the town's nucleus during the school year.

Lacking a football team, Utopia celebrates homecoming during the basketball season. On a January evening John Hillis sat by himself in the front row, as comfortable here as he would be in his family room at home. He wore his old leather high school letter jacket, the year '60 stitched onto his arm. The Runnin' Buffs were getting killed by the Leakey Eagles. (The Lady Buffs had lost earlier in the evening. Their varsity bench consisted of one junior, one sophomore, and the rest freshmen—three of whom had never played basketball before.) While the boys did their best to make up a fifteen-point deficit in the first half, girls wandered in and out of the gym wearing oversized mum corsages in Utopia's maroon and gold colors pinned over their hearts. A few sported corsages nearly as tall as they were, so that the three-foot-long ribbons got caught between the girls' legs as they walked alongside the court with their friends.

At the far end of the bleachers, the Buffalo Thunder, Utopia's school band, stomped their way through "As the Saints Go Marching In." Every once in a while they managed to get a note in key. The Houston CEO's wife had funded the band, and she started off the school year expecting greatness from the ragtag bunch of seventh graders, many of whom had never played an instrument before. She donated the uniforms and instruments, and she expected the kids to look and sound sharp. Now she was happy when anyone showed up to play at all.

Next to the band, Utopia's first cheerleading squad in close to fifty years sat huddled together in a row. The handful of girls ranged in age from prekindergarten through high school and were either knobby-kneed or as round as apples. The younger girls all seemed to favor bright rouge; the older ones were dependent on eyeglasses. Utopia's cheerleaders hadn't yet learned many cheers, but when reminded by a parent they would distractedly wave their pom-poms in the air, knocking one another's pigtails.

At halftime the senior homecoming court waited in the hallway by the locker rooms to be introduced. Kelli Rhodes wore the same white taffeta dress with a black satin sash tied around the waist that she'd worn to the junior prom. The blond girl next to her wore a floor-length green bridesmaid's dress she'd bought last summer for her best friend's wedding. The Pachelbel Canon started playing inside the gym, and the girls linked arms with their fathers, all of whom wore jeans or khakis with boots. Kelli looked anxiously around for her own father, who had disappeared to go smoke a cigarette in the parking lot. Right before her name was called, Ron strolled over and took his daughter's arm. He wore a sharp black suit with a burnt-orange rose in his lapel. "Okay," he said loudly into his daughter's ear. "Let's go put the black man on display."

Out there on the court, Kelli stood next to Ron with her chin held high in the air. Her family—Nancy and Beryl in pantsuits, her older sister, Racheal, in a dark hoodie—sat in the front row waiting to hear the winners announced. A basketball player who hadn't quite caught his breath was named king. Jamie Lynn, Morris's niece, was called out as the queen. Kelli looked almost relieved. In the locker room she quickly changed back into her jeans and Converse sneakers.

Team morale seemed low during the second half. The Runnin' Buffs were over the penalty limit. Morris started hollering at the referee, a preacher from Bandera who happened to be Ralph's nephew, that he was blind and hadn't gotten a call right all night. "Come on, people," one woman yelled from the bleachers. "How about a little more enthusiasm!" She stamped her feet on the floor and clapped her hands, trying to pump up the crowd. "Where are our cheerleaders?" she demanded. "Probably asleep," her husband said. "They're only five years old."

=====================================

CHAPTER 8

Pushing Through a Hot Fog

At the start of her senior year, Kelli dropped her college prep classes and the drama club. She told her newspaper adviser, who'd pushed hard the previous year for Kelli to apply to some out-of-state summer journalism camps, that she was not only turning down the editor in chief position but quitting the paper altogether. The more Kelli grew attached to a future playing music, the more her mother, Nancy, urged her to consider a backup plan. The two were locked in a stubborn loop of the same argument. Nancy worried that Kelli was depressed and unfocused, ignoring scholarship applications and college discussions because she was intimidated by the process. While Nancy fretted, insecure about her own ability to steer her daughter in the proper direction, Kelli retreated in an adolescent huff to fume alone in her room.

Her exasperated parents and teachers and guidance counselor could grind their teeth all they wanted, warning Kelli that she was putting her class rank at risk and sabotaging any chance of getting into a four-year university. But Kelli had given up on school. She wanted to move to Austin to pursue music. She finally agreed to attend an inexpensive community college there, but only with the understanding that it was a low priority.

Relieved of the pressures of college applications, Kelli arranged her schedule so that she was done with school each afternoon by 1:15. She got a job alongside Perla at the café cooking and washing dishes. "Working minimum wage isn't as bad as, say, prostitution, but it does feel a bit degrading," Kelli wrote on her blog. "Twenty-one hours a week I shovel out halfway decent meals just to load up my vehicle with gas . . . at 3 bucks a gallon . . . n somehow I'm supposed to feel some sense of accomplishment . . . well I don't."

One afternoon Perla and Kelli sat down in the café's empty dining room. Working at the café had left them further convinced that they had to get out of Utopia. "People here tip really bad," said Perla. "One shift I made a grand total of ten dollars." The girls hated it when Tacy nudged one or both of them out front to wait tables, a job that didn't suit either of their reserved personalities. Perla in particular felt most comfortable back in the kitchen, where she had only the radio and the hot water and her fifteen-year-old brother, Harlan, who worked alongside her in the kitchen, to worry about. She wouldn't have believed it possible, but the café was actually making her miss her summer job as a dishwasher in a Bandera nursing home. "Though I liked to call myself a dietary aide," she clarified. At least there she made seven dollars an hour. As she slumped into the corner of the booth, Perla's spine settled back into its adolescent hump of dejection. She rested a cheek in the palm of her hand and grimaced at the blooming stain of ketchup on her sweatshirt sleeve. "God, I always smell like french fries when I work here."

As she watched me eat the nachos she'd prepared special for me, Kelli complained about everyone's hysteria that she was torpedoing her future by settling for community college. Perla snorted. At least Kelli's parents accepted that she was going to make her own decision. They didn't have any money to give to their daughter for tuition, but they had offered Kelli three hundred dollars a month to help with her rent. And Nancy had been steadily adding to a box of pots and pans and kitchen utensils. She wanted to give Kelli something to take with her when she moved into her first apartment. Perla would have killed for such support, however grudgingly given. She and her father had been circling each other testily for months as he tried to persuade her not to move to Austin. Perla's family had been hoping their oldest daughter would go to the community college in Uvalde. They wanted her living at home with her younger brothers and sisters and both sets of grandparents. If she had to leave their protective embrace, her father wanted her anywhere but Austin, a city ridiculed in Utopia for its left-leaning politics.

"Every day is an argument," said Perla. "He wants me to go to a Christian college or something. He gave this one military school my cellphone number so they could call me and try to recruit me. I was like, 'Hello?' 'Hey, this is Norwich. So where do we rank on your college list? What are you looking for in a school?' And I was like, 'Nothing there.'" Kelli laughed approvingly. "I was such a bitch," said Perla, with a shy smile of satisfaction. "I don't think my dad really wants me to be in the military, but he keeps bringing it up. My dad is just very conservative and he doesn't want me to go to any college or city that will change my mind from the way he sees things. But going to a Christian school isn't going to make me a better Christian. I guess because he's a preacher, he wants me to—"

Kelli, frustrated by Perla's attempts to explain her father's manipulations, cut her friend off. "If it comes down to it," she said, "you have to be the one who says, 'Fuck you, I'm leaving.'"

Perla blanched and looked down at her hands knotted in her lap beneath the table. Their shared dream of escape was the foundation of their friendship. But when Kelli talked about their future lives outside Utopia, her prickly bravado seemed to make Perla go quiet and pale.

"Sometimes I'm scared that she's the one who's really supposed to make it," Perla said. "Maybe I'll work really, really hard and not make it."

Kelli groaned next to her friend in the booth.

"What scares me is taking that first or second step to making my dream come true," said Perla. "And what scares me even more is that Kelli's going to make it and I'm going to be left behind. Having to start my dream and then having to see my best friend go away with our dream. What I'm scared about is that I'm going to let myself down and I'm going to want it so bad. I don't have a Plan B. If I screw it up, my whole life is a blank."

She and Kelli spent most of their time talking about what their future band would look and sound like. Their other best friend, Chris, who wore the collars of his sherbet-colored Polo shirts turned up and liked to talk about how much money he would make for the girls in promotional deals, had already offered to be the band's manager. The only problem was Perla didn't know how to play an instrument.

Over the summer, Kelli had finally started taking professional lead-guitar lessons. Ron found a blues guitar teacher at a music shop in San Antonio and drove Kelli ninety minutes one way for a weekly thirty-minute lesson. He paid for the gas, Kelli paid twenty-five dollars a lesson out of her café money. Her teacher, Mr. Fox, a bearded white man in glasses with grown children, was charmed by his new student's passion. He said that unlike most of the teenagers he taught, Kelli always arrived with all of her homework mastered. Throughout their brief sessions, she wore an expression of intense focus, staring up at him as if he were a doctor about to give his diagnosis. Kelli didn't write anything down during her lessons, but on the ride home she took her spiral notebook out of her large polka-dotted backpack and scribbled down everything that had come out of her teacher's mouth. At home, she would immediately lock herself in her bedroom and practice for five-hour stretches.

Kelli had been urging Perla for months to join her for lessons. She could arrange it so that Mr. Fox would meet with Perla before or after her turn so her friend could just tag along in Ron's truck. Perla was worried about making the weekly commitment. Her dad had been diagnosed with hepatitis C and was unable to hold down a full-time job, and her mother worked long hours as a home health aide. It was often up to Perla to look after her grandparents when she wasn't at school or working. Whatever money she did make at the café was supposed to pay for her school supplies or clothes or the occasional concert. So whenever she felt badgered by Kelli's urging to sign up for lessons, she said she couldn't afford it. Besides, her parents would never feel comfortable allowing their daughter to take advantage of Mr. Rhodes's willingness to play chauffeur.

Perla knew she was supposed to be inspired by Kelli's progress, but every elated report of a newly mastered chord left her feeling more dejected. So after months of excuses, Perla finally admitted out loud that she was ready to learn how to play the guitar. Once a week, Perla waited for Ron's truck at the top of the steep hill to her family's house. She sat next to Kelli with a thin clump of tip money in her hoodie pocket and stared out the window the whole way to San Antonio.

I asked Perla that afternoon at the café if she ever really pictured herself leaving Utopia in the fall. "I really hope so," she said. "I *want* to want to move. I'm scared, but I really hope so." She took a napkin out of the dispenser and slowly mopped at the congealing ketchup on the table. "I won't bail," she told Kelli, looking up at her best friend. Kelli yanked down hard on the treble clef charm around her neck, holding it in a fist over her sternum. "You better not," she said, shoving a hip into Perla's side.

United once again, the girls moved on to dreaming about the adventures that awaited them. "Austin is so not Utopia," said Perla excitedly. "I feel like it's somewhere I belong. I try to explain stuff to people here, like how guys can wear eyeliner or girls can have mohawks, and they just think I'm weird." With just six months left of high school, the girls' restlessness was reaching a fever pitch. Kelli and Perla pledged to each other that they'd never settle for the same pallid dreams as the rest of their classmates. They didn't want to marry young and make babies in Utopia. And they didn't want to leave town only to end up stuck in some stuffy corporate gig working forty hours a week. "I don't want to be a doctor," said Kelli. "I don't want to be a lawyer. I don't want to be a nurse. I just don't want a normal job." She looked over at Perla for some backup.

"I don't want to work at a restaurant, either," said Perla. "Working at the café is like a suicide job." She looked around at the nearly empty room. The cook sat alone at a table, a cigarette hanging from her lips. "I wish *something* would ever happen in this town," she said.

Kelli sighed and fanned her face. "I just feel like I'm pushing through a hot fog," she said. Kelli's older sister, Racheal, had recently moved back into the trailer house with her two young daughters. Her boyfriend was in jail and she couldn't take care of the kids and make the rent by herself in San Antonio. Home had suddenly gotten a lot more claustrophobic.

Now Michael, who had just turned twenty-one years old, was home from Fort Drum, his base in upstate New York, on leave. He was down on the Army, having been passed over for another promotion. Every time Michael was close to climbing a rank, he found himself in trouble. Last spring he had been demoted after punching a superior officer in the face after the man called him a nigger during warmup exercises. Recently, his off-base privileges had been stripped after he picked up a misfire charge down at the gun range. "I shot my gun when I wasn't supposed to," he said sheepishly. "It was a fully automatic machine gun and they say, 'Pick up a good sight picture,' and that's when you grab it and look down the sights. I didn't have my weapon on safety so I adjusted and pulled back and shot off like five or six rounds. Oh well, that's why we all have flight vests and goggles and helmets, right?" After three years in the Army, Michael was still a private.

When he returned to New York, he would pack up his barracks for his first deployment to Iraq. "We're going to Baghdad, so that's a big hot zone over there," he said nonchalantly on his last night home. After dinner he was going to meet his best friend, Big Lu, in town at Pico. They were going to steal some ice from the cooler in the back of the café and bring it over to the Wiekamp barn. Joey was having a party. Michael seemed more worried about getting the ice than Iraq. "I don't know," he said, flicking a piece of lint from his American Eagle jeans.

"They just told us we were doing security. And security could either be tower guard or gate guard, or we could go out and do patrols outside the wire. I just kind of want to go and get it over with so I can get out."

Lil Scrappy's "Money in the Bank" started playing in Michael's pocket. Big Lu was on the phone. He had been waiting for him at Pico for over an hour and was threatening to just go home. Michael still had to shave and do his hair. "All right, dude," he told his friend. "Dude, I'll be there in a second. Are you serious right now? You're so gay. You're really going to bail on my last night. Dude, I'll be there in like ten minutes. Well, I'll be there, don't worry. All right, peace." Kelli snorted to herself. "Oh please, he's so inconvenienced," she said, after Michael hung up. "That's all they do is hang out at Pico." A month later Michael was in Iraq, posting Facebook status updates like "Michael doesn't have a handle on things" or "Michael woke up, looked around, thought 'Shit, still here.'"

Kelli decided that the only way she could cope with having her sister back home and her brother in Iraq was to harden herself to all family concerns. Throughout her senior year, she'd been trying to muster up the energy to dip a toe into Utopia's weekend social scene. On a whim, she'd gone with Jamie Lynn one night to a party in the nearby town of D'Hanis. But a few minutes after they walked into a stranger's house, some idiot started hooting in the corner telling racist jokes. Kelli found Jamie and told her she wasn't comfortable and wanted to leave immediately. Her friend accused her of overreacting, and pouted to the lunch table at school on Monday that Kelli had made them leave the party early for no good reason.

In the fall a couple of senior boys graffitied the front of the school and hung the Confederate flag from the flagpole. Everyone, from Kelli to the superintendent, knew one of the bozos who did it because he had misspelled the word "seniors." Kelli was used to random redneck episodes, but they still ate at her. She wasn't like Michael. When he had been home on leave, he'd gone over to a buddy's house and the two turned on MTV to watch a reality show. When Michael's friend asked her father what he thought of the show, the man sank grumpily into his chair. "I don't think anything them niggers say is funny," he said in front of Michael. "So I was like, 'Okay, well it's about that time, I'll see you all later,'" said Michael. "You can't be fazed by things like that in Utopia. Sometimes it will be inappropriate, but then on the other hand that's how these people were raised. They've never been taught to call black people African Americans."

Kelli had furiously pounded her fist on the table at her brother's casual response. "But they know it's not appropriate! I'm not putting up with it."

Kelli was the only girl in town Colter could ever picture himself dating. He liked having someone in his life who liked the same music and movies. When they first started talking over MySpace, Kelli thought briefly about the possibility of something more than a friendship with Colter. But then one night, driving home from a concert in San Antonio, he managed to forever turn her off.

Perla was asleep in the backseat. Kelli sat in the front with Colter, determined to stay awake with him on the long drive home. Colter, in an attempt to keep the conversation going, blurted out a dumb joke about Mexicans. Kelli's spine stiffened. She turned to see if her friend had caught Colter's offensive attempt at humor. Colter sat there uncomfortably, wishing his words back. "She gets this look in her eye and you know you said something stupid," he said. "I was like, 'Oh crap, I shouldn't have said that.' I kind of tried to make other jokes and it didn't really work. So I turned on a comedy CD and we both just sat there. Fifteen minutes down the road I was like, 'It's really quiet in here.' And then I was like, 'It's probably that dumb joke you made, Colter. Damn, shouldn't have said that, but oh well.'"

They still talked online every now and then but increasingly their conversations had grown stiff and uncomfortable. Colter had been making noise again about leaving for Arizona to jump into the school's spring semester. But he'd scrapped his haphazard plans around Christmastime. "Five days before I was supposed to leave, there was still a good chance that I was actually going to go," he said. "And then finally I was like, 'Screw it.'" So he told Kelli that his new plan was just to move to San Antonio in the fall and start school there. His paralysis had started depressing Kelli. A polite awkwardness settled between them, both of them realizing their fondness for each other had reached its limits. Colter pretended not to care. "The more we get to know each other, the less we have in common," he said. "Kelli gets offended too easily. She'll joke around for a little but then you'll say something and she gets real pissed off. She takes everything seriously and I take nothing seriously."

Colter met me in San Antonio one Saturday afternoon in February. He looked depressed. That morning his parents had invited Alyssa's boyfriend's family over for barbecue brisket. Horrified by the idea of an afternoon of bonding out at the ranch, Colter opted for a distant double feature instead. We sat under the bright lights at a crowded mall food court waiting for the first movie to begin. A young girl wandered away from her parents to come over and stare up at Colter. When she moved to smooth his gelled hair with her pink plastic Barbie brush, Colter leaned over and talked sweetly with her until her mother motioned her to stop being a pest. The girl waved at Colter, pleased to have made a new friend. He returned his attention to our table and sighed. He had never felt so alone in town.

While the community rallied lovingly around Lindy, they had little patience for the rest of her family. I went to dinner by myself one evening at the café just before closing. I sat down with the waitress and the cook at their smoking table and asked the women for the latest gossip. The waitress told me that Lindy had been back in the hospital but had been released that afternoon. First thing Lindy did when she got home was call one of her friends for a ride to the café. She ate dinner there and promised to be back in the morning. Lindy spent a good portion of her life curled up to a café table. Whenever she walked in the front door, a relieved smile settled over her face. The café often felt more familiar to her than home.

There was a growing sense of disgust down at the café for the way Lindy's family continued to fail her. They were angry at Alyssa for moving her boyfriend into the house. Despite Lindy's protests, the boy was sleeping in Alyssa's room and supposedly bringing beer into the house. They were angry that Clif was gone half the month and a pain in the ass the other half. They were grudgingly pleased to see Colter trying a little harder, but everybody agreed he could still be doing more for his vulnerable mother. The conversation at the café soon widened to include not only the waitress and cook but a nearby table as well.

"They drop her off at the café like a town dog and expect someone to pick her up!" cried one of Lindy's best friends, throwing her chicken taco back onto her supper plate in disgust. "Their mother is dying. And they don't care. She wiped their asses since they were this big, gave them everything they wanted." Another of Lindy's friends, who'd been nodding along excitedly, shook a wrinkled finger in the air. "They're old enough to know better!"

It was easy to feel great admiration for all these women who took such good care of their friend. But did they ever trash her kids. Did people in town, I wondered, ever stop to worry about how Colter and Alyssa were doing? They were young. They were scared. Perhaps they behaved badly because it was hard for them to accept that they could actually lose their mother.

"No, no, no, I'm sorry," said Lindy's friend, shaking her head. "I've seen too much. Just don't get me started. I had Lindy all week and then they were calling Friday and Saturday saying, 'Well, can't you come stay with her for the weekend, we have to go out!' They're ignorant and self-centered and don't care. They're going to care when it's too late, when she's gone."

While she put her rough hands to the sides of her face, as if to contain her rage, her friend smirked. "Then she'll be a saint," she said. "And they'll say how they worked their little fingers to the bone helping their mother." I gasped aloud at the image of Colter and Alyssa being hissed about at their own mother's funeral.

When word had gotten around town that the Padgetts hadn't done anything special for Lindy at Christmas, people worked themselves up into a state. They couldn't believe that Alyssa spent the holiday with her boyfriend's family. And of course Colter spent Christmas alone in his bedroom, staring blankly into a computer screen. When one of the waitresses asked Lindy what she got for Christmas, she was stunned when the woman said nothing. So the waitress got to talking with one of her regulars and the two decided to throw their friend a surprise Valentine's Day party.

On February 12, around suppertime, the waitresses pushed some tables together and arranged pitchers of Kool-Aid and bowls of chips and queso and Obie Milton's homemade chocolate cheesecake next to a pile of presents in leftover Christmas wrapping paper. When Lindy pushed the front door open she stared at the large constellation of her friends clustered in the middle of the restaurant beaming brightly at her.

A young waitress who had graduated in Colter's class had been working on the night of Lindy's surprise party. The girl had thin blue veins running down her pale cheeks and kept her dark blond hair scraped into a ponytail that hung long down her back. As she remembered Lindy's astonished reaction the night of her party, she flapped her bony hand in front of her face when she felt her eyes tearing up.

"Lindy didn't know anything," the waitress said. "She just came in like she always does to get something to eat. Then she's like, 'Oh hi!' you know, saying hi to everybody. And she was like, 'Wow, there's a lot of people here!' And she got halfway in the café and was kind of looking around and we're like, 'It's a surprise party for you, Lindy!' And she kept saying, 'Well, who am I?' and we go, 'You're our friend, Lindy. We love you! We just want to tell you you're special and we love you!' She didn't know why she got a party. She didn't think she deserved it. Lindy went around to everybody and then she came to give me a hug and I've known her for a long time but with all her health drama I don't think she really knew who I was. But she came right up to me and gave me a hug. 'Thank you, I love you.' That was it for me. I had to split or I was going to start crying. So I went back to watch the party through the order window."

Lindy spent the evening with a stunned smile on her weary face, marveling at her candy bouquet and the basket of chocolate hearts and all her friends' simple and tender sentiments scrawled on the large posterboard card.

Everyone in town had gathered at the café that evening—everyone except her family. "Nope," said the waitress with a pinched tone of disapproval. "They didn't even come." She paused for a second. "Well, I don't know if they were invited. But they definitely didn't show."

A couple weeks after the party Lindy tried to explain to me how much the gesture meant to her. "It gives me the chills to think about," she said, sitting in a booth with her best friends while they ate their lunch. "This community has just been . . ." She patted her heart with her hand. "I don't know. They love me."

Colter knew everybody at the café talked badly about him. He had long ago learned to ignore the conversations going on behind his back—and wished his mother had a similar filter. "I have work and Alyssa has school and we have an arrangement planned that people will pick her up," he fumed. "My mom likes to be there. And half the time when we call her and ask if she'd like us to pick her up she's like, 'No, I'd like to stay here.' But people see something and say, 'Oh, they're not doing a good job!' If somebody says something bad about me at the café then she believes them and I'm automatically lying because the person at the café is right. In the eighth grade someone told her they saw me smoking pot in the town square. I wasn't! It's happened time and time again. 'Do you know what the people at the café say about you?' I don't care! They've said everything."

At times Colter said he was unsure if all the care Lindy received in town was worth it if it meant her friends felt at liberty to poison his mother against her own family. "They don't want to get involved in stuff because they care, they want to get involved in stuff because they don't have anything better to do and gossip is the only thing that goes on in that town."

In his calmer moments, Colter was able to appreciate the great reservoir of warmth and compassion that rested within each of his mother's many friends. Without their devoted care and daily cheerleading, the Padgetts would have been lost. Lindy herself would have long ago given in to the depression that had been threatening to submerge her ever since her diagnosis.

But Colter simply didn't have it in him to ever tell anyone thank you, or admit to them that his mother's cancer left him feeling scared and overwhelmed. Perhaps his mother's friends found it hard to extend sympathy in Colter's direction because he was incapable of ever asking for any. He had learned from his father that sarcasm and self-isolation were a man's best defenses in times of crisis. And so he had a tendency to meet gestures of generosity with coldness. When he felt ganged up on, he distanced himself in return.

Lindy seemed tired of playing the mediator between her friends and family. She loved them all, but it was hard having to constantly rely on everyone around her. Her health had been reasonably stable for a few months, her seizures kept to a minimum. So Lindy got up the courage to ask Jessie over at the Hicks House if she might ever be of service in any capacity. She promised to work hard, and not get in anyone's way. She wouldn't expect payment of any kind. Lindy wanted a job, was all. She wanted to experience again what it felt like to be of use.

The Hicks House, whose small staff and homey comfort food were fast making it the chosen place for locals to eat their noon meal, was the perfect place to put her to work. The dining room was small, set up in the home's former front parlor, with ten or so tables crowded close together. Lindy assured Jessie that if she was given a job she'd never put the rest of the staff in the position of having to worry over her health. "I told them, 'I promise nobody would have to take care of me. I'll just sweep the sidewalk and stay out of the way.' Well, after a few days Jessie said, 'Do you want a real job?' I said, 'You're joking me!'" And so Lindy was brought on to help wash dishes and bus tables three days a week, from nine-thirty in the morning until the restaurant closed at three. She earned thirty dollars a shift. She kept half for herself and gave the other half to the Living Waters fund for a Guatemalan orphanage the congregation sponsored.

I went to lunch at the Hicks House one afternoon during one of Lindy's shifts. She'd taken special care on her hair, and made sure to wear her dark jeans and her best silver earrings. When diners called out, "Hey, working girl! Hey there, you!" she'd smile over at them and shake her tiny fist triumphantly in the air, but she was loath to engage in conversation. When people asked after her health, she smiled and excused herself.

After the lunch rush had blown back out the front door, Lindy made a final pass through the dining room, stacking on her quivering arm the last two plates with remnants of the King Ranch chicken special and a tiny parfait dessert dish. She carefully wiped down her final table before tucking her white rag into the back pocket of her jeans. She looked around the clean room, and let out a long exhale of satisfaction.

LUMBERYARD

Utopia Builders Supply, or "the lumberyard," as it is known by locals, is the oldest building in town. The rock-face front is covered with hand-prints and scratched initials of all the coffee drinkers from when they were boys. Every Friday afternoon, the oldest woman in the Sabinal Canyon folds herself with surprising grace into one of the lumberyard's lime-green metal chairs by the cash register. Martha Hans is ninety-nine years old, and she attributes her lean and sturdy frame to a lifetime of helping her husband run their sheep and cattle. Martha likes to linger down at the lumberyard while her only child, June, and June's two best friends go get their hair done at Erma's. After their beauty appoint-ments they join Martha and settle in for their weekly gab session. The women are known in town as the Steel Magnolias.

Martha, wearing a loose cream blouse over a red shirt and cream trousers on this Friday afternoon, has the rangy and angular appeal of Katharine Hepburn. She is a handsome woman, with a sun visor perched sportily on top of her shag of white hair. She sat with crossed legs, closing her eyes dreamily every time the oscillating fan whirred in her direction. A few feet away, her great-grandson Bobby Mauldin rang up a box of nails for a man in a cowboy hat. The customer's five-year-old son sauntered barrel-legged up and down the aisles of the store, as if toward a showdown with the shelf of drill bits. The child wore a gun belt around the waist of his little jeans, a television remote control nestled in the holster. Martha winked, nodding to the boy. "Walkin' big," she said with an appreciative grin.

Before coming home to the lumberyard, Bobby spent a few years working as a firefighter in an Austin suburb, until he tired of the traffic and strip-mall aesthetic. So he moved back to Utopia, married a girl from a neighboring town, and gave Martha a great-great-grandson named Holt. Bobby, in a pair of Levis and a short-sleeved plaid shirt, is the mirror image of his father, Bob, who emerged from the lumberyard's office behind a sliding wooden door to brew a fresh pot of coffee. Bob, who runs the lumberyard with his brothers, Sid Jr. and Tom, took the business over from their father, Sid. Like most people in town, the brothers worked multiple jobs. "We all do whatever," said Bob, a man of few words who might strike one as a bit of a crab if his eyes didn't so regularly crinkle at the corners in boyish amusement. "I've got a land clearing business. I ranch some too. Now that's a real satisfying job."

Bobby, standing beneath the mounted heads of deer and bobcats that were caught on Martha's ranch, nodded at his great-grandmother. "You have to think about how much change she has seen in her life," he said, shouting for the benefit of her failing ears. "Well, I've seen a lot of it," she agreed, tapping her long finger on her chin to jog her keen memory. "I think we have about five churches now," she said, giving me a comical grimace. "Surely something good will happen to us! And about ten years ago we built the senior citizens building, but so many of the older people passed away and the folks that are moving in don't seem very interested in it. They better, though, because they're going to be seniors one of these days too."

Martha grew up twenty-five miles away on a large ranch in Divide country, a swath of land along the Edwards Plateau that used to be all open range. When she turned seventy-five, she moved down to Utopia into a trailer house on June and Sid's property so she could be closer to family. "I told 'em I loved 'em, but I didn't want to live with 'em," she said. "I'm afraid I'd get grouchy." She spoke with mild embarrassment about Utopia's grand plans to throw her a hundredth birthday party in the spring. "There'll be good music, I can guarantee you that," she said. "I love to dance. I say I can still dance if somebody can hold me up."

In a flurry of cooing laughter, Katherine, Lahoma, and June bustled into the lumberyard. They assumed their chairs around Martha, settling down like hens. Katherine, the baby of the bunch at seventy-eight, fanned herself with her hand, gazing up with exasperation at the old shiny pine ceiling. "I suppose we're one day closer to rain," she said. People spoke of the summer's long drought as if it were a wayward child they were used to being disappointed by. Katherine worked with her daughter and husband, Ralph's brother, up Main Street at Boyce Realty. She told her friends that the market was keeping them busy. "We're getting a lot of business now since the tax rate has gone up on twenty-acre tracts," she said. "People are trying to sell. The property taxes are going up and up. I hear they're going up again. That's why you have to keep it on agricultural use. Keep it fenced and have some cows."

June, her white hair arranged demurely into a bun, sighed. She is the shyest of the Magnolias. "It's been a long, long time since we didn't have fences," she said softly. Lahoma shook her head, her large silver lion-face earrings fretting along in tandem. "And now it costs so much to build a fence you can't even build new ones," she said. "So we have miles of bad fences. Just old, old, old, and they'll sag and they'll break and the cows will jump over them."

"You hate to see the land divided," said June, upon news that another family ranch was breaking up.

"It'll probably happen to ours," said Lahoma, her big, pretty eyes watering a little at the prospect. "I'd hate to see it, but maybe it won't happen until after we've all passed." When the fan blew again toward the Magnolias, their hair barely moved in the teasing breeze.

CHAPTER 9

They Sell Soy Milk Here Now

On a cold winter morning, Morris priced a delivery of shredded cheese pouches and prepackaged kids' lunches and loaded them into one of his shiny new refrigerators. Jody Rutherford, the telephone company man, barreled down the aisle looking for the day's first cup of coffee and Sno Ball. He pointed finger guns at each of the new refrigerators. "This one's going to be Bud Lite!" he hooted like a sports announcer. "This one's going to be Miller Lite!"

Morris ignored the man's sarcasm, while the old-timers chuckled softly to themselves in their regular seats. "Morris is all ready for beer, isn't he?" said Baby Ray. "He puts any more coolers in here and we won't have room for coffee anymore."

Jody, or "Motormouth," as Ralph called him, looked around at the latest improvements Morris was making to the store and let out a long whistle. "This is y'all's equivalent of the town changing preachers every few weeks," he hollered. "You're switching this place up on us the way the ladies change their undergarments!"

There was a rumor swirling through town that the business owners in Utopia's precinct, which included the popular Texas summer destination of Garner Park and tourist-heavy towns like Concan, were working on a petition to get booze back on the ballot in the spring election. Locals would have the chance to vote on whether Utopia should once and for all go wet.

Now, Ralph admits to enjoying a glass of red wine in the evening at the house, not that it was anyone's business, but he said he'd hate to see newcomers vote to allow a honky-tonk in his hometown. "These are people who are coming out of the city where they've always had liquor," he explained to me once. "And they think how stupid it is that we don't." In the midseventies Sabinal voted to allow the sale of alcohol (though on-premises consumption was still illegal). Soon enough a drive-through beverage barn opened and became a destination for drinkers in the surrounding area. Last year the nearby town of Leakey had gone completely wet, one-upping Sabinal by allowing restaurants to serve alcohol. Business there was booming.

"When Leakey passed it shocked everybody," Morris told me privately. "All the church groups, all the old-timers. But people are going to drink. It's going to be on the ballot sooner or later. Think about it. You can go anywhere in Utopia and buy drugs. Why in the hell would you worry about buying beer? Let's use some common sense! These kids are obtaining beer and always have been. Somewhere, from some source. Whoever is buying it for them is buying it in Sabinal where no one's watching. If you're selling it here in Utopia, at least somebody's watching."

That morning the coffee drinkers talked over the issue, working the matter over like worry beads. Most everyone seemed to agree that no good could come from Utopia going wet like the rest of the world. "We'll start getting riffraff in here," Ted argued, his pale face flushing pink. "It'll bring beer joints in and that's where there comes fights and," he said, pausing as he pictured the chaos, "lots of other things!"

Baby Ray shook his head sadly. It was the first time I'd ever seen him without his pie-sized smile. "One of these days it'll pass, and I think it'd be a disaster," he said, resting his coffee mug on the baggy leg of his bright blue coveralls. "At least the drunks now have to drive further to get the alcohol. That cuts their drinking down to one day a week maybe. If they bring it in here, it's going to be every day. That's just my opinion, and I drink. Used to, at least. Praise the Lord he took it away from me."

Milton, who'd been listening to Ray with a skeptical knot in his brow, shrugged his shoulders irritably. "I don't drink, but I could care less," he said. The men looked tired of discussing the threat of change, so the superintendent cheerfully shushed the fussing. He reminded the men that every business in town was too close to either a church or the school to allow for the sale of alcohol. The General Store sat diagonally across the street from the Gospel Tabernacle, where one large family gathered to worship while everyone else in town engaged in mildly scandalous fantasies about what their supposedly pentecostal service entailed. Pico was just a few paces from the school. If no one could sell it, no one could drink it. Essentially, the superintendent reasoned, that left Utopia impervious to the election's results.

Morris was quiet throughout the men's discussion. He exhaled loudly as he inspected the front of one of the rectangular boxes of soy milk that he had started unloading into the refrigerator. "This cannot be good for you," he said with a laugh, holding out the box to show the older men. "Regular milk has got about a two-week shelf life. This has got two months."

The coffee drinkers all looked at one another with mystified expressions. "What exactly *is* soy milk?" Ray asked.

"I didn't know they milked soybeans," Milton said.

"Is it like synthetic oil?" continued Ray. "And what is synthetic oil? What's the base of a synthetic oil?"

Ralph came down the center aisle humming to himself, eager to start his second shift at the store.

"They sell soy milk here now," Milton grimly announced. "At least that's what the box says."

Ralph settled into his chair. He'd missed most of coffee yesterday morning because he'd had an appointment in the city with his doctor to get his blood checked.

"Well, what'd he say?" said Milton, asking after Ralph's health.

"She said I'm doing just fine," Ralph said happily.

"*He's* a *she*?" Milton looked stumped as he worked out the particulars of what he'd just heard. He took a sip of coffee to regroup. "Well," he asked in a casual tone of voice, "is she good-looking?"

Ralph cocked his chin and flattened his lips to consider the matter. "Above average," he told Milton. "I like her. I got no complaints."

Morris nodded good morning to his old boss over the click-clacking of his pricing gun. I asked Ralph if it ever touched him to see his successor stocking groceries just as he had done himself for all those decades. Everyone laughed when Ralph hesitated.

"I don't know if I'd say it warms my heart . . . ," he said.

"Better him than you, right?" said Milton.

"That's right," said Ralph. "Done it too many times myself."

Ralph was dismayed to hear how poor business had been for Morris during the months of hunting season. That stretch between November through January used to supply Ralph and Kenneth their best chance at turning a profit. Landowners in town used to depend on the extra income generated from hunting leases. Now so much of the Hill Country had been cut up into smaller tracts or bought up by wealthy people who didn't need a hunter's money. One extraordinarily rich woman outside town recently announced her plan to let the land on her large ranch just go back to nature. Her admittedly idyllic vision for her property was met with wistful frowning from the old-timers. They had fond memories of what had once been a lovingly maintained working ranch. Now that same land was being taken over by brush, and wild hogs and coyotes roamed free. Some of the bigger landowners in town still loved hosting lavish hunts on their property. But they came equipped with the resources to do all their own deer processing on site. That meant little business for Morris down at the General Store.

"You know what they charge on doves now?" Morris asked the coffee drinkers, referring to the many handmade signs up and down Highway 90 advertising dove hunts. "Eighty-five to a hundred dollars, morning and night! Used to be four dollars a day." Everyone laughed in disbelief. "Stupid Yankees just throwing out money," he teased.

"We like their money," said Ralph, crossing one leg over the other as he nodded to himself, stirring his coffee slowly. "Yep, there doesn't even have to be a dove. Just put up a sign."

The problem the men had with so many of these weekend hunters was their lack of respect. They figured a man ought to eat what he killed. "But I would say that in the city ninety percent of the deer meat never hits the table," said Ralph. "It's shoved in the freezer till they're getting ready for next season and then it'll be dumped."

"Look how much deer meat is left here at the store," said Milton. "It's processed, cut, and wrapped, and they just leave it."

"They leave the deer here and don't ever pay for them," Ray explained to me. "Morris takes it because he's just a goodwill guy."

Morris turned to face the men and waved one of his meaty fists good-naturedly in the air. "I'm going to have a big giveaway next year!"

"We used to process a thousand to thirteen hundred deer a season," said Ralph, as the fellows nodded into their cups. "I think right now they process probably five hundred. It used to be our main business. We had to make that money back during deer season. Well, we got so many newcomers now. They don't have to spend it on all the old-timers." He nodded over at Milton sitting to his side on the wooden bench. "We're all dying off, you know?"

"Dead and don't know it," laughed Milton. "One day you wake up and come to the store and your name is on the door!" he said, referring to the stark typed funeral notices that kept the town abreast of any downward shift in its small population.

Milton nodded over at the younger man in their midst. "Morris is doing okay, though. Every Monday morning he gets a load of groceries delivered. Though I don't suppose he's going to end up being a millionaire this way." Morris barked a laugh at the very idea of the General

Store lining his pockets with anything other than used coffee filters. "Maybe with the land, though," said Milton, waggling his eyebrows at Ralph, who snorted in response.

A few years ago Morris found himself, much to his surprise, at the center of a real estate deal with one of the two wealthiest new landowners in town. He told some jokes, made a couple of introductions, shook some smooth hands, and someone handed him a commission. With his easy demeanor and centerpiece presence down at the store, he continued to parlay his relationship with those high rollers into more lucrative deals. On the advice of one of his new business buddies, Morris went and got himself an agent's license. Soon enough he was working out of the General Store on behalf of one of the biggest real estate brokers in South Texas. In the six short years since Morris started moonlighting from the grocery business, he's sold thirty-seven million dollars' worth of land in and around the area.

Morris is gone most afternoons now, leaving either Chance or one of his cashiers in charge. He recently negotiated a deal on a six-hundred-acre ranch some seventy miles away in Sisterdale. A couple of bigwigs out of New Orleans who'd made their fortune in the oil and gas business had offered five million dollars for the property. Morris's commission on that one deal would put to shame his yearly take from the General Store.

"A few years from now he'll be like Lou Waters," Milton jokingly warned the rest of the coffee drinkers, comparing Morris to the retired CEO of trash giant Browning-Ferris, who now owned half of Utopia. "He'll have those pockets filled up with hundred-dollar bills."

Morris laughed, as if the idea was ridiculous, without actually disagreeing about how quickly the tides of his fortune had changed. "Let's just put it this way," he said, his voice bearing a hint of swagger. "I've been very lucky." He rapped a knuckle on the glass of his new cooler. "Most of that money I pump back into this sumbitch to keep the doors to this place open." He looked over at me with my reporter's pad in my lap. "I could write a book," he said. *"How to Get Rich in Real Estate and Lose It in the Grocery Business."* Everyone laughed, Ralph loudest of all. Morris groaned at his predicament. "Problem is I can't find a damn sucker to buy this place off me. Got to find me one of those wealthy newcomers."

"You didn't know Ralph was setting you up for twenty years, did you?" Tony said with a grin.

Morris thwacked his pricing gun against his hearty thigh and laughed. "No, I did. But at that age I didn't have a lot of options."

The coffee drinkers couldn't imagine a General Store run by a new-comer. As far as they were concerned, Morris ought to just go on pour-ing himself into the place until he retired. He then could pass it down to Chance. So the old-timers chuckled along when Morris talked about his wish to sell out, without ever taking him seriously.

Later that morning, after the coffee drinkers had all cleared out, Morris shook his head in mock exasperation, groaning about how lit-tle had changed at the store since he'd started working there all those years ago. Chance leaned up against the Pepsi cooler by the front door, looking bored. "Chance is a good kid," Morris once told me. "Honest as the day is long, but he's got about eight years of maturing ahead of him. He don't want no obligations whatsoever—not to a woman, not to a mama, not to anyone." With his glazed eyes staring down at his boots, it was difficult to tell if Chance was listening to the conversation or simply dozing back there behind his dark lashes. He wore a baseball cap over his thick black curly hair, and the same preppy collared shirt and jeans he'd worn to work the previous day. He was tired from a long night out chasing girls at the dance halls in Bandera.

Back in his bachelor days, Morris had spent countless nights tromp-ing through the same Bandera bars, trying to get a girl he hadn't grown up with to dance with him. His days of running wild came crashing to an end when he'd surprised himself by falling in love. He was twenty-nine years old when he met his wife, a sassy blonde with loose, long Breck shampoo curls and sharp blue eyes. Before he could talk himself out of it, Morris found himself saying "I do" to this no-nonsense schoolteacher from Hondo. It was time for the man to cobble together a grown-up life.

"When we first got married, me and Sydney were living in a little bitty cheesy trailer house," Morris told us from behind the register. He rubbed underneath his ample chin, wincing a little with embarrassment. Morris looked around the store to see if any customers were eavesdropping. He had a story to confess from his newlywed past, but he seemed squirrelly about whether or not he should. After a windy exhale, he went on to describe a lucky discovery during those lean years. "In our backyard there was an old hand-dug well. All the wells in town are real shallow, and this one was filled up with gravel. Sydney wanted me to dig up the gravel, throw some dirt in there, and help her plant some shrubs. I was trying to please the old lady at the time, you know. Newlyweds! I wouldn't do that today. Now I'd go, 'Chance! Go do that!'"

Chance looked up, attesting to this part of the story with a weary nod of his head.

"Anyways," Morris continued, "I was digging down there in the gravel and I found this coffee can and there was a jar in it. Anyways, so it's a pickle jar about this big," he said, placing one of his flattened palms a half foot above the other, "the lid rusted onto it. I opened it up and there was something rolled up down in there."

By this point Chance had lost the drowsy expression on his face. The cashier, Jean, leaned in closer to Morris, delighted that someone down at the store was telling a fresh story for a change. Morris cleared his throat dramatically, emboldened by his suddenly captive audience. "So she's saying, 'Throw it away! It's probably toxic!' Anyways, it was a roll with newspapers around it, and I opened it up—and it was money! Luckily, it was wet, and we started peeling 'em off like old wet newspapers, one at a time, and spreading 'em out on the kitchen table, washer and dryer, counters. It ended up that it was five thousand dollars. And the newest bill was from 1965 or '66. And I'm telling you— *we were dirt-ass poor*. There were hundred-dollar bills in there from the thirties. There wasn't a bank here at the time. I went to take it to a federal reserve bank and it took 'em about a month to verify. It was damaged money, but we ended up getting $4,920. I wish I had it all now, framed. That'd be cooler than shit."

Chance wondered aloud when it'd finally be his turn to find his own pickle jar. Jean laughed and asked the boy how long he'd been working for Morris. Chance opened his mouth to answer but Morris quickly interjected, "Too long! He needs to go out and get a job."

Jean widened her eyes in amused shock. She took Chance by his shoulders and moved him out of the way so she could get to her half-drunk bottle of pop, which she'd stuck in the cooler earlier that morning. She gave the younger man a brisk pat on the shoulder before reminding Morris that Chance already had a job.

Chance had gone to a semester of college at the Corpus Christi campus of Texas A&M. But after he came home for Christmas, he never left. Most people in town assumed that Chance will eventually take over the General Store. But the boy looked sickened when told of his supposed future. "They did not tell you the right thing," he said crabbily, emphasizing each word while Morris and Jean laughed at his vehemence.

A young woman in tight jeans and a T-shirt that stretched unforgivingly over her belly walked up to the register. "Can I have a pack of Marlboro Lights, shorts, in a box?" she said, her eyes hidden beneath her long, lank bangs.

"You're eighteen years old?" asked Morris, with a cocked brow. "Let me see your ID."

"You don't remember me?" the girl said, pouting as she dug for her license in her back pocket. "From back in the day?"

Morris sighed. "The older I get, the younger you all look."

When Morris was in school, word of his Little League baseball skill somehow spread beyond Utopia. A few professional minor league training camps went so far as to invite the young man to attend. But Morris was too interested in girls and hanging out with his friends to commit to anything as serious as an athletic program. A rich uncle living in Chicago, who had shepherded two sons of his own into college basketball programs and was eager not to let Morris squander his natural gifts, sent him an airline ticket. He'd pay for him to move there and attend college for free. Again Morris found himself unable to take advantage of the offer. He did go so far as to accept a track scholarship to a junior college in Central Texas. But he lasted only a month before drifting back home.

"Just the dedication to anything, I didn't think I had it in me," Morris told me, fidgeting at the memory of missed opportunities. "Now I look back and it would have been a breeze. But at that age, any type of commmitment—college, even a four-year pickup truck payment—seemed too scary." So back to the General Store he went, where he'd worked on and off since 1978 and was well treated by Ralph and Kenneth. He took care of the feed and the hardware and all the deliveries as his teens quickly blurred into his twenties.

Morris knew what was expected of him at the store. On two separate occasions he flirted with offshore work in the oil business, but it never took. "I probably had more opportunities to do different things than most people get," he said. "But I don't know, I just grew up here." He frowned, shuddering like a wet dog, as if to rid himself of any lingering regrets. "This is not something I'm real proud of. But I guess I was, well, I guess the word would be chicken-shit to go out into the real world."

When Kenneth told Ralph he was too sick to stay on at the store, the men offered Morris a deal. Sydney was pregnant with their second child. It was time to consider running the show. "They made me an offer that was at that point pretty good," said Morris. "Real good, actually." As Ralph's stepfather had done for them, the older men set Morris up with some money down until he could get his feet under him.

When Morris took over, he inherited not just the coffee drinkers but the credit system that still ate at his nerves every month. "When I started at the store, ninety-eight percent of the accounts were good as gold," he said. "All the old-timers pay by the fifth of every month. The thought of one of them owing somebody money is just ridiculous. But all these young kids today? They get to where they want to drive a new truck before they want to pay their bill. They don't pay the bill one month, and then it's two months, and then they disappear. They're your friends, or your friends' kids. As the years go by, people don't mean to, but just like credit card debt, they get in deep and they can't handle all of it and then your friends owe you money and you don't want to hurt their feelings and you don't say anything."

A couple of months later, Morris invited me to look around the second store he was getting ready to open up the street. Morris's new store had been the talk of the town for months, with everybody speculating as to the man's intentions. "I just kept telling people I was going to open a tattoo parlor, or a strip club, or a beer joint," he said with a smirk.

Originally, the new store was going to offer him the chance to profit from alcohol sales should Utopia go wet. No fool, he kept his plans to himself, without uttering a word to Ralph. He'd figured at the time that he could move the grocery business to the new spot and turn the existing store into a variety and hardware store. If the election went his way, the new General Store could sell beer without violating proximity laws by being too close to any church or the school. After Morris bought the lot, he invited the Texas Alcoholic Beverage Commission up to measure the distance between the site and the school. "Thinking ahead, just in case," he told me. "At that point we were far enough that if the measure ever passed I could sell beer here. Well, since then the school has bought additional properties, which scratches the possibility of this place selling any alcohol." Gone was the need to move the General Store, and Morris was saved the trouble of having to tell Ralph that his morning routine was moving up Main Street whether he liked it or not.

This afternoon we sat on two folding chairs in what Morris had recently christened the Utopia Ranch Outpost. The store wouldn't open for a few more weeks. One of Morris's friends, a newcomer from California—"He's from California but he hates liberals," Morris said approvingly, swatting at my knee with a wink—was setting him up with a modern computer system that would scan bar codes. Morris could leave his pricing gun back at the General Store. Morris winced over the new technology. "I'm just fighting it the whole way," he said. "We've done it the old-fashioned way for so long. I'm not like Ralph, but, well, I'm a little like him. I can't accept that everything will change."

Ralph would never admit as much to Morris, but his feelings were a little bruised when the younger man hadn't consulted him about his plans to open Utopia Ranch Outpost. "Didn't even ask my opinion," Ralph harumphed one morning to the coffee drinkers. "Treats you like a damn stepchild," said Milton. Morris scoffed at the idea that he ought to still run matters of business past his old boss. "If I'd told Ralph he'd just go, 'Awww, enh, I don't know if that's going to work.' When I first bought up this new property he said, 'What'd you buy that for?' I told him some day the town's going to grow and if you're not staying up, you'll be left out in the cold. To give you an example of how set in his ways Ralph is, there was this little tract of land right behind the store. He could've bought it—this was in the eighties—for four thousand. And I told him, 'Don't you think you oughta buy that? We'll need it some day.' And he said, 'Noooooo.' I've added onto the store twice since I've bought it. And now that same piece of land would cost thirty-five to forty thousand." Morris threw his arms up. "Ralph's good as gold, the hardest-working guy I ever saw in my whole life. But he doesn't want to keep up with modern times. Doesn't want to change."

There are those in Utopia who can get to griping about Morris, a whiff of envy rising up in their throats as they roll their eyes over his success in the real estate business. If he wasn't so busy taking clients on helicopter rides over the Hill Country, maybe they could get some fresh produce down at the store. But for all the grudges people in a small town are capable of holding, rare is the public confrontation. To get by in such a cramped community, people put on civil faces and politely nod hello to one another. They smile at shared jokes, ask after family members, and wish one another good mornings and evenings. A town like Utopia is too small to accommodate open hostility for very long. So while someone might bitch a little about Morris on the side, they're also forced to acknowledge his generosity and goodwill.

That year Morris was given Utopia's Lions Club annual Citizen of the Year award. He told me the news with sheepish pride. Clearly tickled by the honor, he nevertheless felt compelled to dismiss it as a "bullshit award." "They gave me this little plaque and it was so embarrassing," he said one morning, before quickly jotting down the name and number of a Lions Club member for me to call. He might not want to brag on himself, but he wasn't against someone else doing so.

It was Morris who made possible the impressive baseball field just north of town. "In 2001, the kids had about nine Little League teams and they were all trying to play at that one field down at the park," he said. Morris applied for every grant he could find, eventually securing around $150,000 in cash. He talked two wealthy families in town into each donating eight acres of property, with the promise that the field would bear their last names on the entry gate. Morris secured $38,000 from another newcomer to light the field. He rallied the locals, who supplied all the labor for free, from the water wells to the electrical wiring to all the welding work.

After a year and a half of fund-raising and planning and construction, after close to a quarter of a million dollars was spent, the lights were thrown on at the new field and the sound of cheers filled the night air.

I asked Morris if he'd forgiven himself for all the choices he'd made as a younger man. He swatted his hand at the idea. "I put that away a long time ago," he said. "When I was young, up until my late twenties, I'd say, I used to wish I'd done things differently." Morris looked down at his ringing phone. Another call for land. "Life goes by way too fast to worry about what you should've done."

That May the votes were counted. The Uvalde newspaper declared that Utopians had decided the fate of the proposed sale of beer and alcohol. One hundred thirty-four voted against the town going wet, only seventy-seven in favor.

The coffee drinkers acted unfazed by the results. "Someone gets it on the ballot every few years, but it never passes," Bud said over coffee a couple of weeks after the election.

Morris, stocking tubs of butter, grumbled to himself. One of the coffee drinkers reminded the grocer that he wouldn't have been able to sell beer anyway. Morris turned and wagged his pricing gun at the coffee drinkers. "All I would have had to do is move the front door by six feet!" he said irritably.

"You had this all figured out, didn't you?" said Bud, grinning up at the red-faced younger man. "We now know who was for it passing, don't we?"

"Not particularly," Morris said, with an unconvincing shrug of his large shoulders. "But being in business, you're kind of shooting your-self in the guts. It would have made the store much more attractive to an outside buyer later on for when I get ready to sell. I made you all a promise that if it passed I'd sell the store to a white man. Since it failed I'm going to go sell it to an Indian or a Vietnamese."

When Morris told his wife that the measure had been shot down by locals, she went ballistic. "She doesn't drink, she never drank a drop in her life," he said. He pointed his fingers at the horseshoe of coffee drinkers. "But she knew that was lost revenue and she expected the lo-cals' support. She told me, 'Throw the coffeepot out! Close all the ac-counts and don't open until seven! Or I'm leaving for Bandera.' Yeah, I'd say she took it pretty hard."

Bud leaned over and whispered in my ear. "There was a few days when Morris didn't show."

For three painful mornings in a row, Ralph waited outside the store, staring dumbly down a dark Main Street. And for three mornings in a row, Ralph shook his head in disgust and got back in his truck to drive home and make coffee for himself alone in his kitchen.

The coffee drinkers snickered over the memory of Ralph's outrage. "He would come into the store later and ask Morris if he had to buy groceries now by appointment," said Bud.

"We figured it was in response to the vote," said Albert.

"It was kind of nice sleeping in," said Morris.

"I kind of liked it myself," admitted Albert, hiding his chuckle in his styrofoam cup.

Morris glared back at the coffeepots. "I don't do this because I enjoy it, you know. It's more out of tradition than anything else."

I asked Morris what made him start setting his alarm again. "Let's put it this way," he said cryptically. "There's some serious negotiations going on."

Bud winked at me. "His wife's probably got herself a new car."

Morris's foul temper seemed to rise with the sun. Later that morning, he fumed behind the register. "I'm getting ready to sell out to a Pakistani!" he threatened to a couple of his friends. "I'm looking far enough down the road. I'll shut this son of a bitch down. I haven't told Ralph that yet. But we are going to have our beer election again. And I'm going to tell everybody, 'Okay, if it passes I'll keep the store. If it fails, I'm going to sell out to a damn foreigner.' See how he treats the local economy! Think they're going to get free coffee from a Pakistani?"

Milton had wandered up front by this point, and his face pickled when he heard the threat. "It'll smell like curry in here so goddamn bad," he said softly to himself.

"See if he'll run three hundred charge accounts!" Morris shouted. "Two hundred of 'em past due!" He took out a calendar and tried to calculate how soon he could realistically lobby to put alcohol back on the ballot. "The ones in town who are morally opposed to it?" he said. "The fruitcakes? Fine. But I heard the other day from a friend that eight or ten people told him that they voted against it because I was the only person in town who was going to profit. You bet your ass those sumbitches I'm mad at."

Morris's friend, who'd been listening with his arms folded in righteous solidarity, couldn't resist an opportunity to fan the flames. "This is a small town," he told me. "There are people in this town who don't want to see you get ahead of them."

Morris laughed sharply. "Anybody who said that probably owes me money! I've done a favor for them at some point or another. I bought their kids' animals at a livestock show. I donated five thousand dollars to 4-H last year—a hundred bucks for every kid who showed an animal. Well, that's gone! It ain't happening. They want to dictate the way I make a living, I'm going to dictate a few things too."

SARGE'S PLACE

The old Boultinghouse ranch, a falling-down shack on about 140 acres of gorgeous land, marks the far northern border of Utopia. Sarge, the youngest of eleven children, lived most of his life in that old house with his beloved sister Tiny, taking care of their parents until they died. Sarge's real name is Raymond Harold, not that anybody in town would be able to tell you that. He picked up the nickname Sarge years ago after being discharged from the Army for an extreme case of homesickness. Some say he lasted three days in the service. Others say six.

Every Veterans Day he stands up proud in the school, saluting the students as they walk through the door. "I never will forget the way he was standing back there," said Ralph. "Greeting everybody like he'd been off to war for forty years. He was just prouder than a peacock in that coat." Sarge likes to think of himself as a war hero, so the town lets him.

His sister Tiny, born Violet Rose, was similarly bound to Utopia. When she was a young woman, a suitor from another town asked for her hand in marriage. Tiny couldn't bear the idea of leaving her home and eventually, tearfully, broke off the engagement. She went on to enjoy a lifelong career as Utopia's most notorious gossip. (She preferred to think of herself in more dignified terms, as a "carrier of information.") Tiny would listen in on party-line telephone conversations, announcing her presence with her trademark laugh—"Whooo-*wheeeee*!"—that rang clear across the canyon. She had a habit of interrupting the most sensitive of conversations ("Excuse me, so you're saying he broke her arm?"). Today, when anyone in town grows overzealous in their pursuit of information, they are met with the same amused scolding: "Okay, Tiny, that's enough."

After their parents died, Tiny and Sarge let the family house slide to cheerful ruin. They didn't put much stock in hygiene, and warned others that soap and water deprived the body of its natural oils. Their sheep and goats and chickens and cats and Sarge's dog, Patsy, whose best trick was pulling him out of the Frio River by the hair while the man pretended to drown, were all welcome in the house. If the siblings ever found a sick animal, they would nurse it back to health with milk in Coca-Cola bottles with nipples. They lived on next to nothing, but not a soul ever left their house without a random gift of a pocketknife or a shawl or a fountain pen.

When Tiny died at the age of ninety, Sarge was so brokenhearted that he glued one of her patent leather baby shoes and her favorite doll's head to the hood of his truck. He drove down Main Street, blubbering for his dead sister, with his dog lying serenely on the roof and sometimes a goat in the passenger seat. "He wouldn't drive but five miles per hour," said Morris. "If he timed it just right, he'd have up to fifteen cars trailing behind him. It would look like a funeral procession." Sarge never did fully recover from the loss of Tiny. He started depending more and more on Morris to bring him groceries or help him around the ranch. It was Morris who eventually decided the eighty-five-year-old man ought to be moved closer to town so everyone could better look after him.

For a while Sarge lived rent-free in a little log cabin behind the café. Every morning one of the waitresses carted him back a pancake breakfast. Morris kept Sarge's pain pills tucked in the store's back safe so he could dole them out judiciously. Sarge liked to keep Morris abreast of his every move. He'd call the store at six A.M. to assure Morris he'd made it through the night, then again thirty minutes later once he'd watched the news.

One of the coffee drinkers brought me by Sarge's to say hello one morning. Sarge was still in his flannel pajama pants watching a morning talk show on his old black-and-white television. His two dogs—Sister, named in honor of Tiny, and a Jack Russell named Bert, after the neighbor across the street who had recently passed—chomped on food spilling out of an overturned bag of dog food. Sarge sat in a wheelchair because of his bad knees. He wore an old burgundy knit cap on his head and dirty socks on his feet. He had an American flag ribbon pinned on his red shirt and a larger flag hanging in his front window. At a commercial break, he rolled his chair over to the refrigerator and unpeeled a wet piece of ham. He spent the next twenty minutes unsuccessfully coaxing Bert to show me how the dog could count to three.

Sarge liked to tell dreamy, meandering stories. He was Utopia's water witch and had picked the spots for many of the wells in town. He explained that he used an old peach-tree limb to locate the source of water and that accepting payment from anyone would have cost him his divining powers. He told me that he missed sleeping with his chickens and that the best cure-all for any ailment was to rub Vicks all over your body and then sleep with a pillowcase over your head. Toward the end of our visit, he offered as a gift a decorative plate hanging on the wall by his calendar, which was open to March from two years prior. A few minutes later he gave me a clock that makes a different birdcall every hour, a gauze bandage, and two lime-sherbet-colored Easter bunny candies. "It'd be my honor if you took something to remember me by," he insisted.

A few months later, Sarge went to the hospital because of another bad attack of pneumonia. The doctor decided it would be best if the man moved permanently into the nursing home in Hondo, a forty-five-minute drive from everything he held dear. Morris took in Bert, and Sister became something of a town dog, looked after by everybody and nobody. Sarge still called the General Store most mornings to assure Morris that he was awake and they're feeding him good. "But I'm thinking I'm ready to come home now."

CHAPTER 10

We Come for Closure

On the second anniversary of Jeff Wiekamp's death, the Army made its pitch to the junior class. Utopia's guidance counselor had dissuaded her friends at various military recruiting offices from making the rounds the previous year, warning that the grieving community deserved space. But that first anniversary had come and gone and it was time to get back to the business of meeting quotas and molding future soldiers. So that morning the handsome recruiter with gel in his hair and a gleaming smile bounced on his toes in front of Utopia's fourteen juniors. His demeanor was part salesman, part coach delivering a pep talk to his disheartened team at halftime.

"Does anybody know what a soldier is?" he asked the group. A rugged boy with acne on his cheekbones and bangs hanging like a slipped toupee across his forehead raised his hand. "Somebody who puts their life on the line and protects our freedom?" he said in a teacher's-pet voice. The recruiter pumped his fist in the air and smiled approvingly. Rubbing his hands together, he pointed at another boy in the classroom. "Why is it that when you see me at Wal-Mart, you go into the women's section to avoid me?" The boy, who'd been drowsily leaning with his chin on his folded arms, sat up straight. "Because you're . . . intimidating?" he guessed, unsure of what the older man wanted to hear. The recruiter laughed at the idea, winking and apologizing to the teenager for targeting him.

"All we are," he told the kids, "are people who volunteered to protect each and every one of y'all. I see you all have a nice new gym. You wouldn't have that if there weren't no soldiers in the world. You wouldn't have air-conditioning in there. There might"—he paused dramatically—"not even be a school." He let that sink in, looking around at the group of students who stared back at him with polite uninterest. He leaned in closer to the kids sitting at their desks and dropped his voice to an exaggerated whisper. "I'm probably the highest-paid person in Uvalde right now," he said proudly. Long ago, "har har," when he graduated from high school, he went to work at his local Kmart making $3.15 an hour. He felt lost, going nowhere. It wasn't until he joined the Army when he was twenty-seven that he found his way. Nearly ten years later he'd seen one of his monthly paychecks reach upward of nineteen thousand dollars after his hearty bonus. "I'm going to Puerto Rico for a vacation in July," he said. "And I'll probably go again in November." The group of teenagers stared back at him, their attention wandering.

"What do you do with your spare time?" he asked a petite Mexican girl in a red T-shirt that said NO WORRIES across the chest. "Read?" she said shyly, her cheeks blushing. The recruiter rolled his eyes at the room and loudly groaned. "No, no, I'm joking with ya, I'm joking," he said. "You ever thought about the Army, dear?" She shook her head, shrugging her shoulders apologetically. He turned away from her, a pensive expression on his face. "I'm not mad at her for that," he assured the other kids. "I have respect for her for being honest."

He pointed his finger at a boy toward the back of the classroom. His words started coming out in a rush. "Okay, you're in the Army. You have a nine-to-five job. Who pays you? The Army! After work you go to the barracks, put on your Nikes, and go to the gym. Playing basketball, you break your leg. Who pays the bill? The Army! Can't go to work for two weeks. Who pays you? The Army! You *cannot* lose money in the Army." He went on about enlistment bonuses for seniors ("You can join the Army as a senior and get a thousand dollars a month until you graduate!"), about paid maternity leave for new mothers, and, strangely, the possibility of medaling at the Olympics.

"Does anybody know that there's a Burger King out there in Iraq? Subway? Pizza Hut? Chilis?"

"Wow, Chilis?" blurted out the guidance couselor, before laughing and covering her mouth. The recruiter grinned appreciatively at her and she motioned for him to continue.

"Air-conditioned showers," he said, "air-conditioned restaurants. We've got indoor pools, Internet cafés, movie theaters." He paused and waved his hands in the air, as if brushing back any preconceived ideas of a war gone bad. "When you see the news, you're seeing the bad things. You're seeing the deaths and . . ." He trailed off, unsure if he should stray from his rousing pitch in front of a group of kids who'd experienced firsthand the loss of one of their own.

"You know," he said seriously, "I carry a religious medallion from my mom that's been in my wallet since I enlisted. My mom gets worried. But that's her issue. I had to move on in life. That's the choice you all are going to have to make next year. I know you all think this is the best time of your whole life." Two girls sitting in front of me looked at each other with puzzled expressions. "But there's a whole world out there," the recruiter continued. "There's a huge, *huge* world out there."

At the end of his presentation, he encouraged the juniors to help themselves to the Army pencils and bumper stickers and keychains he'd spread out across the teacher's desk. "And while you're on MySpace," he called after their retreating backs, "go over to GoArmy.com!" But the kids had already dribbled out into the hallway. They moved like a pack of puppies, clumsy and shoving and harmless, in the direction of the cafeteria.

At lunch, the junior and senior classes ate together at a long table by the windows. They picked suspiciously from trays prepared for them by the two lunch ladies, both of whom were related to students at the school, and drank from large glasses of iced tea they'd gotten from a cooler. Pop music played in the background from a cafeteria mother's computer.

When the boys finished shoveling down their chicken fingers and Tater Tots, ignoring iceberg lettuce mounds, they unfolded their denimed legs from under the table and left in a booted clump. They liked to spend the rest of the lunch period hanging out down by the Sabinal River. Maybe sneak a cigarette. They always invited Kelli and Perla to come along, but the girls usually just drove over to the empty Living Waters parking lot and listened to mopey music in Kelli's car. Today, though, they lingered in the cafeteria, chatting with two girlfriends from the junior class.

"When the Army recruiter was like, 'I know, I know, you think this is the best time of your lives,' I freaked out," said Kayla, a good-natured, blond, blue-eyed volleyball player who planned to follow her older sister to Texas Tech when she graduated next year. "If that's true, then I want to kill myself." Her cousins and parents and grandparents all lived in Utopia. "Utopia is the town where everybody knows everything about you no matter what happens," she said with a cheerful roll of her carefully made-up eyes. Kayla's best friend, Ashley, another volleyball teammate and a star of Utopia's University Interscholastic League math team, nodded at her friend while she unwrapped her ice cream bar. "I had a bad dream that I had to join the military and shave my head and then me and the guidance counselor went and robbed a candy store," she said.

Ashley had the entire schedule of any given week of TV memorized. She spent the spring semester cursing the Hollywood writers' strike for mucking up her lineup. She hadn't settled on a first choice for college yet, but she already knew she wanted to study architectural engineering. Ashley and Kayla described themselves as nerds, but it was hard to picture either of these two seventeen-year-old girls, both of them with long shiny hair and tight jeans, ever being shoved into a locker. That was the remarkable thing about Utopia School. These kids who sat together at their narrow cafeteria table treated one another gently. They could be merciless with an outsider. But once you were part of the family, they accepted you for who you were. Kelli talked about how she had nothing in common with her classmates, but in the end they made her laugh and treated her with decency, and she them.

Sitting around the lunch table, Kelli told her friends that she had decided to major in ethnomusicology at Austin Community College. Everyone looked at her with blank expressions. Perla smiled into her shirt sleeve. "That's pretty much been my parents' and teachers' reaction too," said Kelli.

Just then, a junior named Rosalie swanned into the cafeteria on strappy high heels, a navy and white polka-dotted scarf holding back her bright blond waves of hair. Kelli laughed affectionately when her friend crumpled dramatically onto the cafeteria bench. Rosalie started gushing out news of her wretched geography grade while she fanned herself with her manicured hand. When she caught me eyeing her gold heels under the table, Rosalie cocked a leg out so everyone could take a look at her latest find. "Thrift store," she said proudly. "I don't have a lot of feeling in my feet, I'll tell you that. But girl, I can run in heels. It's a rare day I ever trip and stumble. Like, *lunar eclipse* rare. But this morning Kelli caught me walking down the hallway to the bathroom when I just spiraled over myself like some little starlet."

Rosalie's family moved to Utopia from Houston when she was in the sixth grade. Her great wish in life was to be famous. "Like a hybrid of Drew Barrymore and Anne Hathaway, or maybe I'll be the next Katie Couric," she said. Or maybe she would move to New York City and go to Sarah Lawrence College. She just wanted to see more of the world than Texas.

"Hey, is Colter dating that Sonic girl?" Ashley asked as the friends started gathering the scraps of their lunches. "Alyssa was telling me that this girl came up and jumped into his car. Apparently, she's obsessed with him!" Kelli seemed pleased to hear that Colter had finally found himself a girlfriend. She groaned, though, when talk of his new romance bled into the reality that all the single girls at the table needed to find themselves prom dates. All except Perla, who calmly declared her intention to skip the dance altogether.

Kelli had a crush on a tall, ruddy-cheeked redhead from Knippa, a town thirty miles away that was even smaller than Utopia. The boy was in a graduating class of seven. Kelli had met him the prior year at a regional drama competition, and the two stayed in touch on My-Space. Rosalie, bemused by the young man's corny jokes and affable nature, had taken to calling him the Car Salesman. Her girlfriends declared that Kelli would ask him to the prom at tomorrow's one-act-play performance. "If I feel inclined," said Kelli, covering her blushing cheeks with her hands. She tended to get squirrelly around boys, breaking out into hives as she tried to make small talk.

Kayla's eighth-grade cousin came up to the table and tapped her on the shoulder. "Sorry," Kayla said to her friends as she stood up. "I have to go buy food for Shaylee. She doesn't like the stuff they serve here, so I'm going to take her to the store." Kayla put her arm around her cousin and gave one final thumbs-up of approval for Kelli's crush.

Kids in small towns, kids anywhere really, spend most of high school complaining about how slowly and painfully their lives tick by. Nothing to do. Nobody understands them. The world feels just out of reach until that last warm month of May, when time speeds up, sentimentality kicks in, and some fuzzy pop song is anointed the soundtrack for all that is moving and meaningful in a young person's life. Kelli had started being uncharacteristically nostalgic, calling her friends "besties" and joining them in Utopia's weekend social scene. "I have been waiting for graduation for so long," said Kelli, "and it's weird because life isn't all bad right now. It's actually pretty good."

In the end Kelli mustered up the nerve to ask the Knippa boy to her prom and he said yes. She bought an apple-green floor-length gown from JCPenney. On the afternoon of the prom, Kelli sat in front of the bathroom mirror while Nancy braided her hair and tied it back into a bun, leaving two curled strands hanging down the sides of her face. Her date was twenty minutes late when he finally pulled his white pickup truck in front of the trailer. But she forgave him because he wore suspenders and a tie and made easy conversation with Nancy while Kelli fumbled with the white rose wrist corsage he brought.

Mrs. Waters's daughter, who owns a restaurant on the southern outskirts of town, where locals rarely eat because the portions are small and the prices high, played host for the prom. As the juniors and seniors arrived in the restaurant courtyard, the paparazzi, as the parents and grandparents called themselves, snapped pictures and wondered aloud when their babies had all grown into such fine men and women.

The seniors had decorated the restaurant in a Casino Royale theme with poker and blackjack tables spread around the dance floor. Throughout the dinner of beef tenderloin and cheese potatoes and apple cake, Kelli worked hard at making conversation with her date. She had a hard time concentrating on the food in front of her. Kelli had never been kissed before and she'd decided tonight would be the night. The anticipation was making her sick.

After dinner, a teacher stood up on the foldout dance floor and announced that the time had come to reveal Utopia's prom king and queen. The king was a popular boy whose family owned a large ranch just outside of town. He had shown up at the prom genially sloshed. Then the teacher announced that this year's prom queen was . . . Kelli Rhodes. Kelli's head shot up in the air, and she looked furiously around the room at her friends. What with Perla at home, there were only four senior girls to choose from. But Kelli had been sure it would go to one of the three blondes. Kelli started yelling for a revote. Finally a teacher came up and put her arm around the cringing girl. "Stop it, you be nice!" the woman insisted. "Get up there. Take the crown. Do the dance."

As Kelli looked around the crowd, pretending not to take any enjoyment in the attention, she forced herself onto the dance floor and accepted her tiara. Later Rosalie would tell her that everyone voted for her because she was the coolest girl in the senior class. Of the other three options, Rosalie said, one was a snob, one wanted prom queen too badly, and one was even more of a newcomer than Kelli. "I suppose it's cool that people were nice enough to vote for me," Kelli told me afterward. "But if I get the prom queen curse, if I end up living in a trailer park some day with a bunch of cowbabies, I'll be pissed." A country song came on the speakers and the king grabbed Kelli for the traditional first dance. Kelli didn't know a waltz from a two-step, so her partner was tasked with shuffling her around in a halting circle. At the end, he surprised her with a dramatic spin and Kelli's tiara sailed off her head, landing with a *thwok* on the shiny dance floor.

When the karaoke machine was wheeled out into the middle of the room, the small group of teenagers stood around in a circle, as if the machine was the person they liked too much to ask to dance in front of everyone. So Mrs. Waters broke out her wallet and started offering twenty-dollar bills to anyone brave enough to get up there. Kelli and a few of the junior girls sang a painful rendition of Fergie's "My Humps." Kelli and her date did their best with "Secret Agent Man." The dance floor went unused. Afterward, Kelli went along with the few other kids who didn't really drink to Ashley's house to watch a DVD of *Casino Royale*. Her date's parents had given him an early curfew, so Kelli walked him out to his truck halfway through the movie. When he leaned in to give her a kiss, Kelli wrapped her arms happily around his neck. After a few minutes of making out, the boy sighed into Kelli's ear and told her he felt bad for leading her on. "I don't want you getting attached," he whispered. "You're leaving in a month." Kelli waved off his concern and leaned in for another kiss. "No, I just feel so bad," he protested. Kelli started laughing and took him by the shoulders. "Honey," she said happily, "I'm going to be just fine."

One week later, under a pale pink evening sky, grown men gathered in clumps outside the school gym, dressed up in their best dark jeans. The parking lot was full with row upon row of trucks. Inside the gym's front entrance, the graduates' younger sisters and brothers and cousins tore around the hallway, tagging one another and giving chase, while their mothers slung jackets and purses and camera bags over folding chairs arranged on the basketball court.

Kelli's father, Ron, back in his black suit, waved happily from the front row. Beryl, dressed in a silk pastels, her tender eyes large and slightly surprised behind her glasses, sat next to Ron. Nancy wore a bright spot of lipstick and a little blush on her smiling cheeks. She held the hand of her granddaughter Blossom, who was listing all the reasons she loved her aunt Kelli. Racheal, who wore a black T-shirt tucked into a long floral skirt, with her bob of curly hair pulled back severely with barrettes, sat alongside her family with her baby, Scarlett, in her arms, whispering "hush" into the wriggly baby's ear. And then there was Kelli's guitar teacher, Mr. Fox, who had driven into town for the occasion. He read through the program before twisting in his metal chair to marvel at the boisterous people crowded behind us on the floor and bleachers. Kelli had always told him she came from a small town. But only now, having made the reverse drive from San Antonio to Utopia, did he realize how far she traveled each week.

Before the seniors made their slow, bashful procession into the gym, Utopia's eighth graders made their own pass across the stage, boys awkward in baggy khakis and tucked-in Oxford shirts that ballooned in the back, girls clopping like colts in their first pair of heels. Kathy Wiekamp put her arm around her sister-in-law when Steven's husky son trudged up to shake the principal's and superintendent's hands and collect his diploma. Steven was worlds away in Iraq.

Afterward the twelve seniors took their seats on the riser. The superintendent gave the same speech he delivered every year, reminding the graduates that it was not their last name or their grade point average or their ambition that would determine their destiny. It was their character. And at that point in his speech, as he did every year, he choked up with genuine emotion and pawed at the tears on his large cheeks.

The valedictorian, a serious girl named Christina who was moving to Austin to attend culinary school, gave a somber speech about the nature of nostalgia. And then Kelli, who'd somehow held on to her class rank of salutatorian despite all her efforts otherwise, stepped up to deliver her own last message to the gathered town. She rose from her chair in her gown and black heels, her hair curly and loose and long under her cap, and assumed her place behind the podium. Her voice was a moving blend of softness and strength, and she rarely looked down at her scrap of notes.

Class of 2008. On this eagerly anticipated day, we come for closure. We come to say goodbye to our small town, and look back on the time we've had here. For so many years, we walked the halls of this school wondering when it was ever going to come to an end. We have cruised the short stretch of Main fighting boredom. We have experienced the burdens and the advantages of life in a small town—how each person's story is common knowledge, but how in a time of loss or hardship, the town reaches out with sincerity and generosity. This familiarity among individuals is also present within our class. We all have completely different personalities, but we somehow formed this close-knit group. Full of all the love, hate, laughter, and arguments as in any family.

I find it almost strange that when I moved here, I feared being the odd person out. We all come from different backgrounds. We all have separate stories. We are all changed by our experiences here.

And while this might not be the last time we drive aimlessly down these country roads, it is the end of a chapter and the beginning of our lives. So this is what I want to ask the senior class. Are you the person you want to be? Are you on your way to realizing that dream you dreamed as a child? Are you living up to your—that dreaded word—potential? Potential creates the idea of possibility, the possibility that we may succeed or that we may fail.

The next few years will be life-changing and eye-opening. We have waited so long for them. I hope we find love, whether it comes from another person, or a career, or an art form, or a child. I hope we never stray from the people we hoped to become. I hope we never apologize for our individuality.

We are the class of 2008. This is our life. And we can truly be whoever we want to be.

Kelli paused when she finished her speech and spent a few seconds drinking in the scene before her. "It was me coming to terms with

Utopia," she told me afterward. "This was my experience. It was good. It was bad. I accept the town for what it is." When Kelli crossed the few steps across the portable stage to collect her diploma, Ron gave a loud, deep holler of joy. Perla's father, who sat with his large family one row behind behind the Rhodeses, stood up and whistled with his fist in the air for his daughter's best friend. Nancy took Beryl's hand and they nodded at each other and smiled. Racheal had chosen to wait in the back by the exit when Scarlett started crying halfway through the ceremony. Later, in the parking lot, she took her sister's arm with a sentimental gasp and told her that Kelli had made her cry.

As the few remaining seniors collected their diplomas, pausing during the handshake with a hammy smile for their parents' cameras, Kelli sat holding her diploma in her lap. For the first time in the two years I'd known her, her whole body was loose and relaxed, her lips parted into an almost dumbstruck smile. She listened to the applause of all those people who called Utopia home, all those cowboys and country wives crowded together under the gym lights. And in that moment it felt like everyone had gathered to celebrate her.

After the ceremony, Kelli followed her friends to the annual cookie and punch party at the Methodist church. Then she went with her family and Mr. Fox to Perla's party at the EMS shed. Perla had finally persuaded her father to let her move to Austin. She promised him she would find an affordable apartment with Kelli and get a job and attend the community college there. She was going, not necessarily with her father's blessing, but with his enormous love and concern. At tonight's celebration, Perla's father wore an ecstatic smile spread across his shining face. He shook my hand eagerly, then decided that the occasion called for an embrace. He hovered over the guests, so happy that he seemed to laugh words rather than speak them. He made sure everyone had a cold soda and pushed seconds from the trays of ribs and spicy Mexican rice and potato salad that Perla's mother and aunts had spent all day cooking. We ate off plastic plates, sitting bunched together at two long tables. The conversations were friendly and loud, many of them in Spanish. Mr. Fox told Ron that he was thinking maybe he ought to get himself over to Utopia more often, see if there were more kids in town who would be interested in learning how to play the guitar. Perla and Kelli looked exhausted, like brides on their wedding day who meant to eat but were too busy receiving blessings on their future lives.

After the party, Kelli's parents dropped her off at school to pick up her car. She watched them drive off and then looked up at the enormous night sky. "Town was already dead," she said. "I started crying, alone in my car. All I could think was, 'Holy shit. It's over. I did it. I'm free.' Finally I started up my car and realized it was time to go."

One month later Kelli moved to Austin. On her last night in Utopia, she stood in her driveway looking anxiously into an empty U-Haul trailer. Nancy sat on the bumper in a thin white housedress that fluttered in the warm breeze. They had spent the day practicing parallel parking in their yard and doing laundry and painting an old coffee table that Kelli would take with her to Austin. That night Kelli started untacking the posters of all the boys and bands who had gotten her through high school, before realizing that they didn't belong on the bare walls of her new apartment. She'd leave some things behind.

BANK

It seemed like forever that Utopians had lacked a place in town to put their money—besides pickle jars. The old bank used to sit across the street from the General Store in what was now the Gospel Tabernacle. It closed down in the late 1920s at the beginning of the Depression. So people went to Sabinal or Uvalde or San Antonio to deposit their money, if they went at all. Sixty years later, Sabinal Bank finally opened a branch on the north end of town, across the street from Pico. When it went under, Dolph Briscoe, the former Democratic governor of Texas (1973–79) and wealthy landowner, and his First State Bank of Uvalde rode into town. "If Dolph Briscoe says, 'I don't want the sun to come up in the morning,' people hold tarps up to keep it from shining," one old-timer said, explaining the man's influence in these parts. Briscoe wanted the bank. He got it.

Now, there are many in Utopia who think a bank is an important piece of a proper town. There was even a drive-through at Utopia's First State Bank. Most of the time it worked. But there are many who insist that they would rather drive all the way to San Antonio than put their money into a local checking or savings account. "I don't need everybody in town knowing my business," more than one Utopian told me. It's rude to talk about money anywhere but behind people's backs. So why give them anything to talk about? People who took their money elsewhere irritated Ralph. "They're afraid if they bank here everybody will know what they're worth," he said impatiently. "Which in my opinion is just a bunch of baloney. Those tellers aren't going to go tattling."

Senior teller Carolyn Moore, one of the bank's two employees, has learned not to take people's discretion personally. "If I had a lot of money I could see going elsewhere to do my business," she said. "But I'm so broke all the time, if people know about me it ain't gonna hurt nothing. I could see where people would worry if they thought I went out and jibber-jabbered around town. But I'd never ever—I'd lose my job!"

Carolyn has long brown feathered hair and round eyeglasses and she wished she'd remember to put on lipstick more often. When I asked her how old she was, she shimmied her shoulders a little and puffed at the curls of her hair with her hand. "I'm twenty-two years old," she said. "Oh fine! I'm forty-three years old in June."

Carolyn left Corpus Christi back in 1994 on her uncle's invitation to get out of the city. She arrived in Utopia on May 1. One week later she met her husband, Tommy, at a crawfish boil. Today they have an eleven-year-old daughter named Brandy in the fifth grade across the street. Carolyn closes up in the afternoons at three so she is able to pick her daughter up from school every day. She likes the comfort of sending Brandy to a little school where there aren't any gangs or metal detectors. She likes Utopia the way it is. "But we just keep growing," she said. "When I moved here there was not a car wash, there was not a laundromat. We got a new post office, a new bank, a new antiques store, Morris built the Outpost."

The bank is roomy and dark and quiet. There is a big front office with fancy wooden furniture that Carolyn said nobody ever used, and two back offices for customers who wanted to start new accounts or CDs. When First State Bank opened its branch in Utopia back in 1994, it was run out of an old double-wide trailer just down the street. But then apparently the Governor, as everyone around here still calls Briscoe, wanted to expand. So First State donated the site of the old bank to the library and started construction on the new building. During those many months leading up to its grand reopening in June 2002, Carolyn and the old branch manager, Jeannette, worked out of a twelve-by-fourteen storage shed plopped out front in the parking lot. People in town took to calling it the caboose. "Everybody kept saying that somebody was going to back up to the caboose with their pickup truck, hook onto it, and drive off with the bank!" said Carolyn.

Jeannette retired last Thanksgiving, after working at the bank for seventeen and a half years. Carolyn was a mess on her friend's last day. A customer brought in two Kleenex boxes that were decorated with construction paper cutouts of hearts and suns and sad faces, with colored yarn attached so they could wear them around their necks. "Do you see?" Carolyn said, showing me the box that she still keeps by her teller window. "It says, 'Carolyn's Cry Baby Box.'" The woman sighed. She looked over at her new colleague, a young, attractive Mexican woman who was quiet and efficient. "She's real nice," whispered Carolyn. "But I do miss Jeannette."

CHAPTER 11

I'm Not That Person and I'm Never Going to Be That Person

The rumors were true. The Sonic carhop Colter had tried hard to dismiss all spring, the eighteen-year-old who'd strutted up to his window with his food, had finally made him look at her. Her name was Jamie and she bore a striking resemblance to the actress Kirsten Dunst—blond, pale, thin to the point of being angular, but with a chest that would make Utopia's young cheerleaders faint with envy.

Over dinner one early summer evening, sitting at one of the tables outside Sonic, Colter and Jamie told the story of how they fell for each other three months before. Jamie wore streaks of purple and green eye shadow, a dark yellow T-shirt decorated with psychedelic mushrooms, a miniskirt, and zebra-striped flats. Whenever Colter looked at her, a slightly dazed grin spread across his face. "So she comes up to my car," he told me, "and she says, 'I don't want you to think I'm weird, but you're really beautiful.'" He let out a hiccup of a laugh and looked down incredulously at his half-eaten hamburger.

Jamie coyly covered her head with the hood of her brown sweat-shirt, pulling the strings over her face. She laughed describing Colter's stunned reaction to her praise. "Whatever, he *is* beautiful," she said smoothly, twisting around her index finger the heart-shaped plastic ring she'd gotten from a quarter candy machine. "I can't help it."

Colter crammed some fries into his mouth. "Picture it: I'm waiting for my food and all the sudden there's this girl walking towards me," he said, replaying the events of the evening as if he still couldn't quite believe them himself. "She walks over to my car, says some random strange comment, and then randomly jumps in the back of my car!"

"You have so many fun things back there," said Jamie, her voice soft and rumbly like a cat's. "A hard hat. Your wrench. Ha!" she said, covering her mouth. "That sounded dirty. Whatever. Why wouldn't everyone want to go back there?" She turned to me with a delighted grin. "I would always stand inside the restaurant, putting napkins in the bags when he drove up. And I was like, 'Y'all see that boy? I'm going to get him.' But they didn't think I was *audacious* enough to do it."

Colter looked at me and again threw his hands up in the air. He felt like he was hearing the story of a movie rather than his own life. "So for two weeks she kept coming up and flirting with me . . ."

"Oh God," interrupted Jamie, hiding her eyes with one of her hands as a car pulled into the Sonic parking lot and revved its engine. "There's Nathan and his new gold car . . ."

"Anyways . . . ," said Colter, wincing at the mention of the boy be-hind him.

Jamie sighed dramatically. "He's my recent ex-boyfriend and he's still a little upset," she said.

"*Anyways* . . ."

"Doesn't matter!" Jamie said pertly and turned her gaze back upon Colter.

"Anyways, so then she's like, 'We've talked a lot. We should talk more.' *And she gives me her number.* The first time we talked on the phone was March 3." Colter paused and smiled down at his food.

"He called when I was at work because he knew I wouldn't answer the phone," said Jamie.

"Pretty smooth, huh?" Colter said, giving me a high-five from across the table. "That way it wouldn't be awkward. My message was like, 'Hey Jamie, you told me to call you so I'm calling you and stuff. And yeah, so if you want to call me back . . . but if not that's cool too. Whatever. I guess I'll talk to you later . . . maybe.'"

"So we talked and texted for a while and eventually he said he'd take me to the movies," said Jamie, reaching for his hand. Colter laughed at the only plans for an evening he could think to propose when asking a girl out on a date. "That's all I got!" he said. Since then they'd spent every weekend together and seen every movie playing in theaters within a ninety-mile radius.

Jamie's father owned an electrician business a hundred feet or so from the Sonic. Her mother and older sister helped out there with the books. "My sister was the biggest one who was like, 'Oh, the second I graduate I'm getting out of this town,'" Jamie said with a harsh laugh. "But then she fell into the family business just like she said she wouldn't." Throughout dinner, Jamie fingered a homemade bracelet that said I LOVE MONSTERS—an homage to the energy drinks she and her friends used to pound to make it through the school day. Jamie had gotten wrapped up pretty bad in the Bandera party scene. "There's a lot of meth in this town. A lot of pills." She laughed at my nervous expression. "Come visit anytime!" she said, in the voice of a cheerful tour guide. "We got meth, crank, speed, ice. We got what you need." She nodded over her shoulder at a group of boys huddled around the bed of a truck parked in the back corner of the restaurant lot. "Ooh, that guy's gross," she said, pointing to a boy in a Spurs jersey and a backward ball cap. "He's probably growing Dro out of the back of that truck."

Colter looked at her with a blank expression on his face. "Dro?" she said patiently. "That's really strong weed." Jamie thought it was hilarious that she'd ended up with a teetotaler. Colter didn't drink or do

drugs, nothing since his miserable bender at school that he was determined never to relive. He told Jamie that he'd be forced to leave her if
she fell back into old habits. She wanted to stay clean, but sometimes
she joked that dating Colter was like dating somebody's grandfather.
Instead of hanging out with her friends in their various beat-up apartments around town, she went with Colter to the movies, or watched
TV in his bedroom. Jamie went to see the movies on opening night in
the theaters with Colter, despite the fact that crowds sometimes made
her breathless and panicky. And Colter now watched *America's Next
Top Model* because it was Jamie's favorite show. When she was bored
he gave in to her pleading and sat still while she carefully applied
makeup to his face. Alyssa's boyfriend had moved in months ago, despite Lindy's hand wringing, so nobody bothered Colter when Jamie
spent the night in his room.

I asked Colter if he still planned on leaving for college at the end of
the summer. Jamie flinched, waiting for his answer. "That makes me a
little nervous," she said, her face turning sullen. Colter looked at Jamie
kindly and assured her that whatever decision he made wouldn't have
any effect on their young relationship. "I fucking hate my job," he said.
"I really do. I just want a job where I work inside for once in my life. I
just want to do anything with computers. I'm thinking I'll go to school
in San Antonio in the fall." I asked him where he would live and he
gave a distracted little shrug. "I don't know. I'd have to figure out all
that shit."

Jamie took Colter's hand and looked seriously at me. "I'm supposed
to be going to do something with my life and he's supposed to be going
and doing something," she said. "Our timing is bad." Recently Jamie
had stopped showing up for work at Sonic. She figured she was probably fired. She thought she might also like to go to college one day,
maybe to study psychology. She said she enjoyed the subject, opening
her purse to show me a few popular self-help books inside. But she had
a hard time envisioning herself taking the first basic steps toward a career. "Mostly I just want to sleep," she said with a rueful smile. "I don't
have any goals yet. I don't have any aspirations. I just watch stuff turn

around me. A goal can only lead to failing at the goal." The conversation was putting her in a bad mood.

Just then one of the lenses from Colter's glasses popped out, landing with a quiet splat in the large ketchup smear on his hamburger's paper wrapper. Jamie burst out laughing. She leaned over to kiss her blushing boyfriend on the cheek. "Oh, I love it when that happens," she said as Colter wiped the lens off with his napkin and tried to pop it back into its frame. "Tuck the corner in, honey," she said, her voice filled with teasing affection.

The only other person in Colter's life he could've imagined witnessing such a scene and not making him feel like a loser was Grant. His best friend would be coming home to Texas soon and Colter was eager to introduce him to Jamie. He'd already talked her up a little. "I told him that she's an *existentialist*," said Colter, "and he was like, 'Yeah, that's cool, so is everybody at Yale.'" When Jamie heard that Colter had spoken to Grant about her, she coughed up a giggle and peered up at him. "You talked to your friend about me?" she said, her lashes fluttering. "Oh, you're such a pansy-ass, I love it."

"I talk to everybody about you," said Colter, jerking backward as Jamie reached over to pinch his arm.

"Oh, you're such a Barbie, I love you." Jamie wasn't used to being with a boy of such sensitive nature, so she'd taken to referring to Colter as "Barbie" or her "gay boyfriend" or "Colter Elizabeth."

Colter smiled happily, and shook his head. "My masculinity is either very strong or nonexistent."

After dinner Colter threw away their trash, and with Jamie tucked like a doll underneath his arm, they walked to his car. "Later carburetor!" Jamie called out of the passenger window to me, her voice, bright and innocent, ringing down Bandera's Main Street.

The summer after his sophomore year at Yale, Grant traveled with his astronomy class to Santiago, Chile, where they spent six weeks at one of the world's best observatories. Back in Utopia, Colter got a text message from his friend. "He's like, 'So I'm kind of on the side of a volcano,'" said Colter. "And I'm like, 'Well that's cool, don't jump in there, Joe.'" Colter paused to snicker at his response. "That's a reference to the Tom Hanks movie *Joe Versus the Volcano*. And then I wrote back, 'Dude, you're supposed to be studying astronomy, what are you doing on the side of a volcano? That's on the land!'" Colter, who relayed this story over a cold basket of fries at the café one evening after a long day of road construction, laughed again. Then he sighed. "He never texted me back."

When Grant returned from his adventures in Chile, he started working in the office of a property management company in San Antonio where his mom had just taken a job. One weekend, he drove home to Utopia to meet Colter's girlfriend. The three spent the evening in Colter's small bedroom. The boys played video games while Jamie sat quietly on the bed. Jamie was thoroughly charmed by the boys' high-pitched reunion. "Colter just gets so lit up whenever he's around him," she said. "It almost seems like he has a huge man crush. And Grant is just the cutest thing ever." She tagged along with the boys to the movies in San Antonio. "After the movie," she said, "Grant was like, 'Colter, will you just call me when you get home so I know you all made it back okay?' It was so sweet I almost cried." She went with them to the amusement park Fiesta Texas, where Grant and Colter won matching Batman outfits in a water pistol game and wore them the rest of the afternoon. But Jamie started pouting in the park, complaining that she felt left out. Colter wouldn't go on any roller coasters with her because they scared him.

On Grant's last night in Texas, the four of us met in San Antonio for a movie. At Applebee's afterward, Colter and Jamie sat on one side of the table, Jamie with her hand on Colter's arm, whispering into his ear. Grant sat on the other, reflecting on his sophomore year. He had gotten his first C, in a brutal organic chemistry and lab class. But he finally seemed capable of forgiving himself the rare average performance. His financial aid package was secure. Combined with his scholarships and work-study programs, it turned out that the university was paying him around forty-five dollars a year to attend. That left Grant and Susi responsible for just his books and school supplies. He was trying to double major in physics and astronomy and still planned on going on to medical school. After two years away, he felt like a different person. "I think I learned how *not* smart I was when I got to college," he said. "My confidence was shaken in a healthy way. In high school I thought I was the man, and then I quickly learned there were four times as smart men and women out there as me."

The waiter arrived at the table to take our order. Colter, who was wearing one of Jamie's old Sonic shirts with a tie wrapped loosely around the collar, pointed an aggressive finger at his friend. "Grant's the only one not ready!" he said in a scolding tone as his friend took a hurried glance at the menu.

Grant ordered an iced tea. I asked him why medical school still felt like the right fit for him. "I think being a doctor would give me options—" he said.

"You think it's going to be like watching *Scrubs*?" interrupted Colter.

"No," Grant said agreeably, "but I think it'll allow me to travel and go overseas and do relief or AIDS work. It appeals to me as a profession—"

Colter laughed sharply. "Or you've watched too many episodes of *Grey's Anatomy* and you think you're going to get a lot of girlfriends if you're a doctor."

Grant smiled at Colter, unbothered by the interruptions. "Yeah, and it fits into my life goals of what I'd like to do." Jamie was listening to the conversation at the next table over.

Before Grant left for college he'd always talked about how he'd like to return to Utopia after graduation. "I don't know if at this point that would really fit in," he said, choosing his words carefully. "As much as I was singing Utopia's praises when I left, I've also realized that I wasn't as close to a lot of my friends as I thought I was. I don't miss as many people as I thought I would. I miss Colter. I miss my mom, and I miss Miss Clark. I don't miss everybody in my class like I thought I would. Spending every day with people for twelve years, I'm surprised by how few of those relationships will last. I feel like I was sort of in love with the entire idea of Utopia when I left, and I'm still very attached to it. But it's different. The minute I got to Yale I knew it was right and it's felt right ever since. I wish I could spend more time at home—but I got to go to Chile for six weeks! It was through a grant program, Yale does grants . . ."

Colter laughed into his Caesar salad. "Yale does grants. Grant's at Yale," he said. He nudged Jamie, looking for a reaction to his lame joke, but she ignored him. "I swear," said Colter, "we have the downlows on this side of the table, and the fancy-schmancies are over there."

Grant's mom, Susi, joined us toward the end of dinner. She wanted to spend some of her son's last night in Texas with him and she was anxious to check in on Colter and his progress with college applications. "Colter is going to move to San Antonio and move in with me so he can go to college," she announced to the table with great confidence. "He just doesn't know it yet." She smiled tenderly at Colter, who shuffled in his seat. "I like that plan," Susi said.

"I don't," Jamie said worriedly.

"He'd still be close!" Susi insisted.

Grant kept quiet during the conversation about whether or not Colter would move in the fall. Sometimes it seemed like this was the secret to the boys' steady bond. Grant didn't push Colter about his plans. If he asked his friend about school and got back a one-word answer, he let it go. He neither encouraged nor discouraged any of Colter's decisions. That they had so little in common anymore seemed irrelevant. Their friendship was built on the past, and that was enough for the moment.

"We're like brothers, only closer," said Colter. "That's from *SpongeBob SquarePants,* when SpongeBob lifts up his shirt and their hearts are beating together."

"SpongeBob was one of our great loves," explained Grant.

"Here's a way I can explain our friendship," said Colter. "If you see your mother three times a year, when you see her you don't go, 'Are you still my mother?' If me and Grant don't see each other for six months we're still going to be very, very good friends."

I asked Colter on the way out of the restaurant if he thought he'd ever pony together the change to go visit Grant at Yale.

"I think that'd be awesome," said Grant.

"I invited you to go up last Thanksgiving," said Susi, before turning to me. "Something happened where he couldn't go. But I'll get him up there."

"No, you won't," said Jamie, grabbing Colter's hand and leaning the weight of her body into him. She looked at me and rolled her eyes. "He's going to say he'll do it but then he won't because he's lazy."

"He'll go!" said Susi. "You'll go with me, right, sweetheart?" she asked Colter. She put a comforting arm around Jamie's shoulders. "And I don't want to steal your boy. I just want him to go to college."

Colter didn't say a word.

At the end of the summer, Colter and Jamie met me for dinner at the café. Colter wore a *Teenage Mutant Ninja Turtles* sweatshirt, old suit pants, and flip-flops. Jamie had on a tube top over slim white trouser pants. The rest of the restaurant was in jeans and boots.

Colter, staring miserably into his plate of fries, admitted that this had been a lousy summer. He'd crashed his new car, a used four-door Oldsmobile sedan that he'd bought for a couple thousand dollars after his Blazer died. "I got ran off the road when it was wet outside—"

"By 'ran off the road' he means he was going way too fast," interrupted Jamie, as she crossed her arms in front of her chest.

Colter exhaled sharply. "I was run off the road but I was going way too fast, which I was fixing to say. It was some teenager. I did a full U-turn and hit a pole."

Then he'd lost his job on the road construction crew with two weeks left on the project. He blamed his firing on the fact that he'd had to miss so much work when Lindy had emergency gall-bladder surgery.

"I just don't think he called his boss," said Jamie.

"I did too," he said.

Jamie shook her head at me. "He says he called in and left a message, but in the morning I was like, 'Colter, did you call?' and he was like 'No' and went back to sleep."

"Within twenty-four hours, I had another job," he said defensively. The day after he was fired, he'd gone with his dad into town. Clif started talking with the mechanic and the man mentioned that he was looking for someone to help him turn wrenches. Clif said that Colter wasn't doing anything these days. So the mechanic told the boy to come in that afternoon. After a brief interview, he gave Colter a job as a full-time mechanic's assistant making three hundred dollars a week. At least Colter's new boss let him work on his car's busted H-frame while he was on the clock. Colter sighed, tired by the details of his life. "Sometimes I feel like, 'Great, I finally have a girlfriend, but now I'm a complete loser because I wrecked my car and I still hate my job.'"

Jamie looked up, suddenly worried over Colter's mood. "He's been really down because he's always saying what a screwup he is," she said. "He puts himself so far down."

"It's just that every time I see things going in the right direction I always do something to mess it up," he said.

Jamie shushed him. "Colter, those things happen. Those things happen to everyone. You just have to not take it so harshly." He looked out the window. "Hold my hand! Pretty pretty please? Pretty pretty princess? Colter Elizabeth Padgett!" she said in a playfully stern voice. "Hold my hand!"

He wiped his hand off with a ketchup-stained napkin and took hold of hers.

Jamie kissed his fingers and blanched. "I keep trying to wash his hands but the smell of motor oil won't go away," she said. She had just been turned down by a home health-care agency in Bandera because of a glitch in her background check. She was now looking for a nanny job. Once she started pulling in a paycheck, she said, they could finally start saving some money. When they'd both worked for a few months, they wanted to move into their own apartment in San Antonio or Kerrville.

"To go anywhere else would be good," said Colter. "To do something where I'd have some time to get my entire life planned out and not just feel stuck in a rut." He looked at Jamie and smiled. "After I get home from work at least there's something to look forward to."

Colter had big plans for the fall ahead. He was going to move to San Antonio and go to college. Maybe he would enroll at San Antonio's ITT Technical Institute, while Jamie, who would continue to live at home with her parents in Bandera, commuted to a San Antonio community college. Or maybe they would both keep living at home, save a little money, and then find an apartment in Kerrville. There they'd find jobs and take college courses online.

Jamie, who'd been sniffing at the new mascara she'd taken out of her purse, complaining that it smelled like beer or pen ink, looked up with a worried expression on her face. "But that makes me nervous because I feel like we're putting school on the back burner," she said. "If we both have to work so we can pay for an apartment, then college is going to keep getting pushed further and further on our priorities so we can make the next electricity bill or the next rent check and we'll never do it."

They both agreed that if their young relationship was going to stand a chance, they had to get out of Utopia.

"She can't live here," said Colter.

"Not until I'm nine hundred and four years old," she said.

"And I can't live here," he said. "It'd just be completely horrible. I'm so disassociated from Utopia. How Utopia was when I was growing up? It just doesn't exist anymore. And it's not that it has changed. It's that I've changed." Colter's dad had finally gotten off his case about taking over the ranch. "I guess he realized he just had to give up on it. I'm not that person and I'm never going to be that person." Alyssa, who had decided that she wanted to stick closer to home and would go to the community college in Uvalde, and her boyfriend were thinking about moving permanently out to the ranch after she graduated. Lindy was doing better and she could get by without him. It was time to go.

A few months later, Jamie moved out of her parents' house in Bandera and into Colter's bedroom. She decided that however insufferable life in Utopia would be, it beat haunting her childhood home under her mother's nagging eye. The young couple had plans to fix up the old trailer that sat abandoned next to the Padgetts' house. It had a stove and a dishwasher and electricity. There were a few rotted boards that needed to be replaced, and it was a little rundown, but Colter was sure they could make it nice. They had a bed and their dressers, and Colter had his TV. "We were going to move, but it just seems way more ideal to not pay rent," Colter would tell me that fall. "You know, we're both going to start doing college online next year and then eventually we'll move somewhere else. Whenever we graduate. So, like, in three or four years. It seems like a long time, but it really isn't that long."

But on this summer night at the café, Colter and Jamie talked themselves into believing that their futures were getting ready to open wide. They finished the meal in good spirits. Jamie tickled Colter under his arm to make him smile, and he covered her bare shoulders with his jacket when she complained of being cold. I paid the check and they walked me to my car and said good night. The light from inside the café, where the waitresses swept the floor and stacked the chairs on the tables, was the only glow up and down a shuttered Main Street.

Colter honked Jamie's car horn and headed in the opposite direction from the escape route he'd been plotting his whole life. It was nice to see someone alongside him in the passenger seat. He wasn't alone— and that was something.

The next morning, Colter was back in town, reporting for duty at Motors & More. Anyone cruising Main could see him staring blankly at the engine under the hood of his old sedan, wondering if he had it in him to get it running again.

POST OFFICE

The coffee drinker Bud Garrett was Utopia's postmaster for over thirty years. When he got the job in 1951, working for $2,400 a year, the only piece of furniture in the little office was the apple box he sat on as he sorted mail for people he'd known his whole life. One time he got a letter addressed to Kathy in Utopia, Texas. There were four Kathys in town. So he showed the letter to his favorite Kathy, one of the four Fisher sisters. She opened the envelope and found a birthday card with a twenty-dollar bill tucked inside. It wasn't her birthday, so she returned the card to Bud. He went to the next Kathy and then the next, until he finally found the birthday girl. "You used to know everybody," he said. "You knew the kids. If anybody came to town in a new car, you knew all about it. You pass them nowadays you don't have any idea who they are or where they're going. But it's not only Utopia. It's everywhere."

In 2000, the county built a new post office in town, with air-conditioning and gleaming windows and 1,650 P.O. boxes, only 540 of which are currently being rented. Bud had worked in a tiny building with no windows and just 180 boxes. "Then they come back to build this multi-million-dollar thing where they're spending everything on electricity!" he said. Throwing that type of money around didn't make a lot of sense to a man who came up during the Depression. "In the twenties and thirties you couldn't get a dollar nowhere in town," said Bud. "There just wasn't any money, period. And now they can call around and pick up loads of hundred-dollar bills."

Bud and the rest of the coffee drinkers were talking one morning about how nobody goes to the post office to visit anymore. "Go in, get your mail, then run instead of walk back to your car," said Ralph.

"Somebody told me the postmaster was cussing everybody," Milton said.

Baby Ray looked skeptical. "She's always been good to me."

"Just as nice as she can be to me, too," said Milton. "I guess everybody's just mouthing."

Ralph barked a quick laugh. "Bunch of that hearsay is worth just what it costs."

"You get all kinds of people when you're out there facing the public," said Bud. "The worst is locals when they don't get their pension checks."

Utopia's postmaster, Lettie, a cheerful forty-five-year-old mother of two sons, drives into town each morning from nearby D'Hanis. She started her career as a letter carrier in San Antonio, and has since worked as postmaster in Texas towns like San Juan, Falfurrias, and Pipe Creek. She likes it here in Utopia, though. People are nice, she said, and she doesn't have to deal with a lot of complainers. One morning, after she'd sorted all the mail and placed it in the correct boxes, she started describing to me in vivid detail the season finale of her favorite TV show. As she gasped over the drug-dealing main character's recent adventures, she paused to say hello to a man coming in for his mail. "Hello, Mr. Hampton, how are you?" Lettie singsonged politely. Then she lowered her voice, whispering that she didn't want anyone to confuse her plot summarizing with actual town gossip. Lettie isn't from around here, so she doesn't have much interest in tales of local intrigue.

Back in the day, the post office used to be a regular hub for afternoon socializing. Bud gabbed about the state of the town with the same circle of friends. "Annalee Burns, Henry Fisher, and I used to talk about Utopia growing," he said. "Oil wells came in a time or two, and the highways were coming through. People said, 'Oh hell, it's going to ruin Utopia! It's going to ruin Utopia! Utopia is going to be full of drunks and they're going to sell beer!' So we'd talk about did we want to keep it like it was or did we want it to keep growing. We personally kinda liked it like it was. And Jack Tampke used to come into the post office after dinner quite often and, well, our mail had come and went and I was pretty loose after dinner, and we'd all get on the counter and talk. People would come in and if Jack didn't recognize them he'd say, 'Who in the hell is he and what in the goddamn hell does he want here?'" Bud paused to laugh at his friend's ornery position on strangers. "Now that was just a thought about people back when it began to grow. We were satisfied with what we had and really didn't want a whole new bunch."

These days postmasters aren't allowed to have anybody come visit with them behind the counter at work. After 9/11, the United States Post Office implemented stricter security measures, prohibiting anyone who isn't an employee from venturing beyond the register. Lettie ate lunch alone, peeling her oranges while she participated in an online meeting with other postmasters from distant cities and towns. An electronic beep alerted her if any customers came through the front door. She might know who they are, she might not.

CHAPTER 12

Just Remember Home and
Family and Good Times

Josh went to Iraq the eighth time for love. Like Colter, he had stunned himself by falling hard for a girl. She was stationed at his base in Fort Carson, and that spring, before they both deployed, he brought her home to Utopia to meet his mother.

"He always told me when he brought one home that would mean something," said Kathy. " 'When I introduce her to you, Mom, not just sneak her out of the house or sneak her in the window, you have to worry.' " His girlfriend was a rank below Josh—a specialist to his sergeant—so their relationship was technically forbidden. But they decided there weren't any rules of protocol that would keep them apart. So when she got her orders to deploy to Iraq, Josh decided he better volunteer his own service again as well. He could sock the money away for their future life together, he told Kathy. Besides he would feel better knowing that if they had to be in a war zone, at least they were there together. But first he wanted to show her Utopia.

Whenever her sons visited, Kathy liked to make sure she had all their favorite foods waiting for them in the refrigerator. Jeff had told her that Ashley loved to eat healthy, so Kathy had always made sure to have chicken breasts and salmon steaks for her daughter-in-law. When she asked Josh what she should buy special for his girlfriend, he gave her very specific instructions to buy bottled green tea.

"He said, 'Now when you get to town, you got your phone, show me a picture of it,'" said Kathy. "Before I could buy it he had to make sure it was the right one! So I took a picture, and he said, 'Yes, that's it! Get five of 'em.' I got six. I bring them home, they're the ginseng in the can. Well, apparently she only drinks it from the bottle. He was having a fit. I said, 'Joshua, I'm sure it will be okay.' So what does he do? He opens three of them and pours them into a pitcher and tells her I made them homemade. I told him, 'Joshua, don't lie to her.' But that's what he did. Then the first weekend she was here somebody was making noise, and he come out of the bedroom yelling. 'Joey, not so much noise, quit pounding!' She was sleeping! I've never seen him act like this. He carries her stuff in. He gets her a glass of water when she sits on the couch. He waits on her!"

Kathy's thirty-two-year-old brother, Steven, came home on leave from Iraq at the same time as Josh. On the way back from picking Steven up at the airport her brother had gone uncharacteristically quiet in the backseat. "And by the time we got to 90 and 410 in San Antone, Steven was freaking," said Kathy. "He said, 'You don't realize for the last three months I've drove two miles an hour.' All the cars passing us driving seventy was freaking him out. When we pulled on our road he said, 'We'd be stopping and investigating that patch right there where they had fixed the asphalt. We'd be investigating and checking for IEDs.'"

Steven didn't tell his sister much about his time in Iraq. He didn't want to pollute his life at home with any of the ugly details of his missions. So there was an unspoken agreement at the Wiekamp house that everyone avoided all conversations relating to the war. But Kathy's mother is a Fox News junkie, and she likes to consider herself an expert on current events. So one afternoon she started asking Steven about Iraq. "And she wants to talk and analyze it," said Kathy. "No one in the rest of the family will do that. Negative stuff, I don't discuss. Anything negative? Not anymore. And she started in asking Steven questions about post-traumatic stress and things like that. I pretended like I wasn't listening so I asked Steven a question to get it off the subject." Kathy put in the movie *Alvin and the Chipmunks,* which she'd now decided was one of her absolute favorites, and she spared the men from talking about their internal lives.

Steven wanted the family to gather for a barbecue on his last night of leave. Josh had been unusually calm his whole trip home, staying in with his girlfriend and helping Kathy out around the house instead of cruising Main looking for parties. But it was his uncle's last night and Steven wanted Josh to commiserate over Jäger and Red Bull shots. Steven was leaving for another fifteen-month rotation. And when his contract was up, he would reenlist. "It's what he knows," said Kathy. " 'I'm a soldier and that's what I am.' "

The day after Steven's goodbye party, Josh's girlfriend wanted to go to San Antonio to spend one last night with her large Mexican family. Josh decided to stay in Utopia and help his father trap deer, but told her to go on and take his truck to make the trip. "I swear to God right there I knew it was true love," said Kathy with a laugh. "*She took his truck.* That's his baby."

That night Josh went with his parents to drop a net on some Axis deer. While Randy sat hunched in the deer blind, hidden from view of the animals who would come for the scattered handfuls of corn, Kathy and Josh stayed in the pickup. In the quiet darkness, they waited for Randy's signal that it was time for them to haul the trailer around so they could load up the captured deer. Josh confessed to his mother that he was wrestling with the decision of whether to reenlist after this next deployment. "He was complaining about the Army and I said, 'When you get out, you're going to have the same problem. Whatever job you go to, you can have bosses who are assholes. If that's the reason you're getting out of the Army, don't think it's going to get better,'" said Kathy. "But he seemed like he was ready to get out. Last time he was over there he didn't handle it as well. He's tired." After this last deployment he would take the money and run. He'd given enough to the Army.

A few months later, Kathy sat eating a tuna fish sandwich and potato chips on her family room recliner. She had bright yellow daisies painted on her red toenails, an indulgence from yesterday's trip to the manicurist in Uvalde with some girlfriends. There was a large basket of men's underwear and socks on the sofa that needed folding. Randy passed through the room with a nod and a grunt. He was heading into Sabinal to run some errands. Kathy teased him about her accomplishment that morning. They'd spent weeks trying to outdo each other at a computer game. "Oh, excuse me, but look at high score!" she said. "Hmmm, mmm, beatcha!" Randy smiled sideways at his wife and dropped to his knees to wrestle with Jeff's dog before slipping out of the house without a word. Kathy set her lunch plate at her feet on the floor and turned her attention to the waiting basket of clothes. Josh needed his laundry folded.

Her boy had come home from Iraq early. For the first couple of months over there, he'd been fine. Things between him and his girlfriend were rosy when they arrived at Balad Airbase in northern Iraq. But then his Special Forces team gave Josh orders to move, and he was forced to leave her behind. Almost immediately, he'd started panicking in late night phone calls to Kathy that they were growing apart. "I spent a whole lot of time on the phone with him saying, 'Leave her alone, give her some space,'" said Kathy. The couple soon split. "He was totally blindsided. Josh tends to completely love. And this was the first person that he let himself care about since losing Jeff."

Then Josh got word while he was away on his mission that one of his friends back on base had committed suicide. The soldier had fought over the telephone with his hometown girlfriend. When he hung up the phone, he walked into the bay, pulled out his sidearm, and shot himself in the head.

"After that, Josh called me and said, 'I'm done, Mom. I can't handle any more,' " said Kathy. "There was a lot of talking he did while he was in Iraq. He doesn't sleep. Four o'clock in the afternoon here is three in the morning there. So I'd get a lot of calls and eventually even I was telling him to come home." Josh told his commanders he felt broken, and he left Iraq in midrotation.

The Army gave Josh two weeks of leave before he had to return to Fort Carson to begin the long process of discharging. While he was home, he accompanied Randy and Kathy to Kentucky so they could spend some time with Jared's wife and meet her new baby girl, Emily Morgan. On the trip they stopped in Fort Riley to visit Jeff's widow, Ashley, before she deployed to Iraq.

She had finally gotten her wish. Josh drove his sister-in-law's truck home to Utopia, where it would sit next to Jeff's. Last Christmas, after everyone was done opening their presents, Kathy had looked around and realized that Ashley was gone. The Wiekamps dispersed all over town in search of her. Finally one of Kathy's brothers called the house and said he'd found her crying at the cemetery, slumped alongside Jeff's grave. When Ashley got back to the house, Kathy sat outside with her and told the young woman that it was okay to feel sad, and together they cried a little over the boy they both missed.

I asked Kathy if she thought her daughter-in-law returning to war was a good idea. She said that Ashley was doing much better these days. Kathy explained that the Army had made the grudging decision to redeploy Ashley despite their ongoing concern over the girl's angry grief. "They did send down a medical report that said she was deployable but that they felt she should not carry a firearm," said Kathy. "So I told her, 'You are not going to Iraq and not carrying a firearm. So you figure out a way to not go to Iraq—or you carry a firearm. I don't care which.' "

Kathy exhaled angrily, accidentally kicking over her lunch plate and knocking a few chips onto the carpet. "They were worried she'd shoot herself. I said, 'That's ridiculous, you've had ample opportunity to do that already.' She goes to the range all the time. She could step in front of somebody's bullet if that's what she wanted. I mean, she is suicidal but she can do it any way she wants to. That's stupid to tell her that." Kathy shook her head free of such gruesome scenarios. "She's better," she said firmly. "She's getting better. Alcohol is harder to get there. You can get it, because I had Josh calling me drunk from Iraq. I would tell him, 'Don't you think you shouldn't be drunk some place where they're trying to kill you?' 'Mom! I'm a United States soldier and I'm highly trained and I know what I'm doing.' But it's harder to get there, so that's good at least."

While they were in Kansas helping Ashley pack up her house, Kathy found a box of Jeff's belongings that the Army had sent back from Afghanistan. Back in Utopia, Randy and Kathy got up the courage to look inside. They found one of Jeff's journals. Randy flipped it open and handed it quietly to Kathy. "Well, there's his house," he said in a flat voice, pointing to Jeff's pencil illustration.

"He had drawn a picture of his future house with two baby carriages in front of it," Kathy told me. "Two baby buggies in front." She cleared her throat and stayed quiet for a minute. She smiled sadly and said how much she would have liked to meet her oldest son's children.

Looking through the box that night, Kathy had made a promise to herself that she would set aside any love letter she found that Ashley had written to Jeff. She figured she didn't have the right to unfold those without the girl's permission. "She can tell me stuff, so I won't read her letters to him," said Kathy. But she allowed herself the exquisitely painful pleasure of reading her son's love letters to his wife. "There was a card he had written to her where . . . See, I had always told the kids, to get them through things, that this home was their sanctuary. When they go some place and it's tough and they're scared, just remember home and family and good times. And so he wrote to her, 'This is fast, I've got to go, but I wanted to tell you how much I love you. I'm remembering you cooking at the stove and Riley sitting in the corner and us together as a family. And that's my memory that I'm using to get through Afghanistan.'" Kathy paused and took a shaky breath. "Oh, that was so sweet. And I think that's what all the boys do. They remember the home and the community and the love and support they know that they've got here from everybody."

Soon Josh would return for good to the only place in the world he thought had a chance of making him feel whole again. He told his mom his plan was to use his GI Bill benefits to take some classes at the community college in Uvalde. Maybe major in aviation mechanics, while he helped Randy build their breeding business at home. All he knew is he wanted to come home to Texas, to the comforting embrace of his family and everything in this world he found familiar. "I can't think of any other place that Josh could get as much as he can out of everything than Utopia," said Kathy. "Considering the pain the world can offer you, you need to take the good stuff where you can get it. There are so many times in your life that things are going to be bad that you have no control over. You better enjoy the times you have that are good because life is going to kick you in the teeth no matter what."

Despite all the ugliness Josh had seen out there in this world, and the losses he'd endured, Kathy had to believe that her son's heart could be put back together. "I'll make sure he's all right," she said firmly. "That's my role."

When Josh gets out of the Army, Main Street will look different.

Morris tore down the old brick front of the General Store, which dated back to 1946. He replaced it with bright and shiny finished pine wood that he special-ordered from Fredericksburg. He blasted out space for two wide front windows to finally let a little daylight into the place. "I've been wanting to redo the front for a long time," said Morris. "But we've been waiting on the highway department to decide what they're going to do on these roads. We don't know if the state is ever going to do the sidewalks project. Some of the intelligent locals we have here—you get a chance to have something good done and they always throw a fit. Anyway, I finally got my belly full of waiting." The face-lift gives the General Store a charming fresh look, almost a caricature of what a tourist might imagine a cozy small-town shop ought to look like.

Morris taped a sign on the store's front door warning in black marker that all past due accounts would be immediately closed. The revamped storefront matches the aesthetic of Morris's new real estate office. Across from the register, where there used to be a gloomy entrance to the dusty variety section, there's now a gleaming glass door with Morris's new company's name, Texas Land and Ranch Co., etched proudly in the middle. Morris got his broker's license so that he could start keeping his commissions for himself. He brought in two local boys underneath him to operate as agents. "Big Shyster and Little Shyster," according to the coffee drinkers.

Ralph doesn't have much to say about the changes down at the store. "None a my business," he said into his cup one winter morning.

"That is called progress," Milton said with a harsh laugh.

"Pretty fancy," said Ralph, his voice tight, his mouth creasing into a lemony smile. The men don't understand why the store needed gussying up in the first place, and can't help but think now wasn't the time to be starting a new business, what with the economy heading south. "Sometimes a man can have too many irons in the fire," said Ralph. "With the economy running backwards, real estate is always the first to go. That's what I'm thinking, but I don't know." Morris is doing all right, though, pleased about a $2.5 million offer he'd just received for a property four miles from Utopia. Folks from Colorado looking to give the Hill Country lifestyle a whirl.

In the back by the coffeepots, the same cluster of old-timers sit in their usual spots. All except Hose, that is. A few months back the man's knees started hurting him so bad that he was forced into a wheelchair. Once his legs went out from under him, he gave up on coffee with the guys. He stayed at home listening to his King James Bible cassettes, resting in his old rocking chair with the cowboys-and-broncs seat cushion, staring through the sliding glass doors to his living room, which he'd marked off with bright orange Xs of electrical tape so he wouldn't walk through them. The coffee drinkers sure missed Hose, but only a few of them ever got around to visiting him. A man like Hose wasn't meant to spend his life indoors, and it hurt to see their friend so re-duced. Hose's family eventually decided that it was time to consider an assisted-living facility where he could benefit from full-time care. So Hose moved into a Kerrville nursing home, far from the land he and the generations before him had so dearly loved.

Meanwhile, the coffee drinkers were still trying to accept the fact that America had a new president. The men had endured with corded necks and tensed mouths the long, ugly campaign. They'd been less than thrilled with their choices. Toward the end of the primary sea-son, Ralph took a look at what he considered to be a sorry lot and started insisting he was going to vote for his dog Fudge. The coffee drinkers were sure for a long while that Hillary would scrap her way to the Democratic nomination. But she lost. Then they were certain Barack Obama didn't stand a chance, until they started worrying that he did.

Before the election someone taped up on the wall by the coffepots, next to the postcard of Hillary Clinton's face superimposed on a clas-sic Uncle Sam image, declaring AMERICA . . . I WANT YOUR GUNS, an image of a younger Barack Obama wearing a traditional African shirt juxtaposed with a picture of a rugged John McCain in his pilot uni-form. AMERICA, WHAT IS UP YOUR ASS?! the caption demanded. It was in this context that we spoke about the election. The men had long since written me off as a hopeless Communist and would plug their ears and accuse me of campaigning for the Democrats whenever I came to town. Of all the coffee drinkers, only Bud was voting for Obama. "I don't like this administration," he said angrily a month before the elec-tion. "I lived through the Depression. The Republicans put us in it and I think they've put us in it again. Seventy-five percent of the American people are ready for a change. And I don't see a change in McCain. I see it in Obama. And I'll vote for anybody who promises a change. To me the Democratic Party has always been for the little fellow, and I've been the little fellow all my life and I'm still a Democrat and I'll die a Democrat and I don't give a damn who knows it!"

Milton, who'd long been outraged at Americans for voting George

W., "that goofy bastard," not once but twice into the White House, declared that for the first time in his life he would vote Republican.

"And the reason you're not voting for him is because he's a Negro?" asked Bud.

"That's right," said Milton.

"What has the Negro race ever done to you?" Bud wondered.

"Nothing," said Milton. "I don't particularly hate them. I'm just prejudiced."

"Somewhere in life we've got to adjust to living with Mexicans and Negroes," said Bud. "And maybe you hate to see the white America go. But it's gone."

"I figure I'll die before I have to do that," Milton said stubbornly.

"Well, maybe, maybe. But your kids are going to have to do it. Hell, half of them are married to Mexicans or Negroes now." Bud sighed to himself. "They're people just like everybody else."

Well, at least Bud was happy come election day. Most of the coffee drinkers turned a sour cheek on all the rousing celebrations of hope and history-making that swept the radio and television airwaves after Obama's win. They fussed and grumbled to one another and resisted talk of politics in my presence. "Was there an election?" one of the men asked me, his face shaped into a tight mask of obliviousness.

Not Ralph, who watched the inauguration with something close to admiration. The new First Daughters charmed him enormously, and he promptly picked a beef with anyone who suggested that the First Lady's yellow inauguration-day outfit was anything less than lovely.

Ralph said he knew there toward the end that the election wasn't going to go the Republicans' way. Not with McCain at the helm. "He's just an old-time politician, been up there for a hundred years," he said. "And I think we needed a fresh start, get something different. If the same old game ain't working, change your game plan. McCain wasn't a good speaker. He couldn't get into people's minds and change them. Obama went after the younger bunch. McCain just went to the older folks. And the younger folks outnumber us."

Ralph decided that this young new president deserved a chance and couldn't be expected to fix a floundering country overnight. He sure didn't envy Obama the job he had in front of him. "Oh, he's stirred up this morning," reported Ralph one January morning. "He heard some of those bankers were using the surplus money to give themselves bonuses. Said it was unconscionable! I think he's right, too."

Everyone agreed that America was in a bind. Ray wondered aloud whether we even stood a chance if our fate was left in Washington's greedy and divided hands. "I think when they all go into the Senate in the mornings they ought to take a number. You may be a Republican today and you may be a Democrat tomorrow. And thataway it's all even. You can't say I'ma this party, I'ma this party. Everybody oughta be the same. They all oughta be there for the same reason, and that's for the benefit of the country. Not to get up there and fight and fuss with one another. Talk about it and settle it, listen to what everybody has to say and come up with a solution."

"What they're supposed to be doing is representing me and you," said Milton.

"No matter what party they are," insisted Ray. "I don't care if Obama is a Democrat or a Republican. If he's a good man and he comes up with good plans I'll go with him."

"That damn Rush Limbaugh, sitting there yelling about how he just hopes he fails," said Milton, snorting in disgust. "You know? He just *hopes* he fails."

Enough talk of politics, the coffee drinkers agreed. More importantly, one of the men wondered, why wasn't Fudge sitting out there in the back of Ralph's truck? Ralph rubbed the side of his face and said that Fudge had decided to sit this trip out. The dog had broken the routine, slumping down to the ground when Ralph called for him to come. "Like me, he's getting old," said Ralph. Fudge had been having trouble jumping into the truck, so Ralph bought him a ramp to ease his once springy legs up into the back. The image of his dog dragging his sore bones around sat heavy on Ralph's shoulders. The men all seemed to sigh in unison.

After an hour or so of visiting, Ralph got up slowly and saluted me with a couple of fingers to the side of his cap. He promised to return.

"Some days," he said, with a soft, sheepish grin, "I catch myself hurrying to get through something so I can get back to the store." He shrugged his shoulders, powerless to resist the mighty pull he felt to this place. "This store to me is the town," he said. "When I die they're just going to have to stuff me and stand me in the broom closet."

But for now this was goodbye. He was going home to check on his old dog.

Ralph went humming to himself up the center aisle. He gave Morris a little nod and slipped through the front door into the gauzy bright of a new day.

JUSTICE OF THE PEACE

Bill Schaefer keeps a glass jar of glazed oatmeal cookies on his desk so that anyone who has to come see him can at least enjoy a little snack. At different points in Utopia's history, his large one-room office has served as a grocery store, an antiques market, a café, a feed store, a beauty shop a few times over, and, for a brief period back in the 1940s, a movie house. Slim Boykins owned the place back then, and on Thursday nights he'd arrange up to twenty chairs on the black-and-white tile floor and anybody with a spare quarter could enjoy a Western while the film projector flapped pleasingly in the background. As a child, Bill would sit in this very room with his mouth hanging open watching Roy Rogers or Gabby Hayes save the day. In 1947, he carved his initials on the cement by the front door.

Today Bill, kind and gentle-mannered to the point of almost seeming childlike, is seventy-one years old. He is serving his third term of elected office. When I visited with him, he wore a pearl-button snap shirt and Wranglers, his Silverado hat brim-up on the desk. He grew up just across Main Street from the JP office, the youngest of five siblings, and his daddy ran a Mobil filling station two doors down from where Bill works today. Married by the time he was eighteen, Bill and his wife had five children within five years. Behind him on the wall hangs a wood-framed picture of a baby mountain lion one of his daughters drew for him when she was little. That cub hung in his old tire shop around the corner, and it traveled with him here when his aching shoulders and knees convinced him to look for a job with a chair. Nine years sitting behind a desk and he still hasn't completely caught on to office work. On the subject of email, he shakes his head slowly and leans far back in his chair. "No, well, I don't know what it is. I couldn't tell you even how to touch a computer."

Most of the time Bill's job is pretty easy. The physical space of a town like Utopia, where the constable makes a casual sweep down Main Street on Friday nights, ensures that some sins carried on the wind, whispers of trouble wandering into the perked ears of neighbors. You knock your wife around, you step out on your husband, and people are going to talk. They'll widen their eyes disapprovingly and shake their heads and say old so-and-so is at it again. Sometimes the gossip will mess with the truth, to where reputations are built and destroyed on a wild round of telephone. But people for the most part are used to being left on their own to work out their rage and grievances.

Tragedy skips over no place, though, and Bill has been forced to bear witness. There was the terrible night when he was called to the house of a friend who'd beaten his wife to death. "I knew him all my life," he sputtered. "And knowing this person and knowing what a sweet person his wife was, I don't know, seeing something like that . . ." He trailed off, because there really isn't a way to make sense of such things. He had to confront the aftermath of a young man who shoved a rifle in his mouth and pulled the trigger, and he had to pronounce the deaths of Milton's grandchildren after that beast of a wreck.

"But basically it's not a real hard job," he said, brushing a few leaked tears from his cheeks. Usually he dealt with DUIs and MIPs, kids caught sneaking a few beers on Friday nights. He'd fine them and sentence them to alcohol awareness class and community service. It can be awkward enforcing punishment on kids he is somehow related to or went to church with or whose parents called him at home asking him to bend the rules just this once. And there are those who say that despite Bill's good heart and best intentions, he's been guilty on occasion of letting some of the prominent boys in town shirk their prescribed community service. But he'll cop to making a crime go away just once, after state highway officers made one of their sporadic patrols through Utopia. Four older women got popped one after another as they pulled out of the post office parking lot without their seat belts on. "Well, they come up there to my office," says Bill, hooting at the memory of it all, "here they come. Some of 'em have the oxygen masks on, some of 'em used walking sticks. I told 'em, 'Just go home, forget about it. I'll take care of it here, you just go on home.' "

Mr. Schaefer gave me another oatmeal cookie. He had an appointment with a local who had been arrested for punching a newcomer who owed him money. But before he got down to business, he wanted to share his favorite story about the town he so loved. It involved one of his favorite old-timers, Kelli's grandfather Ed Jones. "I don't know what you heard about him," he said, leaning in close. "I think he was a good, honest man myself." Mr. Schaefer proceeded to tell me about the first friendly face Ed Jones laid eyes on when he was rescued from the German prison camp. "The Americans were coming in and Mellie Ivy, a boy who was raised right up here in Utopia with Ed, was the guy who drove through the fence. He ran this big tank through there and tore the fence down for them boys to get out."

Mr. Schaefer burst into a delighted whoop of laughter. "The war was over! And there was Mellie!" He clapped his hands together at the impossible wonders of our very small world. "Can you imagine?" he said. "Come from a little town like Utopia!"

ACKNOWLEDGMENTS

It was Mark Harris, my editor at *Entertainment Weekly,* who first had the idea. He believed in it enough to wait for me to take driver's ed, get a learner's permit, and then fail my first driver's test. Thank you, Mark, and Rick Tetzeli, for your patience and for thinking a story about a town with a zero-subscription base had a place in the magazine. The ridiculously generous Jeff Giles and Jess Cagle kept me on staff despite the fact that I ran away to Texas. My fierce agent, Betsy Lerner—equal parts overbearing mother and elegant magician forced me to take myself seriously as a writer while muscling this whole project into place. Betsy led me to Chris Jackson, my deeply cool and terrifically sensitive editor, whom I will forever trust and adore. I give a humble curtsy and bow to everyone at Spiegel & Grau, the classiest joint in town.

I clutch my heart thinking about all the good people of Utopia, and even the very few I never did come to like much. It was my great honor to spend time with everybody there, especially the Wiekamp, Rhodes, Padgett, and Potter families. Thank you, Sid and Jacque Chaney, who treated me like a daughter and made me pancakes for supper and always told the best stories in town. Thank you to the Magnificent Miss Alice for her conversation and incomparable fried chicken. Thank you, Diane, Joan, Kathy, and Betty Ann. When I grow up I want to be a Fisher sister. And, finally, I simply can't imagine a better way to start each day than on an old stool, drinking instant, teasing and getting teased by the coffee drinkers. Thank you, gentlemen—Tony, Milton, Ted, Bud, John, Ray, Hose, Henry, Albert, John, Morris, and most especially my friend Ralph—for letting me into your circle. I loved every minute down at the General Store. Goodbye, Fudge.

Thank you, friends and family. Kalimba Bennett first told me that I could write this book. My dad told me that I should. Greg Kirschling and Elaine Valby, tender and thoughtful early readers, made me believe that I was onto something and ought to keep going until the very end.

My beautiful and brave daughter, Ava Bekelech, came into my world during the writing of this book. In her young life, she has aleady known many homes and many towns. Catch your breath, child. Lean on your father, who is good and strong and wise, and who will always offer you a wonderfully soft place to fall. I know this because he caught me years ago and showed me that life is sweet.

Oh Tim! *We did it.*

About the Author

KAREN VALBY is a senior writer at *Entertainment Weekly*.
She lives in Austin, Texas, with her husband and daughter.
This is her first book.

About the Type

This book was set in Sabon, a typeface designed by the well-known German typographer Jan Tschichold (1902–74). Sabon's design is based upon the original letter forms of Claude Garamond and was created specifically to be used for three sources: foundry type for hand composition, Linotype, and Monotype. Tschichold named his typeface for the famous Frankfurt typefounder Jacques Sabon, who died in 1580.